P9-EDN-863

A FIELD GUIDE TO THE BIRDS OF EAST AND CENTRAL AFRICA

A FIELD GUIDE TO THE BIRDS OF EAST AND CENTRAL AFRICA

---

by

JOHN G. WILLIAMS

with 16 *colour plates and*
24 *black-and-white plates by*
the author and
Rena Fennessy

Introduced by
ROGER TORY PETERSON

HOUGHTON MIFFLIN COMPANY BOSTON
THE RIVERSIDE PRESS CAMBRIDGE

To Philippa

Fifth Printing

First American Edition 1964

Printed in Great Britain

INTRODUCTION

by

Roger Tory Peterson

When I first set foot in East Africa in May, 1957, a pleasant, friendly man greeted me as I stepped from the ramp at the Nairobi airport. I had met him several years before in London at the British Museum, and it was then that he urged me to see for myself the bird wonders of East Africa.

Two reporters who also met the plane asked me whether my visit to Kenya meant that I was planning to do a Field Guide to the Birds of East Africa. I replied, " Oh no! But the man who should do such a book is standing here beside me—John Williams." Whether that was the moment when John Williams first conceived the idea of an East and Central African Field Guide I do not know, but we soon talked earnestly of such a book. I urged him to feel free to use my well-known Field Guide system which had proved so practical in both Europe and North America, but I regretted that I could not paint the colour plates because of the overwhelming pressure of other commitments. However, John Williams had already tried his hand at painting the sunbirds, the *Nectariniidae*, a gorgeous galaxy of feathered gems, on which he is the world authority. He decided to undertake the drawings himself and estimated that it would take perhaps a year or two to bring such a work to completion. I knew better, for I had gone through the ordeal several times, and I gave him a minimum of four or five years which proved to be a more realistic estimate.

Africa, unlike that other great bird continent of the Southern Hemisphere, South America, has been blessed with a number of fine ornithological works with numerous illustrations, but most of them are heavy enough to be used as door stoppers. What was really needed was a pocket field guide—something that would give the traveller a dependable introduction to the species he was most likely to see. No man in all Africa was better qualified to tackle the project than John Williams, whose official position is Curator of Birds at Nairobi's Coryndon Museum.

There is no question that he is the sharpest field observer I have encountered in that great continent with the possible exception of Jim Chapin, who during fifty years of his life collected in the forests of the Congo.

I vividly remember my first field trip with John Williams. Only a few hours after my arrival, we took the landrover over the Ngong hills and down to Lake Magadi near the Tanganyika border where we were joined by Sir Evelyn Baring then the Governor of Kenya, and himself a fine field ornithologist. Like other great field men I have known, John Williams was able to identify almost every bird, with amazing certainty, at the snap of a finger. He knew their identification tags, their " field marks." But here I was, thrown into a completely new avifauna. I could only say, when he ticked off another one, " I'll take your word for it, old boy." Our list for that week-end was well over 200 species. John Williams assures me that with a little planning a single " big day " or " century run " in East Africa could easily exceed 250—more species than most active bird watchers see in a whole year in the British Isles or in the north-eastern United States.

In the past, Africa, to the traveller, meant the large game animals and primitive tribes. And the object of going on safari was to shoot. To-day shooting is being replaced by the more civilised sport of photographing —or just looking. The herds of big game are dwindling fast outside the parks and preserves. The once picturesque native peoples, except for the Masai and certain marginal groups, are now so westernised that they are as commonplace in their dress and activities as Europeans. The tourist, on the other hand, will find increasing pleasure in the spectacular bird life. People from temperate Europe and North America who are accustomed to the " little brown jobs " will marvel at the iridescent sunbirds, bizarre hornbills, and gem-like bee-eaters, rollers and touracos. But half the fun is knowing what they are—to be able to put names to things.

John Williams has made it possible to put a name to most of the birds one will encounter, and I predict that the tourist offices will be swamped with requests about the birding spots of East and Central Africa. Already Lake Nakuru, ninety miles north of Nairobi in the Rift Valley is becoming a mecca for tourists from all parts of the world who are drawn by the spectacle of the flamingos. But the marabous, stilts, and waterfowl that populate the shore also merit attention, and so do the ground hornbills, secretary birds, emerald cuckoos and other fascinating birds that haunt the acacia groves. This field guide will give you their names.

Roger Tory Peterson

CONTENTS

CONTENTS

ILLUSTRATIONS

ILLUSTRATIONS

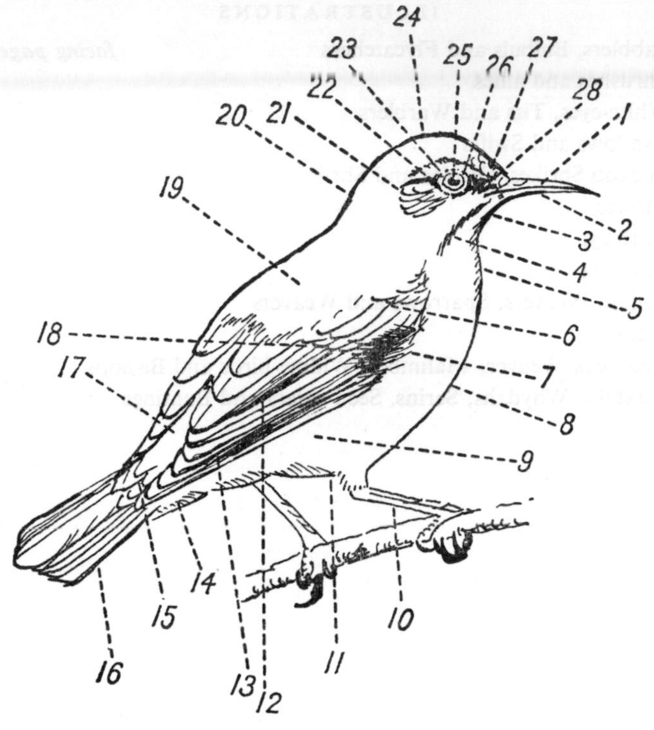

THE TOPOGRAPHY OF A BIRD

KEY TO TERMS USED IN THIS VOLUME

1 Upper mandible
2 Lower mandible
3 Chin
4 Moustachial stripe
5 Throat
6 Wing-coverts
7 Pectoral tuft
8 Breast
9 Flanks
10 Tarsus
11 Abdomen or belly
12 Secondaries
13 Primaries
14 Under tail-coverts
15 Upper tail-coverts
16 Outer tail-feathers
17 Rump
18 Wing-bar
19 Back or mantle
20 Nape
21 Ear-coverts
22 Eye-stripe
23 Superciliary
24 Crown
25 Iris
26 Eye-ring
27 Forehead
28 Lores

HOW TO USE THIS BOOK

Visitors to Africa from Europe and America will find representatives of several bird families well-known in northern climes—birds of prey, ducks and geese, warblers, larks, pipits and wagtails, flycatchers and many others. Groups less familiar will include the ostrich, hammerkop, whale-headed stork, secretary bird, finfoot, jacanas, painted snipe, coucals, turacos, parrots, hornbills, wood-hoopoes, mousebirds, trogons, barbets, honey-guides, broadbills, pittas, babblers and chatterers, bulbuls, cuckoo-shrikes, drongos, helmet-shrikes, oxpeckers, white-eyes, sunbirds, weaver-birds and waxbills. The essential characters of these groups are enumerated in the text and illustrations.

In most instances it will be found possible to identify a given bird by referring to the illustrations and by noting the chief field characters as indicated by arrow-lines. But however certain such identification may appear, it should still be confirmed by looking up the text, where closely allied species are listed and information given on distribution, habitat and habits.

Identification by Elimination: Identifying birds, at least in the early stages, is frequently a matter of elimination. In this process distribution and habitat play a major part. As an example, a large, black-looking sunbird found in Kenya at altitudes over 8,000 feet is almost certain to be the Tacazze Sunbird; below 7,000 feet it is equally likely to be the Bronzy Sunbird.

Voice: As a general rule most birds are recognised by their visual characters; voice and song are of secondary importance, however valuable these may be in drawing attention to birds in the field. Nevertheless there are exceptions to this rule. Several cuckoos would be overlooked were it not for their loud and easily recognised calls, and among the cisticola warblers—a group of "difficult" mainly brown birds—song and habitat have an important role in field recognition.

Written descriptions of birds' calls and song leave much to be desired, and there can be no doubt that the only satisfactory method of depicting voice is with the aid of bird recordings made in the field. Everyone interested in African bird-life owes a debt of gratitude to one of Africa's leading ornithologists, Mr. M. E. W. North, for his work in this sphere. His first record, on which forty-two species of African birds may be heard, has already been released by Cornell University, and further records in this series are in preparation.

Size: A bird's size is not easy to indicate in a species' description so that it means the same thing to everyone. The measurements given in the section "Identification" indicate the average length of the bird from tip of bill to tip of longest tail feather. The following are a few comparative bird lengths which may be useful for those persons familiar with European or North American birds: European Willow Warbler 4½"; House Sparrow 5½"; European Song Thrush 9"; Wood Pigeon 16"; Rook 18". Most of the American Wood Warblers measure between 4½" and 5½"; Cardinal 8½"; American Robin 9½"; and Blue Jay 11½". In addition to size it is important to observe whether a bird is plump-looking like members of the thrush family or slim like the wagtails and bee-eaters.

Habits and Flight: A bird's field habits often provide good clues to its identity. A note should be made as to whether it perches in prominent positions and on vantage points such as telegraph poles and wires, like a stonechat, an augur buzzard or a fiscal shrike; or whether it is a skulker keeping to thick vegetation, like a boubou shrike or a cinnamon bracken warbler. Clues to identity may be found in characteristic habits, such as tail wagging in the wagtails and common sandpiper; or climbing about on branches in the manner of a tit, as is the habit of the red-headed malimbe and some other weavers. Modes of progression offer useful pointers. In the case of ground frequenting species the gait may be a hop or a walk. Among water birds the swimming level may be high in the water like a moorhen, or low like a diving duck, cormorant or darter. When taking off from water a bird may need to run along the surface before rising, like a moorhen, coot or diving duck; or spring clear in one jump like a surface feeding duck. The flight may be undulating as in the case of woodpeckers and honey-guides; rapid but erratic and given to changes of direction, typical of the sunbirds; or direct and fast as in the swifts. The wing-beats may be slow, as in the herons; or rapid as is the case with ducks and parrots. The bird may hover in the air like a kestrel, augur buzzard or pied kingfisher; or indulge in alternate glides on motionless wings and a period of rapid wingbeats, like the swifts.

Distinctive Plumage Patterns and Silhouettes: Aids to identification include pattern and colour contrasts of the entire plumage; the colour of the underparts, whether spotted, banded or immaculate, and the degree and extent of the spotting and banding; the presence or absence of a white rump patch, such as occurs in some species of sandpipers, swifts and wheatears; tail length and whether the outer tail feathers are white or not, and the extent of the white—important in nightjar recognition. The shape of the tail is often significant, whether it is forked and the degree of forking, or whether square, rounded or wedge-shaped, and whether central or outer tail feathers are greatly lengthened, as in many species of sunbirds, widow-birds, bee-eaters and rollers.

Wing patterns should always be noted, especially in the case of waders and ducks. Head markings, especially crown and eye stripes, are important in identifying many perching birds. Such stripes may be pale or dark, and situated on the crown, or above, through or below the eye. There may be pale or white feather rings around the eyes, as in the White-eyes and the White-eyed Slaty Flycatcher.

Subspecies: In treating the problem of subspecies it was essential to concentrate on the primary object of the Field Guide, the identification of bird species in the field. This rule has been relaxed only in those few cases where geographical races are so strikingly different that they may be recognised with certainty and ease. Examples are the various races of the yellow and blue-headed wagtail, and the black-breasted and green-breasted races of the beautiful sunbird. For the rest it is wiser to concentrate on species identification and to leave the vexed question of what constitutes a valid subspecies to the museum taxonomists.

Symbols: The symbols ♂ and ♀ indicate male and female respectively, "M" intimates that the species is a Palaearctic migrant; "M & R" that in addition to being a northern migrant the species also has a resident population in Africa—for example, the avocet and glossy ibis.

RED SEA
Massawa
ERITREA
Asmara
Gulf of Aden
FR. SOMALILD.
Jibuti
Blue Nile
Berbera
Addis Ababa
ETHIOPIA (ABYSSINIA)
SOMALIA
R. Omo
Webbe Shibeli
L. Rudolf
R. Jibuti
L. Albert
UGANDA
KENYA
Mogadishu
Entebbe
Kisumu
Lake Victoria
Nairobi
INDIAN
Mt. Kilimanjaro
Moshi
Kigoma
Mombasa
L. Tanganyika
Tabora
Tanga
Pemba I.
TANGANYIKA
Zanzibar
Dar es Salaam
L. Rukwa
R. Ruaha
OCEAN
L. Mweru
L. Bangweulu
Lindi
NORTHERN RHODESIA
NYASALAND
L. Nyasa
MOZAMBIQUE
Mozambique
Lusaka
R. Zambesi
Zomba
Livingstone
Salisbury
Umtali
Quelimano
MADAGASCAR
SOUTHERN RHODESIA
Bulawayo
Beira
Lourenço Marques
Scale of Miles
0 100 200 400 600

PREFACE

This book is a Field Guide to the Birds of East and Central Africa, and its scope is epitomised in its title. The region specifically covered is eastern Africa and the Central African Federation—Eritrea, Ethiopia, Somaliland, Uganda, Kenya, Tanganyika, Zanzibar and Pemba Islands, Portuguese East Africa, Nyasaland, Northern Rhodesia and Southern Rhodesia. However its value as a field reference work extends far beyond the political boundaries since full distributions of all the species treated are given for the entire African Continent.

The greatest difficulty confronting the author of any book concerned with the birds of East and Central Africa is one of selectivity in a region with such a rich avifauna. A Field Guide embracing every species defeats its own purpose since any but the most advanced bird-watcher will be bewildered by the large choice when attempting to identify some particular bird. To give an example of this superabundance, no fewer than one thousand and thirty-three full species of birds are found in the relatively small country of Kenya.

After careful consideration it was decided that the only way to present East and Central African birds in Field Guide form was to produce two Field Guides. The first of these—the present volume—covers those birds most likely to be seen by the bird-watcher; in other words the common species and those less common birds which draw attention to themselves by their colourful plumage, their spectacular appearance or their loud calls or songs. A total of 428 such species are fully described and illustrated and the essential field characters of a further 324 are enumerated in the text under the heading "Allied Species." In deciding which species to include in the first Field Guide I have been influenced by the lists of birds drawn up by numerous bird-watchers in East and Central Africa over the past sixteen years. To all these many field naturalists I extend my warmest thanks. I am especially indebted to the Rt. Hon. the Lord Howick, General Sir Gerald Lathbury, Messrs. J. D. Macdonald, P. A. Clancey, K. D. Smith, I. H. Dillingham, Colonel H. Cator, Count B. von Rosen, Colonel Richard Meinertzhagen, Messrs. Tony Archer, Ian Parker and Alec Forbes-Watson for East African records; and to Messrs. C. W. Benson, M. P. Stuart Irwin and Reay H. N. Smithers for data on relative abundance and distribution of certain species found in the Central African Federation.

The second—companion—Field Guide deals with those species not covered by the initial volume; it forms part of the author's *Field Guide to the National Parks of East Africa* (Collins, 1967), which is also illustrated by Rena Fennessy.

Acknowledgements: The data upon which this Field Guide is based have been compiled from many sources. They are drawn primarily from field-notes and specimens personally collected in most of the regions covered; from information and specimens supplied by both resident and visiting naturalists; from a study of all available literature, including the Sir Charles F. Belcher Ornithological Library housed in the Coryndon Museum; and from a critical appraisal of bird specimens in the Coryndon Museum collections and of specimens loaned by many museums all over the world.

It is the author's pleasure to record his deep appreciation and gratitude to the many persons—too numerous to mention individually—who have assisted in many ways, both at the museum and in the field.

The Unknown: There are still many places in eastern Africa which have never been explored zoologically. There can be no doubt that there still remain a small number of undescribed species of birds awaiting discovery. In the heart of the Impenetrable Forest of south-western Kigezi, Uganda, there exists a green turaco with very little red on the wings. This bird has never been collected, although seen by two ornithologists of repute besides the author. A very large all black swift has been observed on Marsabit Mountain in the Northern Frontier Province of Kenya; and a greyish, long-tailed bird with red or chestnut under tail-coverts has been glimpsed in the nearby Mathews Range. The author will always be pleased to meet visitors to East Africa at the Coryndon Museum in Nairobi, and advise them about areas where there is a possibility of finding new species.

PUBLISHER'S NOTE

We regret that in the second impression of this book it has not been possible to bring up to date the names of the countries concerned. The many corrections resulting from recent political changes will all be carried out in time for the next impression: in the meantime we offer our apologies and ask readers to observe the following:

For	Tanganyika	*read*	Tanzania
„	Northern Rhodesia	„	Zambia
„	Southern Rhodesia	„	Rhodesia
„	Nyasaland	„	Malawi

OSTRICH: Struthionidae

Largest living bird; flightless; two toes only on each foot.

OSTRICH *Struthio camelus*

Identification: 7-8′. Unmistakable; adult male black and white; female and immature greyish-brown. Races: the Somali Ostrich differs from the North African and Masai races in having blue-grey neck and thighs. In the North African and Masai races the neck and thighs are pink or flesh-coloured.

Voice: Usually silent; in breeding season male has deep booming call which has been likened to a lion's roar.

Distribution and Habitat: Eastern Africa:—North African race, Sudan and north-eastern Ethiopia; Somali race, Somalilands, eastern and southern Ethiopia, north-eastern Uganda and northern frontier districts of Kenya, mainly north of the Tana River; Masai race occurs south of the Tana River in Kenya and Tanganyika. Elsewhere species occurs in North Africa, south of the Atlas mountains to Nigeria, and in South Africa. The ostrich is now extinct throughout much of its former range. Habitat, on plains, open thorn-bush country and semi-desert. The Somali race is locally common in the Northern Frontier Province of Kenya; the Masai sub-species is common in the Nairobi National Park in Kenya and on the Serengeti plains in Tanganyika.

GREBES: Podicipidae

Duck or teal-sized aquatic birds: slender, pointed bills and "tail-less" appearance characteristic of family; expert divers; feet lobed, not webbed; sexes similar.

GREAT CRESTED GREBE *Podiceps cristatus* p. 52

Identification: 18-20″. Duck size with conspicuous chestnut and black frills on sides of head and a black tuft on each side of crown; immature birds lack chestnut and black head frills. The other two grebes found in Africa are half the size of this species.

Voice: In breeding season a low "keek, keek, keek": usually silent.

Distribution and Habitat: Resident, occurs locally from Senegal and Ethiopia to South Africa. In East Africa it is found on fresh-water lakes and dams. Lake Naivasha in Kenya, and the crater lakes of south-western Uganda and Lake Chila, Northern Rhodesia are favoured localities.

LITTLE GREBE OR DABCHICK *Poliocephalus ruficollis* p. 52

Identification: 10″. Small, plump-looking grebe, half the size of a great crested grebe, with dark chestnut-red face and throat. Immature birds lack chestnut on face and throat and are paler than adults.

Voice: A loud, far-carrying and often prolonged trill: a characteristic sound of African fresh-water lakes.

Distribution and Habitat: A common species found throughout Africa in suitable localities. Occurs on fresh-water and brackish lakes, dams, ponds and slowly flowing rivers: rarely on coast. Abundant on all the Rift Valley lakes in East Africa.

Allied Species: The Black-necked Grebe (*Proctopus caspicus*) is a rare resident on inland lakes in East Africa. It is slightly larger than the Little Grebe and has a black head and neck, with a patch of golden-chestnut plumes on each side of the head. The immature differs from the immature Little Grebe by its thinner, more up-tilted bill.

CORMORANTS: Phalacrocoracidae

Dark-plumaged, moderately long-necked water birds with strong hook-tipped bills: small goose or duck sized; swim and dive to capture food, mainly fish and amphibians.

WHITE-NECKED CORMORANT *Phalacrocorax carbo* p. 92

Identification: 36″. Large blackish-plumaged water bird with white cheeks, neck and upper breast: immature birds have entire underparts white, sometimes with indistinct brown spots on chest. Swims low in water with body submerged. Often perches with wings held half open, a characteristic attitude of cormorants and darters. Differs from Long-tailed Cormorant (Reed Duiker) in much larger size, white neck and breast in adult plumage and relatively shorter tail.

Voice: Nesting birds produce a series of guttural croaks.

Distribution and Habitat: Occurs on inland waters throughout East Africa, south to Rhodesias and Nyasaland: also recorded from eastern

Belgian Congo. It is especially numerous on Lake Victoria and on Lakes George and Edward in western Uganda.

Allied Species: The Socotran Cormorant (*Phalacrocorax nigrogularis*) is an entirely bronze-black species which is restricted to the Red Sea coasts. It is slightly smaller than the White-necked Cormorant. The immature has the underparts dusky-white, heavily flecked with greyish-brown. This is an entirely marine cormorant which has not been recorded from fresh or inland waters.

LONG-TAILED CORMORANT OR REED DUIKER

Phalacrocorax africanus p. 92

Identification: 22-24″. Distinguished from White-necked Cormorant by small size, entirely black underparts of adult and relatively longer tail. Immature birds are brownish-white below.

Voice: Silent.

Distribution and Habitat: Occurs commonly throughout the Ethiopian region in suitable localities. It occurs on inland waters and on the coast. It is abundant on lakes in Uganda and Tanganyika and on Lake Rudolf in Kenya.

DARTERS: Anhingidae

Large, long-necked, cormorant-like water birds with long tails. Darters differ from cormorants in having sharply pointed, not hooked bills. Darters habitually swim very low in the water with only the head and neck showing, giving a very good imitation of a snake swimming. This is the origin of the name "snake bird" often bestowed upon this species.

AFRICAN DARTER *Anhinga rufa*

p. 92

Identification: 38″. Resembles a very long-necked, long-tailed cormorant but has slender pointed bill, not a hooked bill. The neck has a characteristic "kink" which is conspicuous both when bird is settled and when it is in flight. Adults have chestnut necks with a white stripe from gape along each side of neck; underparts black. Immature is much paler with buffish-brown belly.

Voice: Usually silent: at nest sometimes utters low croaking grunts.

Distribution and Habitat: Inhabits inland waters, favouring slow-flowing rivers and fresh-water lakes, throughout Ethiopian region in suitable localities. It is common throughout East and Central Africa.

PELICANS: Pelecanidae

Very large water birds with long, hook-tipped bills and a naked pouch suspended from the mandible and upper part of throat.

WHITE PELICAN *Pelecanus onocrotalus* p. 32

Identification: 60-70". Adults entirely white, deeply suffused salmon-pink in breeding plumage, except for black and grey flight feathers. Immature plumage pale buffish-brown, becoming whiter with successive moults. This species is a much larger bird than the pale French-grey Pink-backed Pelican; the two species are often found in the same flock. Pelicans are often observed soaring in thermal currents: the flight is characteristic, leisurely wing beats followed by short periods of gliding; the head is carried well back.

Voice: Silent, except for grunting notes at nest.

Distribution and Habitat: Resident, migrant and spasmodic visitor on larger areas of inland water; rare on coast. Occurs throughout Ethiopian Region. In East Africa vast numbers breed in the Lake Rukwa area in southern Tanganyika; is very common on many other lakes, especially Lakes George and Edward in western Uganda.

PINK-BACKED PELICAN *Pelecanus rufescens* p. 32

Identification: 54". Adults pale French-grey with a very well-developed nape crest. The deep vinous-pink rump and back are conspicuous only when the bird is in flight. Pale grey plumage, large crest and small size distinguish adults from all plumages of White Pelican. Immature birds best identified by small size, about two-thirds that of immature White Pelican.

Voice: Generally silent, but sometimes noisy at nesting colonies, uttering series of guttural croaks.

Distribution and Habitat: Resident and local migrant on inland waters throughout Ethiopian Region; uncommon in coastal areas. Common in East Africa, especially in Uganda.

HERONS and EGRETS: Ardeidae

Tall and graceful wading birds with lax plumage. In flight the head is carried well back on the shoulders with the neck curved: cranes, storks and spoonbills fly with their necks extended.

GREY HERON *Ardea cinerea* (M & R) p. 33

Identification: 36-40″. Distinguished from Goliath and Purple Herons by lacking rufous in plumage; from Black-headed Heron by white neck and crown, the Black-headed Heron's neck and crown are black. The immature Grey Heron differs from immature Black-headed Heron in having dark streaked, not unspotted buffish-white underparts.

Voice: A harsh, loud "raark" when flushed; utters various croaking calls at nest.

Distribution and Habitat: Resident and winter visitor in small numbers throughout Ethiopian Region on inland waters and the coast. It is a much less common species than the Black-headed Heron. Like that species it is sometimes found a long way from water when hunting mole-crickets and frogs. In East and Central Africa it occurs in small numbers in suitable localities, for example Lake Naivasha in Kenya and Lakes George and Edward in Uganda.

BLACK-HEADED HERON *Ardea melanocephala* p. 33

Identification: 38″. A grey, black and white-plumaged heron, slightly smaller than Grey Heron from which it may be distinguished by its black crown and neck: immature has darker head and neck than immature Grey Heron and lacks streaks on underparts. Lack of rufous in plumage distinguishes species from Goliath and Purple Herons.

Voice: A loud nasal "kuark": also a variety of croaking and squarking calls at nest.

Distribution and Habitat: Resident on inland waters and on the coast throughout the Ethiopian Region, common in East Africa. This heron is often found away from water when hunting mole-crickets and grass-hoppers.

GOLIATH HERON *Ardea goliath* p. 33

Identification: 55-60″. This is the largest of our herons; its size, grey upperparts and mainly rufous-chestnut head, neck and underparts distinguish the Goliath Heron from all other herons. The Purple Heron, which is little more than half the size of the Goliath Heron, is a miniature edition in all plumages of the larger bird. The immature Goliath Heron is paler and browner than the adult and has the underparts streaked greyish-white.

Voice: A loud, deep "arrk", usually uttered when flushed.

Distribution and Habitat: Uncommon and local resident in very small numbers throughout the Ethiopian Region. It is found both on inland waters and on the coast. In East Africa favoured localities are Lakes Naivasha and Rudolf in Kenya, Lake Edward in Uganda and the Rukwa region in Tanganyika.

PURPLE HERON *Ardea purpurea* (M & R) p. 33

Identification: 30-36″. A medium-sized, rather slim, grey and chestnut heron with a rufous neck in all plumages. The Grey and Black-headed Herons have no rufous in plumage; the Goliath Heron is a very much larger bird. The immature Purple Heron is paler than the adult and mainly rufous.

Voice: Usually silent, but sometimes utters a short "aark" when flushed or when flying in to alight at nest. Utters various croaks when nesting.

Distribution and Habitat: A local resident in swamps, and in reed and papyrus beds bordering larger lakes throughout the Ethiopian Region. Numbers augmented October to April by winter visitors from Europe and western Asia. In East Africa the species is common in the swamps of southern Tanganyika, Lake Naivasha in Kenya and Lake Kyoga in Uganda.

GREAT WHITE EGRET *Casmerodius albus* p. 33

Identification: 34-36″. Plumage entirely white at all ages. This is the largest of the African egrets being equal in size to the common Black-headed Heron. Legs entirely black; bill black, yellow and black, or entirely yellow. It may be recognised by its large size and noticeably long bill, and its entirely black legs. The Yellow-billed Egret, with which it may at times be confused, is a much smaller bird with a stumpy-looking yellow bill; the black-billed Little Egret has black legs but contrasting yellow toes; the Buff-backed Heron or Cattle Egret, in its all white non-breeding and juvenile plumage, has a yellow bill and yellowish or flesh-coloured legs.

Voice: A croaking "ark," not unlike the call of the Black-headed Heron.

Distribution and Habitat: An uncommon and local species throughout the Ethiopian Region. It inhabits swamps, borders of lakes, flooded areas and the sea coast. It may be found in small numbers in most suitable areas of East and Central Africa, but is most frequent on the coast: many pairs breed in the great heron colony near Garsen on the Tana River, Kenya.

YELLOW-BILLED EGRET *Mesophoyx intermedius* p. 33

Identification: 26″. Plumages entirely white; legs black except for small yellow area above tibia-tarsus joint (*not* a good field character); bill yellow. Much smaller than Great White Egret, but may be confused at a distance when stumpy-looking bill is a better field character than size. Little Egret differs in having black bill and black legs with yellow toes; Buff-backed Heron (Cattle Egret) in non-breeding plumage has yellowish or flesh-coloured legs.

Voice: Generally silent but sometimes utters a short "kwark."

Distribution and Habitat: Resident in French Equatorial Africa, Eastern and Central Africa and South Africa. Locally common in Kenya, Uganda and Tanganyika. Frequents swamps, margins of lakes, flooded areas and the coast. Common on Kafue Flats in Northern Rhodesia.

LITTLE EGRET *Egretta garzetta* p. 33

Identification: 22-24″. All plumages normally entirely white, bill black, legs black with conspicuous yellow toes. Combination of black bill and yellow toes distinguish Little Egret from other egrets and white plumaged Buff-backed Heron. Sometimes this egret has a grey or partially grey plumage phase: this has been recorded several times on the Tanganyika coast. In this plumage it would resemble a Reef Heron (which sometimes has a white phase) but this bird has an orange-yellow bill.

Voice: A brief, hoarse croak.

Distribution and Habitat: Resident throughout the Ethiopian Region, often common. Frequents marshes, swamps, lakes, flooded areas, mangrove swamps and the sea-shore. Occurs in all suitable localities in East and Central Africa.

Allied Species: The Reef Heron (*Egretta schistacea*) has a normal grey phase, a white phase and individuals in particoloured plumage. It differs from the Little Egret in having an orange-yellow bill. It occurs along the coast of the Red Sea. There are unconfirmed reports of its presence on the northern Kenya coast. The Black Heron (*Melanophoyx ardesiaca*) is the same size as the Little Egret and also has yellow toes, but its plumage is entirely slate-black: most frequent in coastal areas of East Africa and common on the Barotse Plain in Northern Rhodesia.

The Rufous-bellied Heron (*Erythrocnus rufiventris*) resembles a paler edition of the Black Heron with dark rufous wings and belly; it occurs very uncommonly in swamps in Uganda and Tanganyika, and commonly in swamps and flooded areas in Northern Rhodesia.

BUFF-BACKED HERON OR CATTLE EGRET *Bubulcus ibis*

p. 33

Identification: 20″. Shorter-legged and more thickset than Little Egret and legs dusky yellow or flesh-coloured. Plumage white with biscuit-buff crown, chest and mantle: in non-breeding and immature plumages entirely white, bill yellow. Often seen in association with big game animals and cattle, frequently some distance from water. The Squacco Heron is also thickset but is a much darker bird than the Buff-backed Heron, appearing mainly white only when on the wing; also it has a black-tipped bill.

Voice: Various harsh croaks at nesting colony, otherwise a silent bird.

Distribution and Habitat: Resident and spasmodic migrant in suitable localities throughout the Ethiopian Region. It is common in most areas of East Africa. Frequents swamps, pasture lands, lake margins and, rarely, the coast. Generally associated with herds of cattle and game animals.

SQUACCO HERON *Ardeola ralloides* (M & R)

p. 33

Identification: 18″. Thickset, rather short-legged heron with deep vinous-buff plumage and white wings; in non-breeding plumage upperparts darker, more brownish-buff; the immature is heavily streaked dark brown, above and below. When settled bird appears uniformly coloured and white wings are conspicuous and striking only when bird in flight. In all plumages much darker than Buff-backed Heron; bill dark-tipped.

Voice: A short, harsh croak, "kaak," but usually silent.

Distribution and Habitat: Resident and winter visitor throughout Ethiopian Region; common in East Africa. Frequents swamps, marshes and lakes, especially those with a thick cover of water plants.

Allied Species: The closely allied Madagascar Squacco Heron (*Ardeola idae*) occurs in East and Central Africa as an uncommon non-breeding visitor. Its breeding plumage (rarely observed in Africa) is white with a creamy tinge on crown and mantle: non-breeding and immature birds resemble large Squacco Herons and have heavier bills and broader dark streaking. It occurs each year in the Amboseli National Reserve in Kenya. The Green-backed Heron (*Butorides striatus*) is a small species (16″) with dark grey crown and mantle and paler grey underparts: it occurs locally in swamps, wooded river banks and coastal mangrove swamps.

NIGHT HERON *Nycticorax nycticorax* (M & R) p. 33

Identification: 24″. A very thickset grey and white heron with upperparts and crown black; legs short and head very large. Immature pale brown with heavy spots of buffish-white on upperparts and wing coverts; below streaked brown and white. Mainly nocturnal in its habits, keeping to thick cover by day so that it is often overlooked.

Voice: A loud, harsh "aark" uttered at dusk while flying to feeding grounds.

Distribution and Habitat: Local resident and winter visitor in suitable localities throughout the Ethiopian Region. Frequents marshes, swamps, lakes, rivers and coastal mangrove swamps where there is suitable cover to suit its nocturnal habits: spends day in shelter of dense reed beds, papyrus swamps or thickly foliaged trees near water. It is common in southern Tanganyika and Lake Kyoga in Uganda: in Kenya it occurs spasmodically in large numbers at Lake Naivasha, and several hundred pairs breed in the great heronry on the Tana River at Garsen.

Allied Species: The much rarer White-backed Night Heron (*Nycticorax leuconotus*) with rufous neck and white back may be encountered in East Africa in the mangrove swamps of Pemba Island, and along the slow-flowing Mara River in southern Kenya: it is common on Barotse Plain, Northern Rhodesia. Two races of the Little Bittern (*Ixobrychus minutus*), the resident African bird with deep chestnut neck and the paler European race occur in suitable reed and papyrus beds in East Africa, alongside the even smaller (10″) Dwarf Bittern (*Ardeirallus sturmii*) with crown, neck and upperparts dark slate-grey. Both species are skulkers in thick cover and are at least partly nocturnal.

HAMMERKOP: Scopidae

A medium-sized brown bird, about the size of a cattle egret, with a superficial resemblance to both the herons and the storks. It is remarkable for its gigantic nest, a stick structure with a side entrance hole, placed in a tree near water.

HAMMERKOP *Scopus umbretta* p. 32

Identification: 22-24″. Entire plumage dusky brown with thick crest—the origin of the bird's name. The immature resembles the adult.

Voice: A series of shrill, piping whistles: at times when several birds are present the noise is considerable.

Distribution and Habitat: Resident throughout Ethiopian Region in suitable localities: local in small numbers in East and Central Africa. It occurs in the immediate vicinity of water, favouring slowly running streams and rivers. Feeds upon frogs and is semi-nocturnal in its habits. In Kenya it may be seen along the Athi River in the Nairobi National Park and at Amboseli.

WHALE-HEADED STORK: Balaenicipitidae

A very large grey water bird, the size of a marabou stork, with a gigantic shoe-shaped bill.

WHALE-HEADED STORK *Balaeniceps rex* p. 32

Identification: 60″. Plumage entirely grey with a huge boat or shoe-shaped bill and a tiny "top-knot" crest. Not to be confused with any other species.

Voice: Produces a chatter with its bill, in the same manner as a marabou stork.

Distribution and Habitat: A very local and uncommon resident in the heart of papyrus swamps in the Sudan, the eastern Belgian Congo, Uganda, and the Bangweulu swamps of Northern Rhodesia (rare). In East Africa it occurs in the Murchison Falls National Park and on Lake Kyoga in Uganda.

STORKS: Ciconiidae

Large, long-legged, long-necked birds with long, usually straight bills: necks extended in flight, not drawn back as in the heron family.

WHITE STORK *Ciconia ciconia* (M) p. 48

Identification: 44″. Identified by white plumage, black flight feathers and *straight* red bill and legs. The Wood Ibis (Yellow-billed Stork) may be confused, but is pink-plumaged and yellow bill is down-curved, the face unfeathered and red, and the tail black.

Voice: Silent: birds in flocks sometimes produce a chatter with their bills.

Distribution and Habitat: A winter visitor to Africa; widespread but appearances tend to be spasmodic, dependent on presence of grasshoppers and locusts which form main diet. Occurs, usually in flocks, on open plains, semi-desert country and cultivated or pastureland. Has been recorded as nesting in Southern Africa. In East Africa common on the Serengeti plains in Tanganyika and the Rift Valley in Kenya.

WOOLLY-NECKED STORK *Dissoura episcopus* p. 48

Identification: 34″. A glossy black stork easily recognised by its white woolly neck and black forehead.

Voice: Usually silent, but reputed to utter harsh, raucous cry when nesting.

Distribution and Habitat: A comparatively rare species recorded over most of the Ethiopian Region except the Somaliland Protectorate. In East Africa most frequent on some of the Uganda lakes and along the Kenya and Tanganyika coast: uncommon and local in the Rhodesias. Occurs, usually singly or in pairs, at the margins of shallow lakes inland and on old exposed coral reefs on the coast.

ABDIM'S or WHITE-BELLIED STORK *Sphenorynchus abdimii* p. 48

Identification: 32″. A metallic-glossed black stork with a white belly and white lower back and rump. Bill deep green to carmine red at base; legs and feet dusky with pink joints. Black neck distinguishes species from Woolly-necked Stork: the larger European Black Stork has black back.

Voice: Sometimes, in flocks, utters a weak peeping call, but generally a silent bird.

Distribution and Habitat: Occurs usually in flocks, mainly on plains or in semi-desert country where it is attracted by grasshoppers and locusts. Occurs over most of Ethiopian Region, breeding in the north and migrating southwards to Transvaal (rare south of this area) South Africa, October to March. In Northern Rhodesia often abundant on migration. In East Africa locally common.

Allied Species: The European Black Stork (*Ciconia nigra*) is a much larger bird, about the size of a White Stork, with a black, not white, back and red bill and legs. It is a scarce winter visitor to East Africa and a rare resident in the Rhodesias.

OPEN-BILL STORK *Anastomus lamelligerus* p. 48

Identification: 36″. Plumage entirely black at all ages; bill long and stout, the cutting edges curving away from each other so that a wide gap is left when the bill is closed: this character is easily observed in the field.

Voice: Generally silent, but sometimes utters weak croak when several birds are feeding together.

Distribution and Habitat: Local resident, sometimes common, in suitable localities throughout the Ethiopian Region, except forested areas and extreme south. It inhabits swamps and marshes, flooded areas and along slowly flowing rivers: distribution is governed by the presence of certain large water snails which form its main diet. In East Africa it is common on lakes in Uganda and southern Tanganyika: several hundred pairs breed at the Tana River heronry at Garsen in Kenya.

SADDLE-BILL STORK *Ephippiorhynchus senegalensis* p. 32

Identification: 66″. Easily recognised by very large size, black and white plumage (in flight the wing feathers are white), and its distinctive red, black and yellow bill. Immature resembles adult but is duller.

Voice: Silent, except for bill chattering.

Distribution and Habitat: Widely distributed in very small numbers throughout the Ethiopian Region, except extreme south and the Somalilands. Frequents swamps, marshes and edges of inland waters, solitary or in pairs or family parties: everywhere uncommon. In East Africa most frequent in Uganda and Tanganyika; rare in Kenya, except at Amboseli National Reserve where several pairs breed. In Uganda it may be seen in both the Queen Elizabeth and Murchison Falls National Parks: widespread in Central Africa, but not common.

MARABOU STORK *Leptoptilos crumeniferus* p. 32

Identification: 60″. A very large stork, grey above and with grey wings; white below with a white ruff at the base of a flesh-pink neck; adults develop a large air-filled pouch which hangs from the front of the neck.

Voice: Generally silent, except for bill rattling, but utters a variety of croaks and grunts at breeding colony.

Distribution and Habitat: Resident and local migrant throughout Ethiopian Region in suitable habitats, but rare or absent in extreme south: a common bird in East Africa. It is mainly a scavenger and associates with vultures at carrion of all sorts: it also occurs near open areas of water, where it feeds on frogs; it is also an important destroyer of locusts.

YELLOW-BILLED STORK OR WOOD IBIS *Ibis ibis* p. 48

Identification: 42″. A pinkish white and black stork; adults in breeding plumage are suffused with deep carmine-pink; bill, down-curved, orange-yellow. May be confused with White Stork, but down-curved bill, bare red face and black tail distinguish it. Immature birds duller and greyer in general plumage than adults.

Voice: Generally silent but utters various harsh guttural calls at nesting colony.

Distribution and Habitat: Resident throughout Ethiopian Region in suitable areas. Common in East Africa. It occurs on inland waters and also locally on the coast.

IBISES and SPOONBILLS: Threskiornithidae

Ibises are characterised by their relatively thin, down-curved bills: spoonbills lose this bill character when the young bird develops the spatulate tip. Ibises and Spoonbills fly with the neck straight out, not tucked in like the herons.

SACRED IBIS *Threskiornis aethiopicus* p. 48

Identification: 30″. White plumage, naked black head and neck, and patch of purple-black plumes on lower back render identification easy. The immature bird lacks the plumes, and the head and neck are covered with mottled black and white feathers.

Voice: Generally silent, but sometimes utters a harsh croak.

FLAMINGOS, PELICANS, HAMMERKOP and STORKS

1
2
3
4
5
6
7
8

1
a
b
2
3
a
b
4
5
6
8
9
10

HERONS and EGRETS

1. **SQUACCO HERON** page 26
   a, *Adult:* Buffish back; white wings very conspicuous in flight.
   b, *Juvenile:* Striped breast; white wings.
2. **PURPLE HERON** 24
   Slender, dark with rufous neck; much smaller than Goliath Heron. Immature paler and sandier.
3. **NIGHT HERON** 27
   a, *Juvenile:* Brown; whitish spots on back and wings.
   b, *Adult:* Thickset; white breast, black back, black head.
4. **YELLOW-BILLED EGRET** 25
   Black legs and toes; stumpy yellow bill.
5. **GREAT WHITE EGRET** 24
   Large, white; black legs and toes; bill yellow or blackish and yellow.
6. **LITTLE EGRET** 25
   Small, white; black legs, yellow toes, black bill.
7. **BUFF-BACKED HERON or CATTLE EGRET** 26
   Buffish plumes; immature and non-breeding birds entirely white; bill and feet yellowish or flesh-coloured.
8. **GOLIATH HERON** 23
   Very large; rufous neck. Immature paler and sandier.
9. **BLACK-HEADED HERON** 23
   Large; black crown and hind neck.
10. **GREY HERON** 23
    Large; pale grey; white crown.

Distribution and Habitat: Resident throughout Ethiopian Region: common in suitable localities in East Africa. Frequents marshes, swamps, pasture land and flood plains.

HADADA IBIS *Hagedashia hagedash* p. 48

Identification: 30″. Entire plumage olive-grey, rather paler on underparts, head and neck; metallic green wash on back and wing coverts: metallic wash conspicuous only under good viewing conditions.

Voice: This species' loud, far-reaching call "hah—hah—hah" is its most distinctive field character, and one of the best known of African bird sounds.

Distribution and Habitat: Resident throughout the Ethiopian Region in suitable places: common in East Africa. Frequents swamps, marshes, flooded areas, rivers with a margin of trees, edges of lakes and pasture-land.

Allied Species: The Green Ibis (*Lampribis olivacea*) is a slightly larger bird with a crested head: it occurs in mountain forest on Mt. Kenya and the Aberdare Range in Kenya, and on the Usambara Mts. and Kilimanjaro in Tanganyika. It has a honking, goose-like call: it is more often heard than seen. The Wattled Ibis (*Bostrychia carunculata*) differs from the Green Ibis in having a throat wattle and conspicuous white wing coverts. It is confined to the highlands of Ethiopia and Eritrea.

GLOSSY IBIS *Plegadis falcinellus* (M & R) p. 48

Identification: 24″. Very dark-looking birds, at times appearing black in certain lights and at a distance: plumage dark blackish chestnut with purple, green and bronze metallic wash: head and neck paler, uniform chestnut: immature and winter-plumaged birds lack the chestnut in plumage but retain more or less of the metallic wash.

Voice: A harsh, heron-like "kaar" at nesting colony.

Distribution and Habitat: Local resident throughout Ethiopian Region: numbers augmented in winter by northern migrants. In East Africa it occurs from time to time on most of the inland lakes and swamps, but its numbers vary greatly from year to year. It breeds at Lake Naivasha in Kenya, in the Lake Rukwa area of southern Tanganyika, and on the Kafue Flats, Northern Rhodesia.

AFRICAN SPOONBILL *Platalea alba* p. 48

Identification: 36″. The characteristic spatulate bill, white plumage and red face and legs are good field characters. The European Spoonbill has black legs. The African Spoonbill may be mistaken for an egret at a distance, but is thicker-set and less graceful than any of the heron family, and flies with neck extended, not drawn back.

Voice: A double "aark—ark," but usually silent.

Distribution and Habitat: Over most of the Ethiopian Region where suitable conditions prevail. Occurs locally in East Africa and Northern Rhodesia in shallow lakes, swamps and marshes.

Allied Species: The European Spoonbill (*Platalea leucorodia*) is a rare winter visitor to East Africa, and breeds along the Red Sea and Somaliland coasts: it differs from the African Spoonbill in having black legs and lacking the red face of the African bird.

FLAMINGOS: Phoenicopteridae

The flamingos are a group of long-legged, long-necked birds which occur in large flocks on brackish lakes: their bills are characteristic, flattened above with the tip bent down at an angle: plumage mainly pink and white.

GREATER FLAMINGO *Phoenicopterus ruber* (M & R) p. 32

Identification: 56″. Plumage white with a pink wash; outer wing coverts and axillaries bright coral red; flight feathers black; bill pink with black tip. Immature plumage duller and bill greyish or pinkish-grey with black tip. This is a larger and paler bird than the Lesser Flamingo and adults may be distinguished immediately by their pale pink bills: adults of the Lesser Flamingo have a dark carmine-red bill.

Voice: A wave of gruntings and murmurations, with an occasional goose-like honk.

Distribution and Habitat: A local resident and non-breeding visitor to brackish lakes, rarely to coastal areas, in the Ethiopian Region. In East Africa occurs in varying numbers on all brackish water lakes and breeds on Lake Elmenteita, Kenya and Lake Natron in Tanganyika. Numbers apparently augmented by winter visitors from the north between October and April.

LESSER FLAMINGO *Phoeniconaias minor* p. 32

Identification: 40″. Plumage deep pink, much brighter than Greater Flamingo; bill dark carmine-red with black tip. Immatures paler and duller. Adults differ from Greater Flamingo by their smaller size, dark red, not pink, bill and much richer general colour.

Voice: The same general murmurations as the Greater Flamingo.

Distribution and Habitat: Frequents brackish inland and coastal (rare) waters, local but widely distributed in Ethiopian Region. In East Africa sometimes present in gigantic flocks on Lake Nakuru (ca. 2,000,000 birds) and Lake Natron, in the Rift Valley. Breeds on the latter lake, and spasmodically at Mweru Marsh, Northern Rhodesia.

DUCKS and GEESE: Anatidae

The Ducks and Geese are an easily recognised group of birds, characterised by webbed feet and by structure of the bill, with its nail-like tip and row of lamellae along the edges.

MACCOA DUCK *Oxyura maccoa* p. 52

Identification: 16″. Diving duck; bright chestnut back and flanks, black head and neck and cobalt-blue bill render male easy to recognise: female drab, best recognised by habit—shared by male—of swimming very low in the water with the tail cocked at right angles. The African Pochard may be mistaken for this species but it swims higher in the water and the male's bill is pale grey not bright blue.

Voice: Usually silent, but male in breeding season produces a great variety of deep, far-carrying frog-like croaks and growls.

Distribution and Habitat: Inland lakes, fresh or brackish water, where there is an abundance of reeds, sedges or papyrus. Resident eastern and southern Africa, but everywhere uncommon. In East Africa it may be found on certain of the Rift Valley lakes, especially Naivasha, Elmenteita and Nakuru, and the Crater Highlands lakes in northern Tanganyika.

WHITE-BACKED DUCK *Thalassornis leuconotus* p. 52

Identification: 15″. A mottled dark brown and fulvous diving duck with a crescent-shaped white patch between the bill and the eye. Has a white back, but this character is seen usually only when the bird is in flight away from the observer. It is tamer than many other ducks and like the Maccoa Duck it is reluctant to fly.

Voice: Usually silent, but sometimes utters a short whistle.

Distribution and Habitat: Local resident on inland waters, often small dams, where there is an abundance of aquatic vegetation. Occurs in Nigeria, eastwards to Ethiopia, south to southern Africa. In East Africa it is common on Lake Naivasha.

AFRICAN POCHARD *Aythya erythrophthalma* pp. 52, 53

Identification: 15″. A uniformly coloured, very dark-looking diving duck with a white patch in wings during flight: bill pale grey. Male may be mistaken for drake Maccoa at a distance, but does not possess chestnut back and bill is pale grey, not bright cobalt blue.

Voice: Normally a silent duck, but sometimes utters a brief quack in flight.

Distribution and Habitat: Ethiopia in the east, Angola in the west, south to the Cape; resident and local migrant. In East Africa its numbers increase from October onwards, the birds leaving again in early December. It occurs on inland waters, especially where there is a good growth of papyrus and sedges.

Allied Species: The northern-breeding White-eyed Pochard (*Aythya nyroca*) is a very uncommon winter visitor to East Africa. It is a small edition of the African Pochard but is more chestnut and has a conspicuous white, not orange-red, eye. The European Tufted Duck (*Aythya fuligula*) is another uncommon winter visitor. Both male and female possess characteristic, drooping crest and black and white plumage, the female duller.

EUROPEAN SHOVELER *Spatula clypeata* (M) pp. 52, 53

Identification: 18″. The large spatulate bill is a good character for both male and female. The male is distinctively coloured rufous, white and black: shoulders of wings blue-grey in flight.

Voice: Usually silent but the male has a guttural croak and the female a weak quack.

Distribution and Habitat: Winter visitor to northern part of Ethiopian Region, in East Africa rarely south of northern Tanganyika. Inhabits inland waters. It is probable that the species nests sometimes in East Africa on lakes in Ethiopia and on Lake Naivasha in Kenya.

Allied Species: Although the Cape Shoveler (*Spatula capensis*) is recorded in other works as a resident in Ethiopia and Kenya, it is most unlikely that this duck occurs at all in East Africa: there appear to be no specimens in collections from north of Southern Rhodesia. This bird may be distinguished in the hand by having dark brown shafts to the flight feathers; in the European Shoveler the flight feather shafts are white.

YELLOW-BILLED DUCK *Anas undulata* pp. 52, 53

Identification: 19″. A rather large, dark grey-brown duck with a very conspicuous yellow bill: speculum metallic green edged with black and white.

Voice: A mallard-like quack.

Distribution and Habitat: Resident, Ethiopia in the east, Angola in the west, southwards to South Africa. In East Africa not uncommon but local: decreasing in numbers: uncommon but widespread in Central Africa. Frequents fresh water lakes, dams, pools and swamps.

Allied Species: Two related European species, the Gadwall (*Anas strepera*) and the European Wigeon (*Anas penelope*) occur as uncommon winter visitors in East Africa. The former is a brownish-grey duck, about the size of a yellow-bill with a chestnut and white speculum. The wigeon is a little smaller with a small, goose-like bill, the male vermiculated black and white above and on the flanks, with chestnut neck and head and cream-coloured crown.

AFRICAN BLACK DUCK or BLACK RIVER DUCK *Anas sparsa* p. 53

Identification: 19″. A blackish-looking duck with large white spots on the upperparts.

Voice: A mallard-like quack.

Distribution and Habitat: Nigeria, east to Ethiopia, south to South Africa. In East and Central Africa thinly and very locally distributed. Occurs on wooded streams and rivers, leaving these retreats for dams and more open water generally at dusk.

Allied Species: Hartlaub's Duck (*Pteronetta hartlaubii*), a large chestnut and black duck with blue shoulders, occurs in similar habitats to the Black Duck and on tiny forest streams. In East Africa it occurs in the south-western Sudan and probably western Uganda.

GARGANEY TEAL *Anas querquedula* (M) pp. 52, 53

Identification: 13″. A small duck with pale blue-grey shoulders in both sexes. The drake has head and neck chocolate-brown flecked with white and conspicuous white band from above eye to nape. Female best identified by pale blue-grey shoulders in flight.

Voice: Usually silent, but reputed to utter a croak-like call.

Distribution and Habitat: Common winter visitor, south to the Rhodesias and Tanganyika in the east, the Cameroons in the west. Frequents both fresh and brackish inland waters. Numbers vary in East Africa; in some years abundant, in others uncommon.

Allied Species: The European Pintail (*Anas acuta*) and the European Teal (*Anas crecca*) are less common winter visitors to East Africa. The Pintail may be recognised by its long tail and long neck; the European Teal is darker than the Garganey and lacks the pale blue-grey shoulders. The drake has a chestnut and dark metallic green head.

CAPE WIGEON *Anas capensis* pp. 52, 53

Identification: 14″. A very pale brownish and white duck without a dark cap and with a bright pink bill. It may be confused with the Red-billed Duck, but that species has a dark brown cap and characteristic patch of orange-buff in wings.

Voice: Usually a completely silent bird, but sometimes utters a short whistle; reputed to quack.

Distribution and Habitat: Widespread through the Ethiopian Region but extremely local. It occurs almost entirely on brackish or soda lakes. In East Africa it is fairly common on many of the Rift Valley lakes, especially Lakes Elmenteita, Nakuru and Rudolf in Kenya.

HOTTENTOT TEAL *Anas punctata* pp. 52, 53

Identification: 11″. The smallest of the East African ducks, dark brown in general colour with a blackish-brown cap; sides of bill blue. It is not unlike a very small red-bill duck at a distance, but is easily distinguished by its blue-sided bill, and in flight by a wide white band in wings.

Voice: A thin, reedy whistle: a low quack at times.

Distribution and Habitat: Occurs widely throughout the Ethiopian Region, but rare in the Sudan. Occurs on both fresh and brackish inland waters. In East Africa common on suitable waters where there is a growth of sedges and reeds.

RED-BILLED DUCK *Anas erythrorhyncha* pp. 52, 53

Identification: 15″. Best identified by a combination of red bill, blackish-brown cap which contrasts strongly with pale cheeks and the large pinkish-buff speculum which is very conspicuous in flight. The other red-billed duck, the Cape Wigeon, has no dark cap and no pinkish-buff speculum.

Voice: A weak whistle, but usually silent.

Distribution and Habitat: Ethiopia in the east and Angola in the west, southwards to South Africa. A common species found on both brackish and fresh inland waters. Common in East Africa, especially on the Rift Valley lakes.

WHITE-FACED TREE DUCK *Dendrocygna viduata* pp. 52, 53

Identification: 18″. Both species of tree ducks, or whistling teal as they are often called, stand more erect than other ducks. The combination of white face and barred flanks is very conspicuous in field.

Voice: A loud, clear whistle, uttered repeatedly.

Distribution and Habitat: Distributed locally, in suitable haunts, throughout the Ethiopian Region. In East Africa its numbers and appearance in any given locality vary greatly: it may be absent for several years and then turn up in abundance. Its numbers are more stable in Central Africa where it is common. It frequents inland lakes and marshes, and the coast and islands off the coast.

FULVOUS TREE DUCK *Dendrocygna bicolor* pp. 52, 53

Identification: 20″. An erect-standing, long-legged duck, tawny-rufous in colour with a number of cream stripes along flanks; in flight white rump conspicuous. Flies with slow wing beats for a duck and legs extend behind tail.

Voice: Loud, two-noted whistles.

Distribution and Habitat: Resident and local migrant from the Chad region and the Sudan and Ethiopia, south to Natal. In East and Central Africa occurs locally on inland lakes and swamps, uncommon on the coast.

PYGMY GOOSE *Nettapus auritus* pp. 52, 53

Identification: 13″. Thickset, teal-sized waterfowl with greenish-black upperparts and bright rufous flanks; white wingbar in flight. Found in pairs or small flocks among water-lilies and other water plants; bright orange-yellow bill of drake very conspicuous. In flight, at a distance, it may be mistaken for a Hottentot Teal if the rufous flanks are not observed.

Voice: A soft two or three note whistle, not often heard.

Distribution and Habitat: A resident, local but sometimes abundant, over most of the Ethiopian Region. Occurs on fresh-water lakes and swamps where there is an abundant growth of water-lilies. In East Africa most frequent on Lake Kyoga in Uganda and in various localities in southern and north-western Tanganyika; an uncommon bird in Kenya.

Common in Central Africa on pools and lagoons with plentiful aquatic vegetation.

KNOB-BILLED GOOSE *Sarkidiornis melanotos* pp. 52, 53

Identification: male 24″; female 20″. Large size, black and white plumage and knob at base of drake's bill are good characters. At close quarters black upperparts are seen to be washed with metallic green and copper.

Voice: Generally a completely silent bird, but sometimes utters a creaking whistle.

Distribution and Habitat: Locally distributed in suitable areas throughout the Ethiopian Region; a migrant in some areas, but movements not understood. Occurs on inland lakes and swamps. In East and Central Africa it is locally common, but numbers and appearances vary; usually present on Lake Naivasha in Kenya.

EGYPTIAN GOOSE *Alopochen aegyptiacus* pp. 52, 53

Identification: 24″. Plumage generally brown with contrasting pure white shoulders conspicuous in flight. Occurs in pairs or in flocks; single birds seldom seen. Often alights in trees, especially over water.

Voice: A loud, strident honking.

Distribution and Habitat: Resident throughout the Ethiopian Region in suitable haunts. Occurs on inland waters and at times, during rains, on open plains. Also found along smaller water courses. Common in East and Central Africa, especially on fresh-water lakes in Rift Valley.

Allied Species: The Blue-winged Goose (*Cyanochen cyanopterus*) is a pale brownish-grey goose, with a brant-goose-like bill and pale blue shoulders. It is confined to the open meadows of the Ethiopian Highlands.

SPUR-WINGED GOOSE *Plectropterus gambensis* p. 52

Identification: 30-36″. A large goose with metallic glossed black upperparts and a white belly: bill dark flesh-red. Female smaller than male.

Voice: Generally silent, but sometimes utters a whistle.

Distribution and Habitat: Resident and local migrant throughout the Ethiopian Region: usually in small numbers and often absent from apparently suitable haunts. In East Africa occurs on most of the Rift Valley lakes; often common in western Uganda and western Tanganyika.

SECRETARY BIRD: Sagittariidae

The Secretary Bird, of which only one species is known, constitutes a very distinct family of the birds of prey. This large, long-legged, long-tailed, grey bird with black "plus-fours" is a great destroyer of noxious snakes and rodents.

SECRETARY BIRD *Sagittarius serpentarius* p. 92

Identification: 40″. A large pale grey bird, with black flight feathers and tibia and long central tail feathers, seen stalking about in open country: long crest feathers conspicuous, especially when blown by wind.

Voice: Generally silent, but in breeding season produces remarkable croaks and even a lion-like cough at nest, often at night.

Distribution and Habitat: Widely distributed throughout the Ethiopian Region, except in forested areas. Frequents open plains, bush country and farmlands. In East and Central Africa it is uncommon but widely distributed: in the Nairobi National Park several pairs may be encountered.

VULTURES: Aegypiidae

Vultures are large or very large eagle-like birds with long wings, rather short tails and relatively small naked or down-covered heads: usually observed soaring or at carrion.

RUPPELL'S GRIFFON VULTURE *Gyps ruppellii* p. 60

Identification: 34″. A large dark brown vulture with a dark back; feathers, especially of underparts and wing coverts, broadly edged with creamy-white, giving a scaly or spotted appearance. Immature bird appears very pale, the pale feather margins wider than in adult. The adult White-backed Griffon has a conspicuous white rump and is more uniformly coloured: the immature lacks the white rump but is a much darker bird than the immature Ruppell's Griffon. The Nubian or Lappet-faced Vulture is a much larger bird with a massive bill. For underside patterns in flight see illustration.

Voice: Produces harsh squarks when squabbling over carrion.

Distribution and Habitat: Senegal, Nigeria and Cameroons, east to

Eritrea and Ethiopia, south through Uganda and Kenya to Tanganyika. Open country, especially where big game animals exist: also in vicinity of inland cliffs.

WHITE-BACKED VULTURE *Pseudogyps africanus* p. 60

Identification: 32″. Large, dark or pale brown vulture with a conspicuous white rump: some examples, apparently very old birds, are pale creamy-brown. Adults may be distinguished by uniform appearance and white rump: immature birds much darker than Ruppell's Vulture. For underside pattern see illustration.

Voice: Harsh, croaking squarks at carrion.

Distribution and Habitat: Senegal, eastwards to Eritrea and Ethiopia, southwards to Transvaal, South Africa. Common in East Africa; local in Central Africa. Soars above big game country: nests in forest or riverside trees, not cliffs.

NUBIAN or LAPPET-FACED VULTURE *Torgos tracheliotus* p. 60

Identification: 40″. A huge, dark brown vulture with a massive bill: folds of naked skin on head and face purplish-flesh. For underside pattern see illustration.

Voice: Silent birds, utter a low squark when fighting over carrion.

Distribution and Habitat: West and North Africa, south to South Africa. In East and Central Africa an uncommon resident and very local: occurs most frequently in the big game areas: occasional elsewhere.

WHITE-HEADED VULTURE *Trigonoceps occipitalis* p. 60

Identification: 32″. This vulture differs from all others in having a striking white crown, white secondaries (in adult) white belly and red bill. The immature bird is best recognised by its white belly, the secondaries being brown or parti-coloured.

Voice: Silent, except perhaps for a hissing squeal at carrion.

Distribution and Habitat: Of wide distribution in the Ethiopian Region but everywhere very uncommon and local. In East Africa most frequent on big game plains in Kenya and Tanganyika.

HOODED VULTURE *Necrosyrtes monachus* p. 60

Identification: 26″. A small, entirely dark brown vulture with a rather short, rounded tail and a thin, slender bill. The immature plumage of the Egyptian Vulture resembles this species but has a distinctive wedge-shaped tail.

Voice: A silent species: no call recorded.

Distribution and Habitat: Widely distributed throughout the Ethiopian Region, found both in open plains and big game country and also in forested areas and native cultivation. A common bird throughout the settled areas of Uganda, less common but far from rare in Tanganyika and Kenya: widespread in Central Africa.

EGYPTIAN VULTURE *Neophron percnopterus* p. 60

Identification: 26″. A small black and white vulture with a distinctive wedge-shaped white tail; bare face yellow; bill slender. Immature birds are brown and may be mistaken for the wider winged Hooded Vulture, but wedge shaped tail distinctive. The Palmnut Vulture or Vulturine Fish Eagle (*Gypohierax angolensis*) may be mistaken for an Egyptian Vulture but has the tail mainly black.

Voice: Silent birds; sometimes make a hissing noise at carrion.

Distribution and Habitat: Absent from the West African forest region, otherwise locally distributed throughout Ethiopian Region, commoner in the north. Not recorded from the Rhodesias. In small numbers only in East Africa, but breeds in Rift Valley. In the north common around human settlements, where it feeds on human excrement. In Kenya and Tanganyika most frequently encountered around Masai encampments.

Allied Species: The Lammergeyer or Bearded Vulture (*Gypaetus barbatus*) shares with the Egyptian Vulture the character of a wedge-shaped tail, but is a much larger bird with rusty-buff underparts. It is rare outside the highlands of Ethiopia. The Palmnut Vulture (see above) has mainly white primaries and a very broad black band on the tail.

FALCONS, KITES, EAGLES, BUZZARDS, SPARROW-HAWKS, HARRIERS and allies: Falconidae

Falcons are characterised by their thick-set build, sharply pointed wings and often extremely fast flight; they generally kill their prey by swooping on it at high speed.

Kites have angular wings and are best distinguished by the more or less deeply forked tails and buoyant flight.

Eagles are medium or large birds of prey with legs feathered to the toes, but harrier-eagles have bare tarsus. In flight heads appear larger than vultures' heads.

Buzzards resemble small eagles but have bare legs and much broader wings: all buzzards except mountain buzzard are often seen perched on telegraph poles.

Sparrow-hawks and allies are smaller than buzzards and have short rounded wings and usually long tails.

Harriers are slimly built hawks with long wings and long tails; flight buoyant: they hunt by quartering the ground a few feet up.

PEREGRINE *Falco peregrinus* pp. 61, 64

Identification: 14-18″. Recognised as a falcon by its heavy but streamlined build and pointed wings; flight direct, rapid wing strokes followed by short glides. Species recognised by dark or medium slate-grey crown which does not contrast with colour of upperparts and heavy black moustache patches. The Lanner Falcon is paler grey with much rufous on crown and nape.

Voice: A rapid, shrill "kek, kek, kek, kek," usually near cliffs.

Distribution and Habitat: Rare resident in suitable localities throughout Ethiopian Region, commoner in north; also winter visitor in varying numbers. Occurs in a variety of habitats, including open country and bush, inland cliffs and native cultivation.

LANNER *Falco biarmicus* pp. 61, 64

Identification: 16-18″. Resembles a pale-coloured Peregrine but distinguishable by rufous or rufous-buff on crown and nape. Underparts whitish-buff, lightly spotted black. The Peregrine has much darker, greyer underparts, barred dusky.

Voice: A shrill "kre-kre-kre" at nesting sites.

Distribution and Habitat: Locally throughout the Ethiopian Region; commoner in northern part of range in Africa. In East Africa local and uncommon, but frequent in Turkana, Kenya Colony. Usually found in the vicinity of inland cliffs, but visits more open country.

Allied Species: The Teita Falcon (*Falco fasciinucha*), a rare species confined to East and Central Africa, south to Victoria Falls, is a small edition of a Lanner Falcon, but may be recognised by its relatively much shorter tail and pale rump. In East Africa it occurs in the Tsavo National Park and at the Amboseli National Reserve. The Saker Falcon (*Falco cherrug*) is like a very large pale greyish-brown Peregrine with streaked underparts and bluish-white legs. It is an uncommon winter visitor to north-eastern Africa. The Bat Hawk or Andersson's Pern (*Machaerhamphus alcinus*) has the silhouette of a falcon: it is mainly dark brown in colour. It appears at dusk and catches bats and late roosting swallows on the wing. It is widely distributed through the Ethiopian Region but is everywhere rare. Voi and Makindu in Kenya are likely localities for this uncommon bird.

AFRICAN HOBBY *Falco cuvieri* p. 61

Identification: 11-12″. Resembles a miniature Peregrine but upperparts much brighter blue-grey and dark rufous below. The European Hobby is paler, buffish-white below and rather larger. Teita Falcon has shorter tail and is very pale on the rump.

Voice: Shrill, piping call notes, "ke, ke, ke, ke, ke, ke, ke."

Distribution and Habitat: Resident Ghana, eastwards to Ethiopia, south through eastern Congo, Uganda and Kenya to eastern South Africa: everywhere very uncommon and local. Frequents edges of forest, native cultivation and savannah country.

Allied Species: The European Hobby (*Falco subbuteo*) is a winter visitor and passage migrant to East and Central Africa. It is slightly larger and much paler than the African Hobby, the underparts being pale buff with black streaks and the thighs rufous.

RED-NECKED FALCON *Falco chiquera* p. 61

Identification: 12-14″. A thickset, grey falcon with a conspicuous chestnut cap and nape, and black and white barred underparts. Seen from behind it may be mistaken for a Lanner Falcon but a view of the barred belly will identify it immediately.

Voice: Shrill "keep, keep, keep."

Distribution and Habitat: Senegal and Gambia, eastwards to Ethiopia, south to South Africa. In East and Central Africa very local in small numbers, almost always in immediate vicinity borassus palms.

EUROPEAN KESTREL *Falco tinnunculus* (M & R) p. 61

Identification: 13-14″. The kestrels are generally less thickset than other falcons: the male European Kestrel may be recognised by presence of black spots on chestnut back; the male Lesser Kestrel has unspotted chestnut back; both sexes of Greater Kestrel have barred upperparts. The female European Kestrel closely resembles female Lesser Kestrel, but the latter is smaller and at close quarters the white claws are distinctive; also it carries its food to its mouth with one foot whilst the feeding European Kestrel holds its prey with two feet in the normal falcon manner. The female European Kestrel may be distinguished from the Greater Kestrel by its black-barred brown tail: the Greater Kestrel has a blue-grey, black-barred tail and creamy white eyes. The East African races of Kestrel are darker than the northern bird.

Voice: The European race is a silent bird in Africa; the African races utter a shrill "kee-kee-kee-kee-kee," usually at their nesting cliffs.

Distribution and Habitat: Resident races occur very locally over much of the Ethiopian Region outside the forest areas: the European race occurs as an abundant winter visitor and passage migrant south to Tanganyika. The northern bird may occur in most habitats outside forest; the resident races are usually found in the vicinity of inland cliffs.

Allied Species: The Fox Kestrel (*Falco alopex*) is an uncommon and local species found from Ghana, eastwards to Ethiopia and in extreme northern Turkana, Kenya Colony. Both sexes are alike: it is larger than a European Kestrel and the entire plumage except black flight feathers is deep coppery-chestnut with short black streaks on upperparts and breast.

GREATER or WHITE-EYED KESTREL *Falco rupicoloides* p. 61

Identification: 14″. Resembles a female European Kestrel at first sight, but may be distinguished by its black-barred, blue-grey tail. At close quarters its white eye is also a good field character. Female European and Lesser Kestrels have a brown barred tail and a brown eye.

Voice: A silent bird, but at nest sometimes utters a weak, kite-like whistle.

Distribution and Habitat: A very local resident in Somaliland, Ethiopia, Kenya, north-eastern Tanganyika, Southern Rhodesia, and South Africa. Occurs in open country and bush country: nests in trees, while the African races of the European Kestrel are mainly cliff nesters.

STORKS, SPOONBILLS, IBISES

1. WOOLLY-NECKED STORK page 29
Woolly white neck and contrasting dark body.

2. OPEN-BILL STORK 30
Black plumage and open bill.

3. ABDIM'S STORK 29
Black and white stork with white rump. Black Stork is larger with black rump and red bill and legs.

4. AFRICAN SPOONBILL 34
Spatulate bill; red face and legs.

5. GLOSSY IBIS 34
Adult: Mainly dark chestnut; metallic gloss.
Juvenile: Darker, less chestnut; appears black at distance.

6. HADADA IBIS 34
Grey plumage; wings washed metallic green.

7. WHITE STORK 29
White, with black on wings; red bill.

8. YELLOW-BILLED STORK or WOOD IBIS 31
Adult: Pinkish-white with black wings and tail; yellow bill.
Juvenile: Body plumage greyish-white.

9. SACRED IBIS 31
Adult: Naked black head and neck.
Juvenile: Neck and head feathered, mottled black and white.

1
2
3
4
5
6
7
8
9

1
2
3
4
5
6 ♀
7 ♂
7 ♀
6 ♂
8

CUCKOOS and COUCALS

1. **COMMON CUCKOO** (African race) page 123
Yellow base to bill: white bars across tail. Migrant European race has upper mandible grey; tail spotted, not barred. Some females and immatures rufous, not grey, barred dusky above and below.

2. **RED-CHESTED CUCKOO** 123
Distinct rufous throat patch: juvenile darker with black throat patch.

3. **BLACK AND WHITE CUCKOO** 124
Conspicuous short white wing bar.

4. **YELLOWBILL or GREEN COUCAL** 127
Conspicuous yellow bill.

5. **DIDRIC CUCKOO** 125
Upperparts coppery-green; tail mainly blackish with white spots —not white with black spots.

6. **EMERALD CUCKOO** 125
Male: Brilliant green plumage and contrasting yellow breast.
Female: Heavily barred underparts.

7. **KLAAS' CUCKOO** 126
Male: Vivid green and white with green chest patches.
Female: Outer tail feathers mainly white.

8. **WHITE-BROWED COUCAL** 126
Clumsy-looking with floundering flight; chestnut wings and whitish eye stripe.

LESSER KESTREL *Falco naumanni* (M) p. 61

Identification: 12″. A small edition of the European Kestrel but upperparts of male bright chestnut without spots; female closely resembles small female European Kestrel but viewed in flight appears pale; at close quarters white claws and method of feeding (Lesser Kestrel carries food to bill in one foot; European Kestrel holds food in both feet in normal falcon manner) will distinguish the two. Lesser and European Kestrels females distinguished from Greater Kestrel by brown barred tails.

Voice: On migration, in huge flocks, utters a sharp chatter.

Distribution and Habitat: Winter visitor and passage migrant to Senegal east to eastern and north-eastern Africa, south to South Africa. Often in huge flocks of many thousand birds on migration. Occurs in a variety of habitats outside forest areas.

Allied Species: The Eastern Red-footed Falcon (*Falco amurensis*) is sometimes found associated with migrating Lesser Kestrels, but is an uncommon bird in East Africa, though in Southern Rhodesia it is commoner than Lesser Kestrel. The male is dark grey with a chestnut abdomen and white under-wing coverts. The female has underparts pale buff, streaked with black.

GREY KESTREL *Falco ardosiaceus* p. 61

Identification: 14″. An entirely grey kestrel with a conspicuous yellow face (bare skin around eyes and base of bill).

Voice: A harsh chatter, and sometimes, usually when nesting, a shrill succession of whistles.

Distribution and Habitat: A West Africa species which extends eastwards to Uganda and western Tanganyika and Kenya. It frequents water-courses where there are trees, wooded areas and native cultivation. Nests in unoccupied nests of hammerkop and may be seen near these structures. Crepuscular in its habits and feeds mainly upon bats.

Allied Species: The darker, slate-grey Sooty Falcon (*Falco concolor*) has the two central tail feathers protruding beyond the others, a character which may be observed in flight: it is a rare species in East Africa, most frequent on the coasts of the Red Sea. Dickinson's Kestrel (*Falco dickinsoni*) occurs in woodlands of Tanganyika and Rhodesias, and also on Pemba Island. It has the underparts grey, the back blackish-grey with a paler head and an almost white rump which is conspicuous as the bird flies.

PYGMY FALCON *Poliohierax semitorquatus* p. 61

Identification: 7½″. A tiny white-breasted hawk with a characteristic shrike-like appearance: this is especially apparent when the bird perches on the topmost branch of some thorn tree. The male has a pale grey back, the female a deep chestnut back. Immature birds resemble the female.

Voice: A shrill series of notes, "ku, ku, ku, ku, ku, ku, ku, ku."

Distribution and Habitat: A local resident in dry bush and savannah country in eastern and southern Africa: does not occur Rhodesias. It is locally common in the Northern Frontier Province and in Turkana, Kenya. It is often seen in the vicinity of buffalo-weaver nests, in which it breeds.

BLACK KITE (European and African races) *Milvus migrans* (M & R) p. 61, 64

Identification: 21-23″. Entire plumage brown to rusty-brown, usually more rufous below: tail conspicuously forked. The resident African races have yellow bills and the head colour not different from colour of upperparts: the European Black Kite has a black bill and a whitish-looking head. Feeds on carrion and also insect pests such as locusts.

Voice: A high-pitched, wavering call, not unlike some species of gull.

Distribution and Habitat: Resident and local migrant throughout the Ethiopian Region in suitable localities: the European race is a winter visitor and passage migrant, mainly to eastern Africa: uncommon in Central Africa. Found in savannah and open country, in cultivated areas, and near lakes and rivers: often in numbers when attracted by carrion or insect swarms.

BLACK-SHOULDERED KITE *Elanus caeruleus* p. 61

Identification: 13″. A thickset, kestrel-sized hawk, pale grey above and white below, with a stumpy, white, slightly forked tail and black "shoulders." Immature birds are darker above with conspicuous white tips to feathers of mantle and wings; below with some rust-brown markings on breast. Behaviour unlike Black Kite, hovers and settles on telegraph wires and poles like a kestrel.

Voice: Usually silent, but sometimes utters a clear piping whistle.

Distribution and Habitat: Resident and local, spasmodic migrant throughout Ethiopian Region. Frequents savannah and open country, cultivation, margins of lakes and rivers and mountain moorland. In East

DUCKS, GREBES and FINFOOT

1. MACCOA DUCK page 36
Male: Bright chestnut with black head and blue bill; both sexes often carry tail cocked up.
Female: Pale cheeks crossed by dark line.

2. WHITE-BACKED DUCK 36
Mottled plumage; white face patch; white rump in flight.

3. AFRICAN POCHARD 37
Uniform plumage; bill pale grey; distinctive female face pattern; white wing patch conspicuous in flight.

4. EUROPEAN SHOVELER 37
Large spatulate bill and blue shoulders in both sexes; male has contrasting white chest and chestnut flanks and belly.

5. HOTTENTOT TEAL 39
Black cap; blue-sided bill.

6. YELLOW-BILLED DUCK 38
Sides of bill bright yellow.

7. GARGANEY TEAL 38
Male: White band on head; blue-grey shoulders.
Female: Pale bluish-grey shoulders.

8. CAPE WIGEON 39
Pale head; pink bill.

9. RED-BILLED DUCK 39
Blackish cap; red bill.

10. WHITE-FACED TREE DUCK 40
White face; barred black and white flanks.

11. FULVOUS TREE DUCK 40
White flank stripes; white rump in flight.

12. PYGMY GOOSE 40
Chestnut flanks; male has orange-yellow bill, female a greenish-yellow bill.

13. PETERS' FINFOOT 86
Long stiff tail; orange-red bill and legs; female and immature paler than male.

14. KNOB-BILLED GOOSE 41
Contrasting black and white plumage; female smaller than male and lacks knob.

15. LITTLE GREBE 20
Chestnut face and throat; immature paler and lacks chestnut.

16. GREAT CRESTED GREBE 19
Black crown tufts and chestnut neck frills.

17. EGYPTIAN GOOSE 41
Brilliant and contrasting white shoulders.

18. SPUR-WINGED GOOSE 41
Black and white; bill flesh-red.

♂
♂
1
♀
3
♀
2
♂
4
♀
5
6
♂
8
7
♀
9
12
♂
10
11
13
14
15
16
17
18

♂
♀
1
♂
♀
2
3
4
5
♂
♀
6
7
8
9
10
11
12

DUCKS in flight

1. **AFRICAN POCHARD** page 37
   White wing patch.
2. **EUROPEAN SHOVELER** 37
   Large spatulate bill; blue-grey shoulders.
3. **HOTTENTOT TEAL** 39
   White wing band; small size.
4. **AFRICAN BLACK DUCK** 38
   White spots on upperparts; frequents streams.
5. **YELLOW-BILLED DUCK** 38
   Conspicuous yellow bill.
6. **GARGANEY TEAL** 38
   Blue-grey shoulders.
7. **CAPE WIGEON** 39
   Pale crown; pink bill.
8. **RED-BILLED DUCK** 39
   Pinkish-buff speculum; dark cap and red bill.
9. **KNOB-BILLED GOOSE** 41
   Black and white plumage; knob at base of bill in adult male.
10. **WHITE-FACED TREE DUCK** 40
    White face; feet extend beyond tail.
11. **FULVOUS TREE DUCK** 40
    White rump; feet extend beyond tail.
12. **EGYPTIAN GOOSE** 41
    White shoulders.

Africa a common species throughout, often abundant when attracted to some particular district by a plentiful supply of food—large insects and rodents: less common in Central Africa.

Allied Species: The smaller and more graceful Swallow-tailed Kite (*Chelictinia riocourii*) is a rare resident species in the northern districts of Kenya, especially Turkana. It may be recognised by its almost tern-like appearance with very long outer tail feathers and a conspicuous small black patch on the underside of the wing in flight. It breeds in colonies in acacia trees in semi-desert country.

VERREAUX'S EAGLE *Aquila verreauxii* pp. 64, 65

Identification: 30-32″. A large black eagle with centre of back and rump white: whitish patch at base of flight feathers conspicuous in flight: silhouette distinctive, see illustration. Immature birds are black with brown tips to feathers above and below. Species may be confused with certain Tawny Eagle plumages at this stage, but build, size and silhouette are distinctive.

Voice: A loud yelping cry, usually at nest.

Distribution and Habitat: A rare and local eagle, resident in the Sudan, Ethiopia, Somaliland, Kenya, Tanganyika, Nyasaland and Rhodesias, and South Africa. This is a mountain eagle, frequenting rocky crags and inland cliffs. It is most frequent in Ethiopia and in Kenya, where several pairs are resident within a hundred miles of Nairobi.

TAWNY EAGLE *Aquila rapax* pp. 64, 65

Identification: 26-30″. A uniformly coloured brown eagle with a rather short, rounded tail: plumages vary greatly from dark brown (uncommon) to brown, rusty brown or pale brown: a rare plumage phase (most frequent in Somaliland) is pale brownish-cream. Immatures usually paler than adults and possess two pale wing bars in flight. Some Steppe Eagles are not distinguishable with certainty in field, but immatures differ in having white or whitish rump, and adults are blackish-brown with golden nape patch. It is the sub-adult Steppe Eagles which are often confused with the Tawny Eagle: it is possible that the two are conspecific. The Brown Harrier Eagle is easily recognised by its large owl-like head and unfeathered whitish legs. Spotted and Lesser Spotted Eagles have white or whitish rumps.

Voice: A raucous yelping cry.

Distribution and Habitat: Resident and local spasmodic migrant throughout Ethiopian Region in suitable areas outside the forest regions. Frequents cultivation, open and savannah areas and mountain country.

Associates with vultures and other carrion feeders at lion kills and around camps. Usually nests in trees.

Allied Species: The Steppe Eagle (*Aquila nipalensis*) is a winter visitor, sometimes common, to east and central Africa. Adults are recognised by their blackish-brown plumage and conspicuous golden nape patch: juveniles by their white rumps and buff-tipped wing coverts. The very similar Spotted and and Lesser Spotted Eagles (*Aquila clanga* and *A. pomarina*) are rare winter visitors to East Africa and difficult to identify; adults are very dark purplish-brown, slightly paler below, usually with some white on the upper tail-coverts. The Spotted Eagle immature has many large white spots on upperparts and a noticeable white V at the base of the tail. The immature Lesser Spotted Eagle is much less spotted and is sparsely marked with white at base of tail: at close-quarters its best field character is a buff patch on the nape. The Brown Harrier Eagle (*Circaetus cinereus*) is easy to identify by its large owl-like head, uniform brown appearance and bare tarsus. This is an uncommon but widely distributed species outside the forest belts in Africa. In East Africa the species seems to be most frequent in savannah country where there are baobab trees.

WAHLBERG'S EAGLE *Aquila wahlbergi* pp. 64, 92

Identification: 22″. A small, rather narrow-winged brown eagle with a short crest on the nape. In flight it may be mistaken for an African Kite, but it has a long narrow unforked tail. At a distance, when size is not a good field character, it may be mistaken for a Tawny Eagle but if settled it may be recognised by its nape crest: if on the wing the relatively long wings and tail serve to identify it. A pale cream-coloured phase occurs, but is rare.

Voice: A two-note whistle.

Distribution and Habitat: Local, generally uncommon, resident over most of the Ethiopian Region except the forested areas and extreme south of South Africa. Occurs in wooded or bush savannah country and along rivers and lake margins where there are trees. In East Africa it is commonest in the woodlands of Tanganyika and locally frequent in Uganda where it occurs in native cultivation. Widespread in Central Africa.

AFRICAN HAWK EAGLE *Hieraaetus spilogaster* p. 65

Identification: 24-28″. A black and white eagle, larger than an augur buzzard: upperparts blackish with white bases of feathers showing through to a greater or lesser extent; underparts white with narrow black streaks on throat and breast: the adult Ayres' Hawk Eagle has heavy black drop-like spots on underparts. The immature African Hawk Eagle is quite unlike the adult, being browner above and unspotted pale rufous below: Ayres' Hawk Eagle immature has the rufous-brown concentrated on breast not over entire underparts, and has whitish tips to feathers of upperparts giving a speckled appearance. In flight the African Hawk Eagle has a black patch at wing joint and flight feathers mainly unspotted white; Ayres' Hawk Eagle has barred flight feathers, and lacks the black patches below wing: see illustration.

Voice: A loud yelping cry at nest and a double or treble whistle.

Distribution and Habitat: A very local and uncommon eagle in suitable localities throughout the Ethiopian Region. It frequents forested and savannah woodlands, usually away from the haunts of humans. In East Africa it occurs in the Tsavo Royal National Park and in the coast forests of Kenya and Tanganyika.

Allied Species: Ayres' Hawk Eagle (*Hieraaetus dubius*) is a smaller bird than the African Hawk Eagle, about the size of an augur buzzard, with heavy drop-like spots on the underparts: it is a rare forest eagle, in East Africa most frequent in the Kenya highlands: it occurs in the forests around Nairobi.

MARTIAL EAGLE *Polemaetus bellicosus* pp. 64, 65

Identification: 30-34″. A very large, massive eagle, brownish-grey above and blackish on the throat; remainder underparts white with a few small dark spots: rounded crest, not always conspicuous. The adult Black-breasted Harrier Eagle resembles the adult Martial Eagle in general colour but is smaller, has unfeathered legs and breast is unspotted: in flight undersides of wings heavily spotted and blotched black in Martial Eagle, unspotted white in Black-breasted Harrier Eagle. The immature plumage of the Martial Eagle has unspotted white underparts and thighs: in this plumage it resembles the immature Crowned Hawk-Eagle, but the latter is slightly washed rufous on chest and has black-spotted legs and thighs.

Voice: Usually silent, but sometimes a short, gulping bark.

Distribution and Habitat: A bird of wide distribution throughout the Ethiopian Region, except the West African forest region. It is, however, uncommon throughout most of its more southerly range where it comes into contact with farming areas. In East Africa it is most frequent in the National Parks, such as Tsavo National Park in Kenya. It frequents savannah and semi-desert bush areas: it is usually encountered perched on top of an acacia or similar tree. It captures prey such as monkeys, hyrax and small antelopes.

CROWNED HAWK EAGLE *Stephanoaetus coronatus* pp. 64, 65

Identification: 32-36″. A massive eagle, the size of the Martial, but with a longer tail and more rounded wings; in silhouette looks like a gigantic sparrow-hawk. Upperparts blackish, with a conspicuous rounded crest—like a halo—and underparts boldly blotched black, orange-rufous and white. The immature bird is paler above and below is whitish, washed with rufous on chest; thighs and legs spotted black. In this dress it could be mistaken for an immature Martial Eagle, but that species has white legs and underparts.

Voice: A variety of musical whistles, rising and falling in pitch and often uttered while flying.

Distribution and Habitat: Of wide distribution in the Ethiopian Region where there are forests and well-wooded areas, but everywhere very uncommon. It is perhaps most frequent in the forests of East Africa and the Belgian Congo. Its presence is usually governed by the presence of monkeys which form its main item of diet.

LONG-CRESTED HAWK EAGLE *Lophoaetus occipitalis* pp. 64, 65

Identification: 20-22″. A blackish eagle with a remarkable long, lax crest giving it an almost cockatoo-like appearance. In flight pale bases to flight feathers form a whitish patch towards the end of each wing. Often seen perched on a telegraph pole. The black phase of the Augur Buzzard has no long crest and has yellow, unfeathered legs: the legs of the Long-crested Hawk-Eagle are feathered.

Voice: Shrill series of whistles—"kee, ee, ee, ee, ee, ee, ee."

Distribution and Habitat: Throughout the Ethiopian Region in suitable localities: common in many parts of East Africa, less frequent Central Africa. The species occurs in open park-like country, wooded areas, the edges of forests, native cultivation and on farmland. It feeds almost entirely on rodents and other agricultural pests and is a most beneficial bird.

LIZARD BUZZARD *Kaupifalco monogrammicus* p. 61

Identification: 14-15″. A thickset pale grey hawk with banded black and white underparts but throat white with a conspicuous vertical black streak; rump white. The Gabar Goshawk is not such a thickset hawk and has the throat grey without a black streak. Black throat streak best field character.

Voice: A clear, ringing whistle, followed by a quick succession of notes, "chu, chu, chu, chu, chu, chu, chu."

Distribution and Habitat: Widely distributed over most of the Ethiopian Region, south to Natal. In East Africa common in Uganda, the coastal forests of Kenya and most of the savannah woodlands of Tanganyika. Frequents open park-like country, cultivated areas, woodlands, edges of forests, semi-desert bush. Common and widespread in Central Africa.

BLACK-CHESTED HARRIER EAGLE *Circaetus pectoralis*

pp. 64, 65

Identification: 27-28″. The Harrier Eagles and the Bateleur all have large, lax-feathered, owl-like heads and unfeathered legs. The Black-chested (or breasted) Harrier Eagle has dark grey upperparts and chest and a white belly; tail with three white bands and a pale tip. Unspotted white underparts and under wing-coverts distinguish species from adult Martial Eagle which has black spotting on belly and below wings. Immature plumage of Black-chested Harrier Eagle entirely pale rufous-buff, quite unlike adult dress. Some augur buzzards, when perched, facing the observer, have a slight resemblance to the adult Black-chested Harrier Eagle, but may be distinguished by their yellow, not bluish-white, legs and red tails.

Voice: Silent birds as a rule, but sometimes utter single or double note shrill whistle.

Distribution and Habitat: A local resident in small numbers from the Sudan, Ethiopia and Eritrea, south to South Africa; Angola. It occurs in fairly open woodlands, cultivation, park-like country and semi-desert bush country. In East Africa it is most frequent in the Rift Valley and in the northern parts of Kenya and Uganda. Feeds mainly upon snakes and lizards.

Allied Species: The Brown Harrier-Eagle (*Circaetus cinereus*) is entirely dark brown and is quite distinct from the much paler and more rusty-plumaged immature Black-chested Harrier Eagle. It is a local species in small numbers in East and Central Africa. In Kenya and Tanganyika it especially favours savannah country where there are baobab trees. Two species of Banded Harrier Eagles occur but are very rare in East and Central Africa; they have black and white banded underparts. The Banded Harrier Eagle (*Circaetus cinerascens*) has one broad blackish band across the tail, the Southern Banded Harrier Eagle (*Circaetus fasciolatus*) has three to five dark tail bands.

GRASSHOPPER BUZZARD *Butastur rufipennis*

p. 61

Identification: 16-17″. When perched the Grasshopper Buzzard resembles a large edition of a kestrel; in flight it looks like a harrier with very rufous wings, but no white rump. In the north of its range it may be mistaken for a Fox Kestrel, but that bird is mainly rufous in colour and lacks the Grasshopper Buzzard's dark grey back.

Voice: A silent bird as a rule: sometimes utters a single plaintive whistle, "keeee."

Distribution and Habitat: A breeding species from Senegal, eastwards to Ethiopia and Somaliland: a non-breeding migrant southwards to the dry areas of eastern Kenya and north-eastern Tanganyika between November and March. Occurs in acacia and semi-desert country. At times it is seen in numbers during December and January in the Tsavo National Park, Kenya.

BATELEUR *Terathopius ecaudatus* pp. 65, 80

Identification: 24″. Identified in all plumages by its remarkable short tail which measures only 4 inches. On the wing the adult is unmistakable, with contrasting black underparts and white undersides of wings; back, rump and tail chestnut, rarely rufous buff. The immature is entirely dark brown and may be distinguished from the Brown Harrier Eagle by its very short tail.

Voice: A sharp, barking cry.

Distribution and Habitat: Widely distributed throughout the Ethiopian Region outside the forest areas of West Africa. In East and Central Africa it is one of the commoner eagles, especially in the Northern Frontier and Turkana districts of Kenya, and the savannah woodlands of Tanganyika. It is generally seen on the wing, soaring high overhead —a habit which may well explain its continued abundance! Occurs in semi-desert and open country, bush and savannah woodlands: less frequent in cultivated areas.

AFRICAN FISH EAGLE *Cuncuma vocifer* pp. 65, 80

Identification: 30″. The adult fish eagle is a most strikingly coloured bird with white head, chest, back and tail, rufous-chestnut on the belly and shoulders and black wings. The immature is brown with a black-streaked breast. The Palmnut Vulture or Vulturine Fish Eagle differs in having completely white underparts and a broad black band across the tail; it has no rufous in the plumage.

Voice: The far-carrying call of the fish eagle is one of the characteristic sounds of the African wilds. It is a wild, almost gull-like cry. When calling the bird throws the head back, even in flight.

Distribution and Habitat: From Senegal and Ethiopia, south to South Africa: numerous in many places. Occurs always in the vicinity of

VULTURES

1. EGYPTIAN VULTURE page 44
Whitish plumage; bare yellow face; slender bill. Immature brown. In flight: wedge-shaped tail.
a, *Adult*
b, *Immature*

2. HOODED VULTURE 43
Brown plumage; slender bill. In flight: broad wings without distinctive pattern; short rounded tail.

3. WHITE-BACKED VULTURE 43
Wings, back and breast uniform, not spotted; white rump. In flight; single broad white band along fore edge of wing.

4. RUPPELL'S GRIFFON VULTURE 42
Spotted on back, wings and breast; no white rump. In flight: three white bands on underside wings.

5. WHITE-HEADED VULTURE 43
White crown; white secondaries patch; red bill. In flight: white belly, white head and white wing patch—large in adult, small in immature.
a, *Adult*
b, *Immature*

6. NUBIAN or LAPPET-FACED VULTURE 43
Huge size and massive bill; bare, wrinkled purplish head. In flight: short white wing bar and white thigh patches.

1
1
a
b
2
3
4
5
5
a
b
6

1
2
3
4
5
6
♂
♀
7
8
9
10
11
12
13

BIRDS OF PREY, settled

1. AFRICAN HOBBY page 46
Dark blue-grey upperparts; deep rufous belly.

2. RED-NECKED FALCON 46
Chestnut cap and nape; barred belly.

3. LANNER 45
Rufous-buff nape patch; back pale grey.

4. PEREGRINE 45
No rufous-buff nape patch; crown, nape and back dark grey.

5. LESSER KESTREL 50
Male: Chestnut back not spotted.
Female: Smaller and paler than European Kestrel; *see* text.

6. EUROPEAN KESTREL 47
Male: Chestnut back spotted with black.
Female: Tail barred black and brown; eyes brown.

7. GREATER or WHITE-FACED KESTREL 47
Tail barred black and blue-grey; eyes white; sexes alike.

8. GREY KESTREL 50
Uniform grey plumage; skin around eyes yellow.

9. LIZARD BUZZARD 57
Black throat streak; black and white barred belly.

10. PYGMY FALCON 51
Small size and shrike-like general appearance; white underparts.

11. GRASSHOPPER BUZZARD 58
Mainly rufous flight feathers; rump dark, not white.

12. BLACK-SHOULDERED KITE 51
Black shoulders; white underparts.

13. AFRICAN BLACK KITE 51
Forked tail; yellow bill.

water—lakes, swamps, rivers, flooded areas and the coast. In East and Central Africa it is plentiful in suitable localities. It feeds almost entirely on fish but will at times take large rodents.

STEPPE BUZZARD *Buteo vulpinus* (M) pp. 80, 81

Identification: 18″. Buzzards, as a group, may be recognised by their broad wings whilst in flight. The Steppe Buzzard is a brown or rufous-brown species with rufous edgings to the feathers of the upperparts: underparts very variable: may be blotched or streaked or barred brown: tail brown or rufous-brown usually with many narrow dark bars. This buzzard greatly favours telegraph poles as vantage perches, as does the Augur Buzzard: the Mountain Buzzard never or very rarely perches on poles, even where telegraph lines pass through forest country. The Augur Buzzard in all plumages may be distinguished by its white mottling on the secondary feathers of the wing (see illustration), larger size, and in the case of adults the rich chestnut, unbarred tail. The Mountain Buzzard is always blotched blackish-brown below and lacks rufous in the plumage, but may be slightly tinged yellowish-buff. It is smaller than the Steppe Buzzard and is entirely a forest species, while the Steppe Buzzard favours open country. The Mountain Buzzard hunts by soaring, chameleons being its food, when it utters a characteristic mewing call: the Steppe Buzzard hunts from a perch where it can scan the ground for rodents and large insects.

Voice: In its winter quarters a silent bird, rarely heard to utter a shrill, tremulous whistle.

Distribution and Habitat: A winter visitor in varying numbers to eastern and southern Africa: commonest in East Africa. It appears in September or October and leaves again in March. It favours open country and semi-desert districts: in the open moorland country of Kenya it is often abundant, perched on the telegraph poles which cross the country.

Allied Species: The Mountain Buzzard (*Buteo oreophilus*) is without rufous in plumage and keeps to mountain forests: it does not perch on telegraph poles but hunts on the wing. It is a local species in East Africa, confined to high level forests. The Eastern Steppe Buzzard (*Buteo menetriesi*) has the underparts entirely deep rufous; it is a rare winter visitor to East Africa. It has the same habit of perching on telegraph poles as the Steppe Buzzard. The Honey Buzzard (*Pernis apivorus*) is an uncommon winter visitor and passage migrant in East Africa, rare in Central Africa, most evident in spring. It has a longer tail and narrower wings than the true buzzards: its plumage is very variable: widely separated dark tail bars are conspicuous. It has a characteristic, lethargic flight.

AUGUR BUZZARD *Buteo rufofuscus* pp. 80, 81

Identification: 20-24″. The adult Augur Buzzard may be recognised by its dark slate-grey upperparts, bright, unbarred chestnut tail, and greyish-white and black barring on the closed wing; below it may be entirely white, white with a black throat and upper breast or entirely black, the melanistic phase. The normal immature has the underparts streaked or blotched with black and the tail is barred black and brown; the melanistic immature is brownish-black, also with a barred tail. When flying the broad wings and chestnut tail of the adult render identification easy; both the white and the black-breasted forms have white underwing coverts. The adult melanistic form might be mistaken for an adult Bateleur, but has a much longer tail.

Voice: A ringing, wild, far-carrying "guang-guang."

Distribution and Habitat: Resident from Somaliland, Eritrea, Ethiopia and the Sudan, south to South Africa; also in Angola. Common in the highlands of Kenya and Uganda, local in Central Africa. Frequents open moorland country, mountains, inland cliffs and cultivated areas. Perches on telegraph poles and suchlike vantage points. A most valuable bird as it preys almost entirely upon rodents: those birds seen near chicken runs are not hunting the fowls, but the rodents attracted by chicken food.

LITTLE SPARROW HAWK *Accipiter minullus* p. 81

Identification: 9-11″. Above grey with a distinct white rump; throat white; remainder underparts white, narrowly barred grey and rufous. Immature plumage brown above with white underparts with dark brown drop-like spots on breast and flanks. The Little Sparrow Hawk is a miniature edition of the much larger African Goshawk in all plumages except for its white rump. Adult male Gabar Goshawk has grey throat and upper breast. The Shikra lacks the white rump.

Voice: Silent woodland species: at nest sometimes utters a sharp "kee, kee, kee."

Distribution and Habitat: A resident forest and woodland hawk throughout the Ethiopian Region, excepting Ghana to Gaboon in West Africa, but everywhere uncommon and local.

Allied Species: The Western Little Sparrow Hawk (*Accipiter erythropus*) is slightly larger than Little Sparrow Hawk and has chest and upper breast rufous. It occurs in western Uganda, west to Cameroons, south

BIRDS OF PREY, in flight

1. **PEREGRINE** page 45
   Pointed wings; black moustache patches; greyish belly; nape dark.
2. **WAHLBERG'S EAGLE** 55
   Uniform brown plumage; tail relatively long and narrow.
3. **LANNER** 45
   Pointed wings; black moustache patches; buff-white belly; rufous nape patch.
4. **TAWNY EAGLE** 54
   Uniform brown plumage; tail relatively short and rounded.
5. **BLACK KITE** 51
   Rusty brown plumage; deeply forked tail.
6. **BLACK-CHESTED HARRIER EAGLE** 58
   Breast and under wings unspotted white.
7. **MARTIAL EAGLE** 56
   Breast and under wings spotted black.
8. **LONG-CRESTED HAWK EAGLE** 57
   White wing patches.
9. **CROWNED HAWK EAGLE** 57
   Underparts blotched black, rufous and white.
10. **OSPREY** 70
    Black under wing patches; white belly.
11. **VERREAUX'S EAGLE** 54
    Silhouette distinctive, wings narrowing sharply at body; plumage black.
12. **HARRIER HAWK** 70
    Black tail with broad white band.

1
2
3
4
5
6
7
8
9
10
11
12

1
2
3
4
5
6
7
8
9
10

BIRDS OF PREY, settled

1. **BLACK-CHESTED HARRIER EAGLE** page 58
   Large lax-feathered head; unfeathered legs; unspotted white breast.
2. **AFRICAN FISH EAGLE** 59
   White head and tail; chestnut belly.
3. **AFRICAN HAWK EAGLE** 55
   Feathered legs; white underparts with narrow black streaks. Immature unspotted, pale rufous below.
4. **LONG-CRESTED HAWK EAGLE** 57
   Long crest; white wing patch.
5. **BATELEUR** 59
   Very short tail. Immature all brown.
6. **TAWNY EAGLE** 54
   Uniform brown plumage; no nape crest.
7. **MARTIAL EAGLE** 56
   Black spotted breast. Immature completely white below without spots.
8. **CROWNED HAWK EAGLE** 57
   Underparts blotched black, rufous and white. Immature whitish below with black spotted legs and thighs
9. **VERREAUX'S EAGLE** 54
   Black with contrasting white back and rump patch.
10. **HARRIER HAWK** 70
    Black tail with broad white band.

to Angola. The Rufous-breasted Sparrow Hawk (*Accipiter rufiventris*) is 12-14 inches in length and has entire underparts rufous, or barred rufous and white, paler on the throat. It is a forest hawk most frequent in the highland forests of East Africa, rare in Central Africa.

GREAT SPARROW HAWK *Accipiter melanoleucus* pp. 80, 81

Identification: 18-22″. A very large sparrow hawk, about the size of a European Goshawk: upperparts slaty-black; underparts white with black patch above thighs on flanks. In melanistic phase underparts black except for white throat. Immature plumage brown above; below white, buff or deep rufous, heavily streaked black. Tail appears long in flight. Sometimes preys upon pigeons and farmyard poultry.

Voice: A sharp, far-carrying, "keep, keep, keep," uttered especially when nesting.

Distribution and Habitat: A local and rare resident in forested and wooded areas throughout most of the Ethiopian Region. In East Africa it is frequent in forests of the Kenya Highlands.

SHIKRA *Accipiter badius* p. 81

Identification: 11-13″. A pale grey hawk without a white rump; underparts barred pale rufous or rufous and grey. The immature is also pale grey above, not brown as in most other species of "sparrow hawks," and has underparts blotched pale rufous. Lack of white rump distinguishes the Shikra from the Little Sparrow Hawk and Gabar Goshawk: the African Goshawk has blackish-slate upperparts, not pale blue-grey.

Voice: A high-pitched "keek, ee, ee, ee, keek."

Distribution and Habitat: Resident species throughout most of Africa except West African type forest regions and southern South Africa. Occurs especially in park-like country, semi-desert bush, acacia thickets and riverine forest, savannah woodlands and in East Africa in coast forest. In East and Central Africa a common species in woodland savannah.

Allied Species: The Ovampo Sparrow Hawk (*Accipiter ovampensis*) resembles a Shikra and although a rarer bird it has much the same distribution. It may be identified by the conspicuous white spots down the centre of its tail feather.

AFRICAN GOSHAWK *Accipiter tachiro* p. 81

Identification: 14-17″. A medium-sized sparrow hawk, the female much larger than the male. Upperparts dark slate-grey, barred below brown and white with rufous wash; female paler and less barred below than male. Immature dark brown above with dark heavy-spotted underparts. Lack of white rump distinguishes this species from Gabar Goshawk and Little Sparrow Hawk. A much darker bird above than the Shikra which has a pale blue-grey mantle; Ovampo Sparrow Hawk is pale above and has white spots in centre of tail feathers. A juvenile female African Goshawk could be mistaken for a juvenile male Black or Great Sparrow Hawk, but African Goshawk has spotting of underparts heavier and more drop-like, not thin streaks.

Voice: A shrill "wud, wud, wud, wud, wud," often uttered by bird whilst flying.

Distribution and Habitat: A local forest species widely distributed in Ethiopian Region, from Sierra Leone and Ethiopia southwards to South Africa. A bird of forests and well-wooded areas: common in East Africa in suitable forest country.

Allied Species: The Cuckoo Falcon (*Aviceda cuculoides*) occurs in West Africa, the Belgian Congo and Uganda and Kenya, south to South Africa. It is an uncommon and local forest species. Adults have very broad rufous or dark brown barring on underparts and a short but conspicuous crest. In flight the Cuckoo Falcon has heavy, rather slow wing-beat; undersides of wings mainly rufous: in African Goshawk underwing coverts white or buff with black markings.

GABAR GOSHAWK *Micronisus gabar* p. 81

Identification: 12-14″. A pale grey hawk with a white rump and grey and white barred underparts: a melanistic phase is not uncommon, almost entirely dull black with grey bars in wings and tail. Female much larger than male. A male Gabar Goshawk can be mistaken for a female Little Sparrow Hawk, but has the throat and upper breast uniform pale grey, not white. The African Goshawk, Shikra and Ovampo Sparrow Hawk do not possess the white rump. Immature has brown streaked chest and brown barred belly and flanks.

Voice: A high-pitched "ki, ki, ki, ki, ki, ki."

Distribution and Habitat: Occurs throughout the Ethiopian Region in suitable localities outside the West African forest region. It occurs in wooded and thornbush country, acacia woodland and park-like savannah. It is common and widespread in East and Central Africa.

PALE CHANTING GOSHAWK *Melierax poliopterus* p. 81

Identification: 19″. A very upright-standing pale grey hawk with closely barred belly; legs and base of bill conspicuous bright reddish-orange. The immature is brownish grey above, with broad brown streaking on the chest and rufous brown barring on the belly. Both adults and young have a white rump which is very conspicuous when the bird flies.

Voice: A curious piping call which may be mistaken for the call of some species of small hornbill.

Distribution and Habitat: A resident in dry bush and acacia country in East Africa from Somaliland, southwards through eastern Kenya to central Tanganyika. This is a well-known bird of the semi-desert bush areas of eastern and north-eastern districts of Kenya: it is especially frequent near Lake Magadi and near Isiolo.

Allied Species: The Dark Chanting Goshawk (*Melierax metabates*) which occurs in western Kenya, Uganda and Tanganyika is rather dark brownish-grey above with a black and white barred rump, not a white rump. This species occurs southwards to South-West Africa and Southern Rhodesia.

MONTAGU'S HARRIER *Circus pygargus* (M) p. 80

Identification: 16-18″. Harriers are the long-winged, long-tailed hawks which one sees flying a few feet above the ground, quartering an area in a systematic manner. In this species adult male mainly pale grey above with a narrow black wing bar and red-brown streaks on the belly. The female is brown with a white rump and streaked underparts; the immature bird lacks the streaks on the underparts. The female and juvenile plumages of the Montagu's Harrier are not distinguishable in the field from those plumages of the Pallid Harrier. The adult male differs from the other pale grey harrier found in East Africa—the Pallid Harrier—in having a black wing bar and rusty streaks on the belly. In the Pallid Harrier the underparts are immaculate white, slightly greyish on the chest, and there is no black wing bar.

Voice: A rather kestrel-like "kek, kek, kek," rarely heard in East Africa, except sometimes at harrier roosts.

Distribution and Habitat: Winter visitor and passage migrant to suitable localities outside the forested areas throughout eastern, central and southern Africa. In East Africa appears in September and October and departs northwards in March and April; especially common during spring passage. Frequents open country, swamps, lakes and moorland.

PALLID HARRIER *Circus macrourus* (M) p. 80

Identification: 17-19″. Male unmistakable with pale blue-grey upperparts, contrasting black flight feathers and white belly. Montagu's Harrier male has narrow black wing bar and rusty-brown streaks on belly. Female and young brown with contrasting white rump, not distinguishable in field from female and immature Montagu's Harrier.

Voice: Silent in winter quarters.

Distribution and Habitat: Winter visitor and passage migrant to Africa, south to Cape Province, South Africa: a common winterer and passage migrant in East and Central Africa. Occurs in similar habitats to Montagu's Harrier, favouring open plains, moorlands and large swamp areas. Both this species and Montagu's Harrier feed largely on grasshoppers and in some areas, tree frogs.

EUROPEAN MARSH HARRIER *Circus aeruginosus* (M) p. 80

Identification: 19-22″. A large brown harrier without a white rump: adult male with grey tail and blue-grey secondaries and black primaries; the female and immature lack grey in plumage and have creamy crowns and shoulders. The juvenile plumage is dark chocolate-brown with bright buff, almost orange, crown and throat. Females of Pallid and Montagu's Harriers have white rumps. The African Marsh Harrier has no blue-grey tail or wing patch, and the female and immature are uniformly coloured without the creamy-buff head and shoulders.

Voice: In Africa generally a silent bird, but when at harrier roosts sometimes utters a squeaky, kite-like whistle.

Distribution and Habitat: Winter visitor and passage migrant in Africa south to Angola, Tanganyika and Northern Rhodesia. In East Africa its numbers vary from year to year: sometimes it is a common species, in other years it is far outnumbered by Pallid and Montagu's Harriers. It occurs on open plains, moorlands, swamps and marshes and on inland lakes.

AFRICAN MARSH HARRIER *Circus ranivorus* p. 80

Identification: 18-20″. A uniformly dark or rufous brown harrier without a white rump: adult males indistinctly streaked dark rufous on underparts. Adult male differs from the European Marsh Harrier in having tail and wings barred black; females and immatures are uniform dark brown without the creamy head and shoulders of the European species.

Voice: A weak mewing cry, uttered by male when approaching nest.

Distribution and Habitat: Uncommon local resident from the Congo, Uganda and Kenya, south to Angola and South Africa. In East Africa it is most frequent in south-western Uganda, the highland moorland and swamps of Kenya and southern Tanganyika. It occurs on open plains, wheatlands (in Kenya it often nests in the middle of a field of wheat), swamps, marshes and the margins of lakes.

HARRIER HAWK *Polyboroides typus* pp. 64, 65

Identification: 24-27″. A long-legged, blue-grey hawk, not unlike a large edition of the chanting goshawk: tail long, wide and black, narrowly tipped white with a broad white band; face bare, bright lemon yellow or pinkish-yellow. Feathers of nape long, forming a lax crest. Belly barred black and white. The immature may be dark brown, rufous, or rufous buff: birds in this plumage best identified by lax crest and rather floppy flight. Sometimes seen raiding weaver-bird colonies, when it hangs by the legs, upsidedown, slowly flapping its wings while it raids the nests.

Voice: A drawn-out, quavering whistle, often uttered in flight.

Distribution and Habitat: A local resident throughout most of the Ethiopian Region. In East Africa it is fairly numerous in the Kenya coastal forests, and in western Uganda. It occurs in forest and wooded areas, park-like country, savannah woodland, especially where there are baobab trees and in cultivated areas where trees have not been felled. Sparsely distributed in Central Africa.

OSPREY *Pandion haliaetus* (M & R) pp. 64, 92

Identification: 20-23″. A large blackish-brown bird of prey with contrasting white underparts and long, narrow wings with characteristic angle and black carpal patches; head whitish with slight crest. Always seen near water. Feeds upon fish which it captures by plunging feet first into the water.

Voice: Generally silent but sometimes utters several short whistles, especially when two birds are competing over a single fish.

Distribution and Habitat: Occurs throughout the Ethiopian Region as a passage migrant and winter visitor: a few pairs breed in isolated areas. In Kenya several pairs nest on islets in Lake Rudolf. Occurs always near water, including inland lakes and rivers, and the coast.

GAME BIRDS: Phasianidae

This family includes the quails, francolins, guinea-fowls and their allies. All are chicken-like, terrestrial birds with moderate or short tails: sexes usually alike in African species.

COQUI FRANCOLIN *Francolinus coqui* p. 84

Identification: 8-10″. The term "francolin" is reserved for those species with feathered throats: those species called "spurfowl" have bare, unfeathered throats. This is a partridge-sized bird with outer tail feathers showing rufous or chestnut in flight: underparts barred black and white; legs dull yellow. Female with greyish or rufous upper breast. The Coqui Francolin is best identified by its barred underparts—in some races the barring is confined to the breast and flanks, in others the barring extends all over the belly—and chestnut in tail during flight.

Voice: A shrill "qui-kit, qui-kit," heard most often at dawn and in the evening.

Distribution and Habitat: A local resident throughout much of the Ethiopian Region, outside the West African type forest areas, wherever suitable conditions prevail. In East Africa it is most frequent in savannah woodlands of Tanganyika and in the coastal bush and forests of Kenya: widespread in Central Africa. Occurs in coveys, which are usually difficult to flush, in grasslands where there is some bush cover, savannah woodlands and hillsides where there is bush cover.

CRESTED FRANCOLIN *Francolinus sephaena* p. 84

Identification: 10-11″. Another bantam-sized francolin: underparts whitish-buff with a little indistinct mottling on the breast; sides of neck with triangular chestnut spots: outer tail feathers black; tail usually carried cocked at an angle over the back. The Stone Partridge also has this habit but is a smaller and much darker bird. The Crested Francolin appears as a rather pale-looking francolin with conspicuous white streaks on the back and a wide necklet of chestnut spots on the throat.

Voice: A very loud, far-carrying "tee-dee-jee, tee-dee-jee," uttered over and over again: birds especially noisy at dusk and dawn.

Distribution and Habitat: A resident species, sometimes very common, in the southern Sudan, Somaliland and Ethiopia, south to South Africa. Local in Central Africa. It is a bush country bird, often abundant in thickly bushed dry water courses of northern and eastern Kenya, and in semi-desert country.

Allied Species: Kirk's Francolin (*Francolinus rovuma*) differs from the Crested Francolin in having chestnut spots on the belly. It occurs in Somaliland and parts of the Kenya coast, south along the Tanganyika coast area to Portuguese East Africa and Nyasaland.

GREY-WING FRANCOLIN *Francolinus afer* p. 84

Identification: 11″. The name Grey-wing Francolin is not altogether suitable as the species has some rufous at the bases of the flight feathers. In Kenya it is better known among sportsmen as the "Ulu Francolin." This is a rather thickset francolin with the throat white, the chest and flanks blotched chestnut and the belly mottled black and whitish: outer tail feathers black in flight. The Redwing Francolin has entirely rufous flight feathers, sometimes dusky at tips, a conspicuous rufous patch on the back of the neck and the belly buff with dark markings, not mottled black and white. Shelley's Francolin has heavier black markings on belly.

Voice: A shrill "tid, ji, ji, ji, ji, ji."

Distribution and Habitat: Resident in Ethiopia and southern Sudan, southwards to Cape Province, South Africa: a local species, usually in hilly areas over 4000 ft. In East Africa occurs in highlands from Mt. Moroto on the Kenya/Uganda border to Mbulu in north-eastern Tanganyika. Occurs in small coveys and pairs in grass and scrub country, open forests, wooded water courses and bushy ravines.

Allied Species: Shelley's Francolin (*Francolinus shelleyi*) has mainly rufous underparts with a wide band of round black spots on the chest in the two Kenya alpine races. It occurs in the alpine zone of mountains in Kenya and on Mt. Elgon on the Uganda border, and in south-western Uganda, south through Tanganyika to Natal, South Africa. The Ring-necked Francolin (*Francolinus streptophorus*) occurs on rocky and bushy hillsides in western Kenya and locally in Uganda and north-western Tanganyika. It has the back and front of the neck barred black and white, forming a ring which contrasts with the rest of the plumage.

RED-WING FRANCOLIN *Francolinus levaillantii* p. 84

Identification: 12-13″. This is a small chicken-sized francolin, mainly rufous-buff in colour with reddish flight feathers and a conspicuous rufous patch on the hindneck; chest blotched deep rufous. The Greywing Francolin differs in having a black and white mottled belly.

Shelley's Francolin is mainly deep rufous below with round black spots on the chest or heavier black markings on belly.

Voice: A shrill "kee-el-de-we," repeated over and over again.

Distribution and Habitat: Local resident western Kenya and Uganda, south to highland areas of Transvaal, Natal and Cape Province, South Africa. This is a highlands species, found chiefly on hillsides where there is bush and grass cover. In East Africa it is most frequent in the western highlands and the Cherengani range in western Kenya: in Central Africa in Nyika Plateau, Nyasaland, and Balovale and Mankoya districts, Northern Rhodesia.

HEUGLIN'S FRANCOLIN *Francolinus icterorhynchus* p. 84

Identification: 11-12″. A medium-sized, rather dark francolin with dusky upperparts; below pale buff with black mottling on the chest and black spots on the belly: male possesses two spurs on each leg. Appears as a dusky francolin with a black spotted belly. Often observed perched on the top of termite hills.

Voice: a shrill, three-note call, uttered usually at dusk.

Distribution and Habitat: Local resident French Equatorial Africa, north-eastern Congo, southern Sudan and Uganda. It is most frequent in savannah woodlands of north-western Uganda in areas where there are many termite hills. It perches freely on these termite hills and in trees.

HILDEBRANDT'S FRANCOLIN *Francolinus hildebrandti* p. 84

Identification: 14-15″. Sexes unlike: the male having white underparts, heavily blotched with black; the female pale rufous-brown on the belly. This is a chicken-sized francolin with dark, finely vermiculated upperparts and red legs. When pairs or family parties are encountered the striking difference in plumage between the sexes is a good field character.

Voice: A three-note, loud, "kok-kok-kok" repeated over and over again, often very rapidly. Calls mainly towards dusk.

Distribution and Habitat: A very local and generally uncommon species in hilly country in East Africa. Occurs in central, eastern and south-western Kenya, southwards to Northern Rhodesia and adjacent parts of the eastern Congo. It is found in well-wooded hill country, scrub-covered hillsides and sometimes on hillsides where the only cover is a little grass and rocks. It is perhaps most numerous in the wooded Loita Hills of Kenya.

Allied Species: Clapperton's Francolin (*Francolinus clappertoni*) occurs in dry areas of Nigeria, eastwards to Sudan and northern Uganda and the Mt. Elgon area of western Kenya. It is of small fowl size, dark in colour without pale shaft streaks on upperparts. On the wing the buff on the inner webs of the primaries contrasts strongly with dark outer webs and forms a pale wing patch, very like the wing patch of the Yellow-necked Spurfowl for which this francolin could be mistaken.

SCALY FRANCOLIN *Francolinus squamatus* p. 84

Identification: 10-12″. A medium-sized dark-coloured francolin with very conspicuous red legs; plumage above and below broadly streaked dark brown. A well-known forest francolin called "redleg" by Kenya sportsmen.

Voice: A rapid, guttural "kew-koo-wah, kwe-koo-wah."

Distribution and Habitat: A resident in forest and thick bush in the vicinity of forest in Cameroons and Gaboon, West Africa, eastwards to Ethiopia, southwards through Uganda, Kenya and Tanganyika, and the Congo to north-eastern Northern Rhodesia. A very local bird, absent from many apparently suitable localities. In the eastern highlands of Kenya and northern Tanganyika this is a common species. Its presence in forested areas is usually betrayed by the birds' noisy calls towards dusk. After rain this and other species of forest-haunting francolins may be seen on forest paths.

Allied Species: Two species of forest francolins occur in forest areas of Uganda and westwards: these are Nahan's Forest Francolin (*Francolinus nahani*) and the Forest Francolin (*Francolinus lathami*). Both species have black underparts with conspicuous white spots: the former has the upperparts dark brown with black bases to the feathers, without white shaft streaks. The Forest Francolin has brown upperparts with distinct white shaft streaks. Like other forest game birds these species are usually noted on forest paths after rain. Both occur in Bwamba forest, western Uganda.

JACKSON'S FRANCOLIN *Francolinus jacksoni* p. 84

Identification: 13-15″. Male larger than female. A rich brown francolin with white-margined chestnut neck and belly, throat white; legs and bill red. This is a mountain forest bird confined to Kenya. It may be recognised by the combination of red bill and legs, and chestnut underparts. The Scaly Francolin which occurs alongside has red legs, but its plumage is mainly dark greyish-brown, without chestnut. Shelley's Francolin has a black and white mottled throat band and round black spots on the chest and yellowish-brown feet.

Voice: Birds call loudly at dusk, prior to roosting in bamboo clumps and forest trees: the call notes are harsh "grrr, grrr, grrr."

Distribution and Habitat: Confined to mountain forest on Mt. Kenya, the Aberdare Mts., the Kinangop plateau and the Mau Forest in Kenya Colony. In parts of the eastern Aberdare forest the species is abundant. Mountain forest and mixed forest and bamboo are the bird's normal habitat.

Allied Species: The Handsome Francolin (*Francolinus nobilis*) of the Ruwenzori and Kivu mountain forests, western Uganda and the Belgian Congo, is about the same size as Jackson's Francolin with a rich purplish-chestnut back and grey crown: below the feathers are dark chestnut, edged with grey; throat greyish-white. It occurs in bamboo and mountain forest and is shy and seldom observed. The Chestnut-naped Francolin (*Francolinus castaneicollis*) is another large francolin with a white throat and a great deal of chestnut-red in the plumage and red bill and legs. It may be distinguished from Jackson's Francolin by its buff-white belly. It is confined to mountain areas where there is plenty of cover, in Ethiopia and Somaliland.

RED-NECKED SPURFOWL *Pternistis cranchii* p. 85

Identification: 13-14″. This is a very variable species which may have the underparts vermiculated grey and white, with or without chestnut streaks, or the belly feathers may be black, edged with greyish-white. All races have greyish-brown upperparts with dark shaft stripes and a bare red throat and red legs. The Grey-breasted Spurfowl has an orange throat, chestnut-margined feathers of flanks and back, and a grey chest with dark shaft stripes. Swainson's Spurfowl has a red throat but blackish-brown legs.

Voice: A loud, shrill "kraaek, kraaek," uttered from thick cover, either early in the morning or just before the birds take up their roosts at dusk.

Distribution and Habitat: A resident in wooded districts in East, Central and southern Africa; Angola. In East and Central Africa black-breasted races occur in coastal districts Kenya Colony south to eastern Northern Rhodesia, Nyasaland, where locally abundant, and the Mashonaland plateau in Southern Rhodesia. Races with grey underparts, with or without chestnut streaks, occur in western Kenya and Uganda, south through Tanganyika to the Rhodesias. Occurs in wooded and savannah country, park-like country and hillsides where there is plenty of cover. In many parts of its range it is a shy and retiring bird which would often be overlooked were it not for its noisy call.

Allied Species: The Grey-breasted Spurfowl (*Pternistis rufopictus*) has a very restricted distribution in dry thorn-bush country around Lake

Eyasi and the Wembere Steppes, northern Tanganyika: it is also reputed to occur in south-eastern Uganda. It has an orange throat and chestnut-red streaking on back and underparts. Swainson's Spurfowl (*Pternistis swainsoni*) occurs widely in the Rhodesias: it resembles one of the grey-breasted races of red-necked Spurfowl but has blackish, not red legs.

YELLOW-NECKED SPURFOWL *Pternistis leucoscepus* p. 85

Identification: 13-14″. This is a fowl-sized francolin, greyish-brown above with pale vermiculations and streaks, and buff-streaked dark brown underparts; throat conspicuously bare, bright yellow merging to orange-red at base; bird stands high on its legs. Generally pale colour and yellow and reddish throat best field characters.

Voice: A loud, grating "graark, grak, grak," especially in the early morning and at dusk.

Distribution and Habitat: Locally common resident Somalilands, Eritrea, Ethiopia, north-eastern Uganda, Kenya and northern Tanganyika. Frequents open bush country, edges of forest and woodland, and dry thornbush country. This is the commonest francolin in Kenya and northern Tanganyika. It is numerous in all the Kenya National Parks.

HARLEQUIN QUAIL *Coturnix delegorguei* p. 85

Identification: 6½″. Male easily recognised by mainly black underparts and black and white throat markings; female has pale rufous-grey underparts without spots, streaks or barring. This is the commonest of the African quails, in East and Central Africa subject to extensive spasmodic migratory movements, when it may become extremely abundant locally in open grasslands.

Voice: A four note whistle, "pleet, pleet—pleet pleet."

Distribution and Habitat: Widely distributed resident and local migrant throughout Ethiopian Region, except West African forest areas. Frequents open grasslands where its presence may be detected by its plaintive call-notes. Occurs at sea level up to 8,000 ft. and over. In seasons of good rains very common on the Athi Plains, near Nairobi, Kenya Colony.

Allied Species: The European Quail (*Coturnix coturnix*) occurs as a passage migrant and winter visitor to the Sudan, Eritrea, Ethiopia, northern Uganda and northern Kenya. This bird and its African race, the Cape Quail, differ from the female Harlequin Quail in having a brown or chestnut throat patch (males) or spotted chest and flanks (females). The Cape Quail is a local resident from Ethiopia southwards to South Africa; absent from Southern Rhodesia: it is a highlands species, usually over 7,000 ft., in East Africa, Nyasaland and Northern Rhodesia. The tiny Blue Quail (*Excalfactoria adansoni*), length 5 inches, is a most handsome bird, blue-grey and chestnut; the female is rufous-brown with black barred underparts. It inhabits neglected cultivation and damp grasslands: uncommon local resident in East Africa, more frequent Nyasaland and Northern Rhodesia; rare in Southern Rhodesia.

STONE PARTRIDGE *Ptilopachus petrosus* p. 85

Identification: 10″. A small game-bird, dark brown mottled with pale buff; centre of abdomen creamy-white. Best identified by its characteristic habits: occurs only on rocky hills and cliffs, usually in small parties; holds its tail cocked up so that it has a remarkable resemblance to a small bantam fowl.

Voice: A shrill, piping "weet, weet, weet, weet," especially at dusk.

Distribution and Habitat: Resident of local and patchy distribution from Senegal and Northern Nigeria, eastwards to Ethiopia and northern Uganda and northern Kenya. Occurs in dry thornbush country on rocky slopes and cliffs. Very shy as a rule and easy to overlook. The best method of locating the species is to listen for its call towards dusk. In Kenya it may be found in the broken, rocky hills north of Isiolo.

HELMETED GUINEA-FOWL *Numida mitrata* p. 85

Identification: 20-22″. General colour black, spotted all over with white; head and neck sparsely feathered with bony horn protruding from crown; blue and red wattles at base of bill. Almost indistinguishable in the field from the Tufted Guineafowl which has tuft of whitish nasal bristles at the base of the bill; wattles usually entirely blue in this species, but some races have red and blue wattles. Usually seen in pairs or large flocks.

Voice: A loud cackling call, frequently repeated.

Distribution and Habitat: A local resident, abundant where not shot, Kenya (southern and eastern districts), southern Uganda, eastern and southern Tanganyika, eastern Northern and Southern Rhodesia, Nyasaland and Portuguese East Africa to eastern Cape Province. Occurs in bush country, dry thornbush areas, neglected cultivation, park-like country and savannah woodlands.

Allied Species: The Tufted Guinea-fowl (*Numida meleagris*), which is considered conspecific with the Helmeted Guinea-fowl by some authorities, differs in having a tuft of whitish bristles over the nostrils at the base of the bill. It occurs in north-eastern Africa, from the Sudan and Ethiopia, south to Uganda and the northern half of Kenya.

KENYA CRESTED GUINEA-FOWL *Guttera pucherani* p. 85

Identification: 18-22″. This is a chicken-sized guinea fowl, black with bluish-white spots; neck and face bare, cobalt blue and dark red; head without helmet, crested with long curling black feathers. The closely allied Crested Guinea-fowl differs in having the feathers at the base of the neck purplish-black, without spots.

Voice: The usual call is a weak clucking: this is easily imitated and will bring the birds very close to a hidden observer. At times the birds also produce a harsh "churrrr, tuk, tuk, tuk," perhaps an alarm call.

Distribution and Habitat: A local resident in forested and thickly wooded areas in southern Somalia, Kenya east of the Rift Valley and north-eastern Tanganyika and Zanzibar. The birds occurring in the Jombeni mountains in the Northern Frontier Province of Kenya are a giant race, over fifty per cent larger than typical coastal birds. The species in most areas is shy and seldom seen unless heavy rain has driven them to the relative dryness of forest paths and tracks. It is most frequent in the Kenya coastal Sokoke Forest inland from Kilifi.

Allied Species: The Crested Guinea-fowl (*Guttera edouardi*) differs from the Kenya Crested Guinea-fowl, which has blue-spotted neck feathers, in having a collar of black, or chestnut and black adjoining the bare neck. It occurs in western Kenya and Uganda, south through Tanganyika, Portuguese East Africa, Nyasaland, and the Rhodesias to the eastern Transvaal, Natal and Zululand. Occurs in the southern half of its range in deciduous thickets and dense scrub and riverine forest: farther north, in Kenya and Uganda it also occurs in rain forest.

VULTURINE GUINEA-FOWL *Acryllium vulturinum* p. 85

Identification: 23-24″. A most handsome, long-tailed guinea-fowl with feathers of upper mantle and chest long and striped white, black and cobalt-blue; breast brilliant cobalt-blue; head and neck bare, blue, with patch of downy chestnut feathers on nape; head appears small for the bird's size, giving it a vulturine appearance. Usually occurs in flocks: cobalt-blue plumage conspicuous in field.

Voice: A series of loud, shrill cackles and a loud "kak, kak, kak, kak."

Distribution and Habitat: A local resident in dry thornbush country, semi-desert areas and dry forest in the Somalilands, eastern Ethiopia, eastern Kenya and north-eastern Tanganyika. Numbers fluctuate greatly, species at times very uncommon; in other more favourable years abundant.

CRAKES, RAILS, MOORHENS and COOTS: Rallidae

The Rails and their allies are generally marsh or water-haunting birds with rounded wings and apparently weak flight, with legs dangling. Toes long and slender; tails short and often carried cocked up. Crakes have relatively short and thick bills, rails have long slender bills; moorhens and coots have heavy, thickset bodies and small heads and often swim.

BLACK CRAKE *Limnocorax flavirostra* p. 93

Identification: 8″. Plumage entirely slaty-black, with contrasting apple-green bill and pink legs. Less skulking than most crakes and rails, and often seen feeding among water-lily leaves at the edge of reed and papyrus beds.

Voice: A shrill "r-r-r-r-r-r-r-r-r, yok" and various clucking sounds. Until one gets to know the call of the Black Crake really well it is possible to mistake the trill of a Little Grebe for the call of the Black Crake.

Distribution and Habitat: Occurs throughout the Ethiopian Region where a combination of water and fringing vegetation exists. It is abundant throughout East and Central Africa. In the Amboseli Game Reserve, Kenya, these crakes have become extremely tame and may be observed at close quarters with ease.

Allied Species: The Kaffir Rail (*Rallus caerulescens*) is a widespread resident in rank vegetation in permanent swamps in East and Central Africa, but is shy and seldom observed. It is 11 inches in length with a long slender bill; upperparts dark brown with black and white barred flanks. The European Corn Crake (*Crex crex*) is a passage migrant and winter visitor to East and Central Africa, occurring in dry open grasslands. Seldom observed unless flushed at one's feet. Plumage buff-brown with blackish streaks on upperparts; throat greyish. Rufous wings very conspicuous when bird in flight. In Kenya mainly a passage migrant and most records are birds which have killed themselves by flying into telegraph wires. The African Crake (*Crex egregia*), 9 inches, has dark olive and black upperparts and black and white barred flanks and belly. It is a resident locally migratory, throughout East and

BIRDS OF PREY, in flight

1. BATELEUR *page* 59
Very short tail in all plumages.
a, *Adult*
b, *Immature*

2. AFRICAN FISH EAGLE 59
White head and tail.

3. PALLID HARRIER 69
Male: No black wing bar: underparts white.
Female: White rump: *see* text,

4. MONTAGU'S HARRIER 68
Male: Broken black wing bar; rufous streaked belly.
Female: White rump: *see* text.

5. EUROPEAN MARSH HARRIER 69
Male: Grey wing patch; grey tail.
Female: Cream-buff head and shoulders.

6. AFRICAN MARSH HARRIER 69
Barred primaries and tail: head and shoulders dark brown or streaked, not buff.

7. STEPPE BUZZARD 62
Tail narrowly barred; broad wings; underparts markings vary greatly, *see* text.

8. AUGUR BUZZARD 63
Broad wings; bright chestnut tail. In melanistic phase undersides of wings mainly white. Immature has underparts streaked or blotched and tail barred.

9. GREAT SPARROW HAWK 66
White below with black thigh patches. Melanistic phase black below with white throat. Immature heavily streaked black.

a
1
b
2
♂
4
3
♂
♀
6
♂
5
♀
7
8
9

1
2
a
b
3
4
5
6
7
8a
8b
8c

BIRDS OF PREY, settled

1. **GABAR GOSHAWK** page 67
White rump; barred belly; banded tail. Immature has chest streaked with brown.

2. **LITTLE SPARROW HAWK** 63
White rump; lightly barred underparts. Immature brown; underparts whitish with dark spots.

3. **GREAT SPARROW HAWK** 66
a, *Adult:* White underparts with black thigh patch: melanistic phase has underparts black with white throat patch.
b, *Immature:* Upperparts brown, more or less edged rufous; below whitish or pale rufous with heavy black streaks.

4. **PALE CHANTING GOSHAWK** 68
White rump; reddish-orange legs; unbarred tail. Immature brown with streaking on chest and rufous barring on belly.

5. **AFRICAN GOSHAWK** 67
Dark slate-grey upperparts including rump. Immature whitish below with dark spots.

6. **SHIKRA** 66
Pale grey upperparts, including rump. Immature also pale grey above, below blotched pale rufous.

7. **STEPPE BUZZARD** 62
Feathers upperparts edged rufous; tail usually heavily barred.

8. **AUGUR BUZZARD** 65
Barred wing patch in all plumages. In adults tail rufous with only a subterminal dark band. In immatures tail is usually barred.
a, *Immature*
b, *Adult*, pale phase
c, *Adult*, melanistic phase

Central Africa: it occurs both in rank grass in dry areas and in rank vegetation near water. It is a shy bird and its presence is usually indicated by its call, a high-pitched, chittering trill.

WHITE-SPOTTED PYGMY CRAKE *Sarothrura pulchra* p. 93

Identification: 5½″. The Sarothrura group of crakes, or Flufftails as they are sometimes called, are difficult to observe and identify in the field: some species frequent marshes and grasslands; others are forest dwellers. Their presence is usually indicated by their calls. The present species, which is typical of the group, has the head, neck, chest and tail rich chestnut; the remainder of the plumage in the male is black with white spots; the female is barred black and buff above and below.

Voice: A bell-like note, repeated over and over again, "goong-goong-goong-goong."

Distribution and Habitat: The White-spotted Pygmy Crake occurs in West Africa, eastwards through the Belgian Congo to the Sudan, Uganda and western Kenya. It is a bird of swampy forest, where it would often be overlooked were it not for its call. It is common in the forest around Entebbe in Uganda, but seldom seen.

PURPLE GALLINULE *Porphyrio porphyrio* p. 93

Identification: 18″. Larger than a coot with long bright pink legs; back deep green merging to bright purple-blue on wings and head and underparts; face and throat washed bright blue; bill and head-shield bright red; juvenile dusky bluish-grey with horn-coloured legs. Climbs among reeds and sedges in water; shy. In flight dangling red legs conspicuous. Knob-billed Coot is slaty-black with white frontal shield and grey legs. The moorhen is much smaller with white flank streaks, red frontal shield and green legs.

Voice: A loud, harsh grunting call.

Distribution and Habitat: Resident and local migrant throughout Ethiopian Region except West African forest area, the Sudan, and northern and central Ethiopia. Common in suitable localities in Kenya, Uganda, Tanganyika and Central Africa. Frequents dense swamps and papyrus and reed beds, especially where there is an abundant growth of water-lilies.

Allied Species: The much smaller Allen's Gallinule (*Porphyrula alleni*), 12 inches, is olive green with blue underparts and a blackish head; head shield green, legs dark red. This species is widespread in Ethiopian Region, except Somalias, but is shy and retiring and generally overlooked. It may sometimes be flushed in rank grass at the edges of swamps.

MOORHEN *Gallinula chloropus* p. 93

Identification: 13″. A thickset, blackish-slate bird of aquatic habits. Smaller than Knob-billed Coot with a red frontal shield, not white; and green, not grey, legs. White streaks along flanks; some white feathers below tail. Jerks tail while walking or swimming. Immature paler and browner than adult. Bill red, with yellow tip. The Lesser Moorhen is smaller and has the entire lower mandible yellow.

Voice: A harsh "kr-aa-rk."

Distribution and Habitat: Throughout most of the Ethiopian Region where suitable conditions exist. Widely distributed and usually common in East and Central Africa: common on Lake Naivasha in Kenya. Inhabits swamps, marshes, lakes, ponds, streams, dams, and slow-flowing rivers.

Allied Species: The smaller Lesser Moorhen (*Gallinula angulata*) is distributed locally throughout the Ethiopian Region, but is a much shyer bird than the Moorhen and is infrequently observed. It appears to be commoner in Central Africa than in Kenya and Uganda. In addition to its size it differs from the Moorhen in having the lower mandible entirely yellow, not red at the base. This is a good field character.

RED-KNOBBED COOT *Fulica cristata* p. 93

Identification: 16″. Large thickset water bird, blackish-slate in colour with white bill and frontal shield having two dark red knobs at the base of the shield. Often gregarious. Blackish plumage and conspicuous white bill and shield distinguish species from Purple Gallinule and Moorhen. Flight laboured and weak with greyish legs dangling. Swims well and has characteristic bobbing of head whilst swimming.

Voice: A harsh, deep-sounding "kwork" and various other grunting calls.

Distribution and Habitat: Resident and local migrant throughout greater part of Ethiopian Region, from Ethiopia to South Africa, but not western Africa. Locally common in East and Central Africa. Frequents lakes and swamps and dams where there is an abundance of aquatic vegetation and reed and papyrus beds.

Allied Species: The European Coot (*Fulica atra*) is a winter visitor to the Sudan as far south as Khartoum. It differs from the African bird in lacking the two red knobs at the base of its head shield.

GAME BIRDS

1. **COQUI FRANCOLIN** page 71
Underparts strongly barred black and white; legs yellowish.
2. **CRESTED FRANCOLIN** 71
Chestnut neck spots; white streaks on upperparts.
3. **GREY-WING FRANCOLIN** 72
Black and white mottling on belly; no rufous neck patch.
4. **RED-WING FRANCOLIN** 72
Rufous patch on hind neck.
5. **HEUGLIN'S FRANCOLIN** 73
Black spotting on underparts.
6. **HILDEBRANDT'S FRANCOLIN** 73
Finely vermiculated upperparts and red legs. Sexes dissimilar; underparts male whitish with black blotches; underparts female pale rufous-buff.
7. **SCALY FRANCOLIN** 74
Uniform colour; red legs. Inhabits forests and thick bush.
8. **JACKSON'S FRANCOLIN** 74
Red bill and legs; mainly chestnut underparts. Inhabits mountain forest.

♂
1
♀
2
3
4
5
6
♂
7
♀
8

♀
1
♂
2
3
4
5
6
7b
7a
8

GAME BIRDS and BUTTON QUAIL

1. **HARLEQUIN QUAIL** page 76
   Male: Black and white throat markings; black belly.
   Female: Underparts uniform, no heavy black spotting and no chestnut throat patch.
2. **STONE PARTRIDGE** 77
   Belly creamy-white; tail carried cocked up; inhabits rocky hills.
3. **BUTTON QUAIL** 116
   Rump not darker than remainder upperparts.
4. **HELMETED GUINEA-FOWL** 77
   Conspicuous bony helmet; no tuft of whitish bristles over nostrils.
5. **KENYA CRESTED GUINEA-FOWL** 78
   Lax black crest; blue-spotted neck feathers.
6. **VULTURINE GUINEA-FOWL** 78
   Upper mantle and chest feathers long, striped blue, black and white.

7a. **RED-NECKED SPURFOWL** 75
   (Race with vermiculated grey underparts). Bare red throat; red legs.

7b. **RED-NECKED SPURFOWL** 75
   (Race with black and white underparts). Bare red throat; red legs.

8. **YELLOW-NECKED SPURFOWL** 76
   Bare yellow throat.

FINFOOTS: Heliornithidae

The finfoots are aquatic, swimming birds with a superficial resemblance to a grebe or small cormorant, but possess a long tail of stiff feathers and bright orange-red legs and feet. They frequent densely wooded streams and rivers where there is an abundance of cover along the banks.

PETERS' FINFOOT *Podica senegalensis* p. 52

Identification: 18-21″. A duck-sized aquatic bird with brown upperparts, a long stiff tail and orange-red bill and legs. The male is larger than the female and has the neck slate-grey; in the female and immature the front of the neck is whitish. Species swims low in the water; female and young resemble immature Great Crested Grebe until red legs and long tail are observed.

Voice: Usually silent, but sometimes produces a shrill "keeee."

Distribution and Habitat: Local resident in suitable localities throughout East and Central Africa. Also occurs Congo, West Africa and South Africa. Found mainly on perennial rivers and streams with thickly wooded banks: in Kenya, and probably Tanganyika, also occurs in coastal creeks where there is a thick cover of mangroves.

CRANES: Balearicidae

The Cranes are large, stately terrestrial birds, superficially resembling storks, from which they differ externally in having the nostrils in a long groove, and the hind toe short. The various species inhabit open country, cultivated areas and marshes. Voices loud, trumpet or goose-like. Long neck and legs extended in flight. Gregarious outside breeding season.

CROWNED CRANE *Balearica regulorum* p. 92

Identification: 40″. Upperparts slate-grey, paler on neck and underparts, wings appear mainly white in flight with black primaries and chestnut secondaries; crown with a black, velvety cushion with a conspicuous tuft of straw-coloured, bristle-like feathers behind: bare cheeks and neck wattles white and red. The Crowned Crane can be mistaken only for a closely related species the Sudan Crowned Crane, which is smaller with a blackish neck.

Voice: A loud, honking call "ah, aahow, ah, aahow," which has been likened to the honking of Canada geese. Call uttered usually in flight.

Distribution and Habitat: A local resident, common in Kenya and Uganda, from Kenya and Uganda and eastern Congo, southwards to Central Africa to South Africa. Occurs on open plains, marshes, swamps and cultivated land.

Allied Species: The closely allied Sudan Crowned Crane (*Balearica pavonina*) is smaller than the Crowned Crane and has a blackish, not a pale grey neck. It occurs in Ethiopia and the Sudan, west to Senegal and northern Nigeria. It is reputed to occur as a vagrant in northern Uganda. The Wattled Crane (*Bugeranus carunculatus*) is a large species (50 inches) mainly pale grey in colour with a white neck and two white feathered pendant wattles from chin: it occurs in two isolated populations, one in the highlands of Ethiopia, the other in southern Tanganyika and Central Africa where it is commoner than the Crowned Crane. Favoured localities for the species are near Salisbury, Southern Rhodesia and the Kafue Flats and Bangweulu in Northern Rhodesia.

BUSTARDS: Otididae

Large or very large terrestrial birds with three-toed feet and long necks; mainly buff with fine dark vermiculations. Frequent open plains or desert or dry bush country. Gait a stately walk. Behaviour varies, sometimes very shy, running or crouching at the first sign of danger; at other times completely fearless of humans. Flight powerful with slow, deliberate strokes.

KORI BUSTARD *Ardeotis kori* p. 92

Identification: 30-40″. Male much larger than female. Upperparts and neck vermiculated black and greyish-buff; top of head crested. Feathers of neck very lax giving the effect of a thick-necked bird. Best identified by large size, lack of chestnut at back of neck, crested head and lax neck feathers. Jackson's Bustard has the back of the neck reddish-chestnut.

Voice: Less vocal than many other bustards, but at times gives a loud, far-carrying "kah, kah, kah."

Distribution and Habitat: A local resident Ethiopia, the Somalilands,

Kenya and Uganda, south to South Africa. Uncommon in Central Africa. Occurs in open or semi-open plains country or open dry country bush. Perhaps most frequent in Kenya Colony, where widespread and common in the Northern Frontier Province near Isiolo and on Mt. Marsabit.

Allied Species: Denham's or Jackson's Bustard (*Neotis denhami*) is about the size of a female Kori Bustard but has the back of the neck bright reddish-chestnut. It occurs in the Sudan and Ethiopia, south to Northern Rhodesia. It frequents open plains and game country. In East Africa it is frequent on the Mara River plains in southern Kenya: in Northern Rhodesia it is reputed common in Bangweulu. The Arabian Bustard (*Ardeotis arabs*) is a little smaller than a Kori Bustard with white tips to the wing coverts; in the Kori Bustard the wing coverts are white with black tips. It occurs in the northern parts of the Turkana district, Kenya; elsewhere in the Sudan, Eritrea and eastern British Somaliland. Heuglin's Bustard (*Neotis heuglinii*) is smaller than a Kori Bustard, with the crown, sides of face and chin black in the male. It occurs in the Somalilands, eastern Ethiopia and northern Kenya Colony; at times common in the little-known Dida-Galgalla Desert north of Marsabit, Northern Frontier Province, Kenya.

WHITE-BELLIED BUSTARD *Eupodotis senegalensis* p. 92

Identification: 24″. A white-breasted bustard with a very conspicuous blue-grey neck; male with inverted black V-patch on throat. Upperparts finely vermiculated orange-buff and black. The female Buff-crested Bustard has a white chest but is black on the belly and under tail coverts. Females of Black-breasted and Hartlaub's Bustards have white or pale buff underparts with black markings on the chest, but lack all trace of blue-grey on the neck.

Voice: A very loud, far-carrying "oo-warka, oo-warka."

Distribution and Habitat: Local resident from Senegal, eastwards to the Sudan, Ethiopia and Somaliland, south to Kenya and eastern and central Tanganyika. It occurs in semi-desert bush country, open and bush-covered plains and big game country. Common in the Nairobi National Park, Kenya.

Allied Species: The Little Brown Bustard (*Heterotetrax humilis*) is a very small bustard, the size of a Yellow-necked Spurfowl with buff upperparts and a white belly. It occurs locally in dry bush country in British Somaliland.

BLACK-BELLIED BUSTARD *Lissotis melanogaster* p. 92

Identification: 24″. Underparts of male black, of female pale buff with black vermiculations on chest; tail and rump vermiculated brown and warm buff. Hartlaub's Bustard male differs in having the rump and tail black-looking in the field, not pale buffy-brown. Female of Hartlaub's Bustard has heavy black markings on the chest; the female Black-bellied Bustard has the chest lightly vermiculated black and buff.

Voice: A single note "mm-wark."

Distribution and Habitat: Local resident in East and Central Africa, frequenting open plains, grasslands, and light savannah woodlands and bush. In Kenya, on the grassy plains of the eastern highlands it is now less common than Hartlaub's Bustard: previously the Black-bellied Bustard was the commoner species.

Allied Species: Hartlaub's Bustard (*Lissotis hartlaubii*) occurs locally in northern and eastern Uganda, Kenya and southwards to central Tanganyika. It is most frequent in the eastern Kenya Highlands and the Mt. Marsabit area of northern Kenya. The Buff-crested Bustard (*Lophotis ruficrista*) is a smaller bird (slightly larger than a fowl) with black underparts in both sexes and a drooping pinkish-buff crest. It occurs in dry bush country and dry open woodlands throughout East and Central Africa. It is locally common in the arid bush country of the Northern Frontier Province of Kenya.

STONE CURLEWS or THICKNEES: Burhinidae

The Stone Curlews or Thicknees (also called Dikkops) are a group of medium-sized sandy or grey-coloured plover-like birds with large heads and very large yellow eyes: mainly nocturnal in habits and some species often seen on roads at night: legs long and hind toe absent.

SPOTTED STONE CURLEW or THICKNEE *Burhinus capensis* p. 93

Identification: 17″. Upperparts sandy-rufous with black mottling giving the impression of heavy spotting: below pale buff to white on belly with black streaks on throat and chest. The European Thicknee and Senegal Thicknee are streaked above, not spotted. The smaller water

Dikkop is finely vermiculated black and grey above with dark streaks.

Voice: A loud, far-carrying curlew-like whistle, uttered usually after dusk.

Distribution and Habitat: A widespread but local resident throughout East and Central Africa. Frequents open bush and lightly wooded areas, dry rocky river-beds and broken ground. During the day usually observed resting in the shade of acacia bushes; more active at dusk and at night. Frequents roads at night-time and many are killed by motor vehicles.

Allied Species: The European Stone Curlew (*Burhinus oedicnemus*) is tawny or greyish-tawny above with heavy black streaking, and a white bar along the shoulder of the wing. It is a winter visitor to the northern districts of Kenya and Uganda. The Senegal Stone Curlew (*Burhinus senegalensis*) is also streaked above but has no white bar along the shoulder of the wing. This species and the Water Dikkop are often found in the vicinity of rivers and lakes, while the European Stone Curlew and the Spotted Thicknee frequent drier areas. The Senegal Stone Curlew is a local resident species in the northern parts of Uganda and Kenya. The Water Dikkop (*Burhinus vermiculatus*) is a smaller and greyer bird found along rivers and the shores of lakes throughout Kenya, Uganda, Tanganyika and Central Africa. It is very common on the Tana River in Kenya.

JACANAS or LILY-TROTTERS: Jacanidae

The Jacanas or Lily-trotters are curious long-legged water birds, somewhat resembling rails or plovers, with very long toes. Their enormous feet enable them to walk and feed on waterlily leaves and floating aquatic vegetation. Their nests are sodden platforms of water-weeds and their eggs are remarkable for their very high gloss.

AFRICAN JACANA or LILY-TROTTER *Actophilornis africanus*

p. 93

Identification: 9-11″. A bright chestnut, plover-like bird with a large bluish head-shield, nearly always seen walking about on floating water vegetation. At close quarters the bluish-white bill and head-shield are conspicuous. The Lesser Jacana is half the size of the African Jacana and has no head-shield and little chestnut in plumage.

Voice: A series of chittering call-notes.

Distribution and Habitat: Widely distributed and often common in suitable localities throughout East and Central Africa. Occurs on open waters where there is an abundance of aquatic floating vegetation, especially water-lilies.

Allied Species: The Lesser Jacana (*Microparra capensis*) is a dunlin-sized species, also with long legs and toes. It has very little chestnut in the plumage, the upperparts being grey with a purplish-black patch on the back at the base of the neck. It has the same range as the African Jacana but is a much rarer bird and often more skulking in its habits, frequenting patches of dense marsh grass.

PLOVERS: Charadriidae

The Plovers are small or medium-sized birds of the wading bird type, although some species occur on dry plains. They are more thickset than the sandpipers and their allies, with thicker-looking necks and relatively larger and more thickset heads.

RINGED PLOVER *Charadrius hiaticula* (M) p. 96

Identification: 7½″. A plump little plover with a broad black band across its white breast. White wing-bar conspicuous in flight. Bill orange or orange-yellow with black tip; legs orange-yellow. Immature birds have dusky brown breast band, often incomplete in front, and resemble Kentish Plovers. They may be distinguished by their yellowish, not black, legs. The Lesser Ringed Plover has no white wing-bar and its legs are pinkish-flesh, not orange or yellow.

Voice: A melodious whistle "too-lee."

Distribution and Habitat: Winter visitor and passage migrant to coast and inland waters East Africa; in Central Africa frequent Nyasaland and Northern Rhodesia but only one record for Southern Rhodesia.

Allied Species: The Little Ringed Plover (*Charadrius dubius*) is an uncommon winter visitor to inland waters in East Africa, south to central Tanganyika. It is smaller than the Ringed Plover and lacks the white wing-bar in flight. At close quarters yellow eye-ring and pinkish legs are good characters. The Kentish Plover (*Charadrius alexandrinus*) is a very uncommon non-breeding visitor to the East African coast. It has a small blackish patch on each side of the upper breast, not a complete black band. The White-fronted Sand Plover (*Charadrius marginatus*) occurs as a breeding bird on sandy parts of the East African coast and sandbanks of the larger lakes and rivers in Central Africa. It is pale tawny brown above with a white forehead: underparts white with a rufous wash on the chest. The very local Chestnut-banded Sand

BUSTARDS, CORMORANTS, CRANES, etc.

1. **AFRICAN DARTER** page 21
Pointed bill; white neck stripe.

2. **LONG-TAILED CORMORANT** 21
Small size; relatively long tail.

3. **WHITE-NECKED CORMORANT** 20
White neck; relatively short tail.

4. **WAHLBERG'S EAGLE** 55
Short nape crest.

5. **WHITE-BELLIED BUSTARD** 88
White belly: blue-grey neck.

6. **BLACK-BELLIED BUSTARD** 89
Male: Black belly; tail and rump pale brown, not black.
Female: Belly buffish-white; light vermiculations on chest.

7. **OSPREY** 70
Clear white belly; black head markings.

8. **KORI BUSTARD** 87
Neck feathers lax; no chestnut patch at base of neck.

9. **CROWNED CRANE** 86
Straw-coloured crown; black velvety forehead; white and red face wattles.

10. **GROUND HORNBILL** 150
Black with white primaries; red face and throat; terrestrial, in distance resembles domestic turkey.

11. **SECRETARY BIRD** 42
Long central tail feathers; lax crest; black tibia; terrestrial.

1
2
3
4
5
♂
6
7
♀
8
9
10
11

1
2
3
4
5
♂
♀
6
7
8
9
10
11
12

PLOVERS, RAILS and ALLIES

1. **LONG-TOED LAPWING** page 101
White front; carmine-red and black bill. Lives on floating aquatic vegetation like lily-trotter.

2. **WATTLED PLOVER** 100
Red and yellow eye wattle; yellow legs.

3. **BLACKHEAD PLOVER** 100
Black crown and crest; red eye wattle.

4. **RED-KNOBBED COOT** 83
Uniform blackish plumage; white bill and frontal shield with two red knobs.

5. **WHITE-SPOTTED PYGMY CRAKE** 82
Head, chest and tail bright chestnut-red.
Male: Back and belly black with round white spots.
Female: Back and belly barred black and buff.

6. **PURPLE GALLINULE** 82
Bright red bill and frontal shield; pink legs.

7. **AFRICAN JACANA** 90
Bright chestnut plumage; bluish-white bill and frontal shield. Inhabits floating aquatic vegetation.

8. **MOORHEN** 83
White flank streaks; bill red with yellow tip.

9. **SPOTTED STONE CURLEW** 89
Heavy spotted upperparts; nocturnal, often on roads after dark.

10. **AVOCET** 101
Upturned bill; black and white plumage; blue-grey legs.

11. **BLACK-WINGED STILT** 102
Very long pink legs; black and white plumage; straight bill. Immature birds much greyer than adults.

12. **BLACK CRAKE** 79
Uniform slaty-black plumage; apple-green bill; pink legs.

Plover (*Charadrius venustus*) is a resident on Lake Magadi in southern Kenya and Lakes Natron and Manyara in northern Tanganyika. It resembles a Ringed Plover but has a narrow chestnut, not a broad black, band across the chest.

KITTLITZ'S SAND PLOVER *Charadrius pecuarius* p. 96

Identification: 6½″. This species may be recognised by its dark upperparts, the white forehead band which is prolonged round the back of the neck to form a white collar and its pale underparts richly washed orange-buff: bill black, legs grey.

Voice: A clear, plaintive whistle, " pleeep."

Distribution and Habitat: A resident species throughout East and Central Africa in suitable localities. It occurs on sandy or mud flats on the coast and on inland waters. It is often found in small flocks on grassy flats on the margins of inland lakes and is usually very tame and without fear of man.

THREE-BANDED PLOVER *Charadrius tricollaris* p. 96

Identification: 7½″. In general appearance not unlike a slim Ringed Plover but with two black bands across the breast, not one. Upperparts dark olive-brown with a white forehead and a white ring on the crown; bill orange with black tip; legs coral pink.

Voice: A plaintive "wik-wik," usually uttered when flushed.

Distribution and Habitat: Widespread resident throughout East and Central Africa on lake shores, dams, streams, rivers and rain pools. Uncommon on the coast, but does occur at times along edge of tidal lagoons.

Allied Species: Forbes' Plover (*Charadrius forbesi*) is a rare species recorded from Northern Rhodesia and the western districts of Uganda and Tanganyika. It is a little larger than the Three-banded Plover and the forehead is dark olive-brown, not white.

MONGOLIAN SAND PLOVER *Charadrius mongolus* (M) p. 96

Identification: 8″. In non-breeding plumage this is a pale greyish sand plover with a white forehead and white underparts and a patch of grey on each side of the breast. In breeding dress, which is rarely observed in East Africa, the upperparts are washed with tawny with a black band on the forehead and black ear-coverts: a band of pale chestnut across the breast. This species is a miniature edition of the Great Sand Plover, which is intermediate in size between the Mongolian Sand Plover and the Grey Plover. The first field character when size cannot be recognised is the relative size of the black bill: in the Mongolian Sand Plover the bill appears small for the size of the bird; in the Great Sand Plover the bill appears relatively large.

Voice: A whistling call-note, but usually a silent bird.

Distribution and Habitat: A non-breeding visitor to the coastal areas of Kenya, Tanganyika and Zanzibar and Pemba Islands. Very uncommon on inland waters: a single record for Northern Rhodesia. Occurs usually in very large flocks, often associated with shore-birds such as Sanderlings and Curlew Sandpipers. In Kenya very common on the extensive mud-flats of Mida Creek, south of Malindi.

GREAT SAND PLOVER *Charadrius leschenaultii* (M) p. 96

Identification: 10″. A rather large, greyish plover with white underparts and a patch of pale grey at each side of the chest. Intermediate in size between Mongolian Sand Plover and Grey Plover. In summer plumage the upperparts are washed with orange-tawny, there is a black band across the forehead and the ear-coverts are black; breast with a broad band of pale chestnut. The best character for distinguishing this species from the Mongolian Sand Plover, apart from size, is its relatively larger bill, which appears big for the bird's total size.

Voice: A one or two-note whistle, but usually silent.

Distribution and Habitat: A non-breeding visitor to the coast of Kenya and Tanganyika: it is reputed to breed on the coast of Italian and British Somaliland. It occurs both on mud flats and on sandy beaches, usually in small parties or single birds. The species is much in evidence during the spring migration at Mida Creek on the Kenya coast.

Allied Species: The Caspian Plover (*Charadrius asiaticus*) is an uncommon winter visitor and passage migrant to East and Central Africa. It occurs in localities away from water, favouring grassy plains. It is much addicted to grass-covered airfields. It is 9 inches long, pale brown above, white below with a broad pale chestnut or pale brown band across the chest; face and eye-stripe white. This species occurs in flocks of a dozen or more birds: in flight, at a distance, they resemble golden plovers.

GREY PLOVER *Charadrius squatarola* (M) p. 96

Identification: 11-12″. In spring plumage black below and mottled silvery-white and black above. Winter and immature plumaged birds have upperparts more uniform greyish-brown and white below: black axillaries conspicuous in flight in all plumages.

PLOVERS

1
2
a
3
b
4
a
5
b
a
6
b
7
8
9
10
11

1
2
A
B
3
4
5
6
7
8
9
10

SNIPE, GULLS and ALLIES

1. **PAINTED SNIPE** page 103
Flies like rail with legs dangling; wings rounded with buff spots; bill down-curved; conspicuous white eye-patch.

2. **AFRICAN SNIPE** 104
Very long straight bill; striped crown; flight sluggish. *Note:* in hand African Snipe easily distinguished from European Common Snipe by very slender, mainly white outer tail feathers.

3. **TEMMINCK'S COURSER** 110
Plover-like buff bird inhabiting open plains; black patch on belly.

4. **PRATINCOLE** 111
Tern-like with long forked tail; black bordered buff throat patch.

5. **WHITE-WINGED BLACK TERN** 115
White fore-edge of wings and white tail contrast with black body plumage. Winter and immature grey and white with blackish nape patch.

6. **GREY-HEADED GULL** 114
Occurs mainly on inland waters; pale grey and white gull with grey head.

7. **SOOTY GULL** 114
Occurs mainly on coast; blackish head and white nape; immature paler and white nape patch absent.

8. **GULL-BILLED TERN** 115
Heavy, gull-like black bill; forked tail.

9. **CURLEW** 109
Very long decurved bill; no crown stripe.

10. **AFRICAN SKIMMER** 116
Remarkable bill with elongated lower mandible; gregarious; immature paler above.

A, Outer tail feather of African Snipe.
B, Outer tail feather of European Common Snipe.

Voice: A far-carrying, plaintive, "tlee-oo-ee."

Distribution and Habitat: Non-breeding visitor throughout East and Central Africa. Most common on coastal mudflats of Kenya and Tanganyika but also occurs on inland waters in small numbers. Birds in full summer plumage may be seen on the Kenya coast in April and early May.

CROWNED LAPWING or PLOVER *Stephanibyx coronatus*

p. 96

Identification: 11″. Upperparts uniform pale greyish-brown; top of head black with a white ring on crown; below, chin white merging to pale brown on breast, bordered black; abdomen white; bill red with black tip; legs red.

Voice: A noisy, scolding whistle, frequently repeated.

Distribution and Habitat: A locally common resident throughout East and Central Africa, which also occurs in Angola and South Africa. It inhabits short grassy plains, open bush country, grassy airstrips and sometimes cultivated areas.

Allied Species: The Bronze-winged or Violet-tipped Courser (*Rhinoptilus chalcopterus*) has a superficial resemblance to a Crowned Plover. It may always be identified by its more upright stance and the blackish-brown patch on the chin and below the eyes. It is nocturnal in its habits and if seen by day is usually resting in the shade of some bush or small tree. Any bird seen on the road at night which looks like a Crowned Plover is likely to be the Violet-tipped Courser.

SENEGAL PLOVER *Stephanibyx lugubris*

p. 96

Identification: 9″. This is a long-legged, rather small grasslands plover with greyish-brown upperparts and chest and a conspicuous white patch on the forehead. It closely resembles the larger highlands species, the Black-winged Plover, but may be distinguished in flight by its half black under wing-coverts; the Black-winged Plover has entirely white under wing-coverts.

Voice: A most melodious, two- to four-note whistle.

Distribution and Habitat: Locally distributed in suitable areas in West, East and Central Africa, south to Natal. It is usually found in areas below 5,000 ft. whilst its near relative the Black-winged Plover usually frequents areas over 6,000 ft. The Senegal Plover is especially attracted by recently burnt-over grasslands and by bush areas which are being cleared and burnt for native cultivation. In East Africa it is a common species along the Kenya coast in open bush country, and in the open grassy plains of western Uganda. It is a common plover in the Queen Elizabeth National Park, Uganda.

Allied Species: The Brown-chested Wattled Plover (*Anomalophrys superciliosus*) is the same size as the Senegal Plover: it has the front half of the crown rufous, the hinder half black, and a yellow wattle in front of the eye: underparts grey on throat and breast with a chestnut patch on the lower breast. It is a rare species in East Africa, recorded from western Kenya, Uganda and western Tanganyika. It frequents both marshy areas and plains.

BLACK-WINGED PLOVER *Stephanibyx melanopterus* p. 96

Identification: 11″. Upperparts greyish-brown becoming grey on neck and head; forehead white; chin white, merging to grey on the throat and to black on upper breast; remainder underparts white; under wing-coverts white. From the smaller Senegal Plover it may be distinguished by its entirely white under wing-coverts which are conspicuous in flight and when the bird raises its wings on alighting.

Voice: Usual call a loud "cee-chee-chee-reek," quite unlike the plaintive whistle of the Senegal Plover. Often very noisy when its breeding grounds are invaded.

Distribution and Habitat: This is a highland species, in East Africa occurs usually above 7,000 ft. It ranges from the highlands of Ethiopia and the eastern Sudan southwards through Kenya Colony to eastern South Africa. From Central Africa there is a single record of the species in Southern Rhodesia at Sabi River. It is an abundant species on the Kinangop plateau in Kenya Colony.

SPURWING PLOVER *Hoplopterus spinosus* p. 96

Identification: 10½″. A striking black, white and greyish-brown plover. Differs from closely allied Blacksmith Plover in having back entirely pale greyish-brown. The Blacksmith Plover has a large black patch on the mantle. Wings and tail strongly patterned black and white. Has small spur on bend of wing but this is not generally conspicuous in field.

Voice: Usually silent unless disturbed on nesting grounds, when they have a very loud and shrill "yak-yak-yak" call.

Distribution and Habitat: Resident in West Africa, eastwards through the Sudan to Ethiopia and Somaliland, southwards through eastern Uganda and Kenya to central Tanganyika. It frequents the vicinity of water and marshes, preferring areas of short grass. It occurs alongside the

Blacksmith Plover in some parts of Kenya, for instance at Lakes Naivasha, Elmenteita and Nakuru.

BLACKSMITH PLOVER *Hoplopterus armatus* p. 96

Identification: 11″. A conspicuous species with contrasting black, white and pale grey plumage. Differs from the allied Spurwing Plover in having the crown white, a large black patch on the back and the cheeks and sides of breast black.

Voice: A loud, ringing "tik, tik, tik" call, resembling two pieces of metal being knocked together.

Distribution and Habitat: Occurs locally from the southern half of Kenya south to Angola and South Africa. A local resident in Central Africa, most frequent in the vicinity of swamps in Northern Rhodesia. The species occurs in areas near water, both brackish and fresh. It is common near the Rift Valley lakes in southern Kenya.

WATTLED PLOVER *Afribyx senegallus* p. 93

Identification: 13″. A large plover with pale olive-brown plumage, a black chin and black streaked throat, a white forehead and a large and conspicuous red and yellow wattle in front of the eye: bill greenish-yellow with black tip; legs yellow.

Voice: A shrill "peek-peek."

Distribution and Habitat: In East Africa the Wattled Plover is a local resident in western Kenya, Uganda and Tanganyika, southwards to the Zambesi River. It is widely distributed in the Rhodesias but rare in Nyasaland. It frequents open grassy areas, generally adjacent to water.

Allied Species: The White-headed Plover (*Xiphidiopterus albiceps*) has long yellow wattles in front of the eyes, brown and white plumage, black shoulders and a white crown. It occurs in Uganda, Tanganyika, Nyasaland, and the Rhodesias. This is a bird of sandbanks in the larger rivers such as the Zambesi, Sabi and Limpopo. In Tanganyika it sometimes occurs in the vicinity of lakes and swamps but is most uncommon.

BLACKHEAD PLOVER *Sarciophorus tectus* p. 93

Identification: 10″. This is a rather small dry-country plover with pale greyish-brown upperparts, a black crown with an upturned crest; chin white but cheeks, neck and streak down middle of breast black; a small red wattle in front of eye. Bill red with black tip; legs maroon red.

Voice: A shrill two or three-note whistle, heard usually at dusk or at night.

Distribution and Habitat: Resident in arid thorn-bush country from Senegal eastwards to Ethiopia, Eritrea, the Somalilands and Kenya Colony. Species mainly nocturnal in its habits and when encountered during the day is usually seen in pairs in the shade of acacia trees. Partial to grassy airstrips where these exist. In Kenya it is common in the arid bush north of Garissa and in the vicinity of Lake Baringo in the Rift Valley.

Allied Species: The much larger Spot-breasted Plover (*Tylibyx melanocephalus*), 13 inches, also has a black crown with a short crest: above it is ashy-brown with a green wash; below throat and neck black, and white breast also streaked black. It inhabits the highlands of northern and central Ethiopia.

LONG-TOED LAPWING *Hemiparra crassirostris* p. 93

Identification: 12″. A distinctive, long-legged plover with the habits of a lily-trotter, generally observed on floating aquatic vegetation. Face, front half of crown, throat and upper breast white; remainder of breast and upper part of belly black; abdomen and under tail coverts white; a great deal of white in the wings conspicuous in flight. Bill carmine red with black tip; legs deep maroon red.

Voice: A loud metallic "tik, tik."

Distribution and Habitat: A local resident from Lake Chad and the southern Sudan to Uganda, Kenya, Tanganyika, Nyasaland and Northern Rhodesia. It usually frequents areas of water where there is an abundance of floating vegetation but in some localities (at Entebbe, Uganda and the Kafue Flats, Northern Rhodesia) it may be seen on the shores of rivers and lakes. It is numerous and very tame in the Amboseli Game Reserve in southern Kenya.

AVOCET *Recurvirostra avosetta* (M & R) p. 93

Identification: 17″. Contrasting black and white plumage, thin, black upturned bill and blue-grey legs enable this species to be identified with ease. Immature birds and birds frequenting soda lakes have black plumage more or less suffused with pale brown. During flight legs extend beyond tail. Wades in shallow water and feeds in a graceful manner with a side-to-side scything motion: sometimes swims, especially when a hatch of aquatic insects is in progress. In East Africa sometimes seen in very large flocks, hundreds and sometimes even thousands strong.

Voice: a loud "kleep" or "kloop," uttered on the wing.

Distribution and Habitat: A winter visitor in large numbers to East Africa, where there is also a small and very local (Rift Valley lakes) breeding population. In Central Africa very uncommon resident species. Avocets frequent fresh and brackish water lakes, exposed mud-flats, estuaries and sand banks. In East Africa often very abundant in winter on lakes Naivasha, Elmenteita and Nakuru and a regular breeder at Lake Magadi.

Allied Species: The European Oyster-Catcher (*Haematopus ostralegus*) is a very uncommon visitor to the coast of Kenya and Tanganyika and islands off the coast. Its black and white plumage, characteristic orange bill and pink legs make it unmistakable. The Crab Plover (*Dromas ardeola*) is a non-breeding visitor to the East African coast. It is black (or in the immature, greyish) and white with blue-grey legs; head large and black bill rather short and thick. At a distance when flying the general black and white plumage and trailing blue legs can give the impression that the bird is an avocet, but at closer quarters the two cannot be confused. It is usually present on the vast expanse of mud and sand flats of Mida Creek on the Kenya coast.

BLACK-WINGED STILT *Himantopus himantopus* (M & R) p. 93

Identification: 15″. Unmistakable: in flight very long pink legs trail 6-7 inches beyond tail. Plumage black and white, or in the case of immature birds, black, white and grey. Black undersurface of sharply pointed wings conspicuous in flight.

Voice: A shrill, yelping "kyip, kyip, kyip."

Distribution and Habitat: Uncommon local resident and abundant winter visitor in East Africa: less common in Central Africa. Species frequents fresh and brackish inland waters but is uncommon on coast. In Kenya it is a numerous bird on the brackish waters of Lakes Nakuru, Elmenteita and Magadi, and on the fresh water of Lake Naivasha.

PAINTED SNIPE: Rostratulidae

This very distinctive bird combines the field appearance of a snipe and a rail. When flushed from thick sedges at the edge of water its slow flight, rounded wings and dangling legs give a very rail-like impression. It is further remarkable in that the female is more brightly coloured than the male. It is the female who initiates courtship and the male who incubates and hatches the young.

PAINTED SNIPE *Rostratula benghalensis* p. 97

Identification: 10-11″. When flushed dangling legs and rounded wings (with large round buff spots) present an appearance nearer rails than snipe. Female larger and more brightly coloured than male which has chestnut on back of neck and throat: white ring around eye, extending as streak behind eye, conspicuous when bird observed on ground. Bill slightly down-curved and reddish-brown in colour.

Voice: Usually completely silent birds even when flushed, but reputed to utter a guttural croak.

Distribution and Habitat: Resident and spasmodic local migrant throughout Ethiopian Region in suitable places. Local in East and Central Africa and nowhere really common. Frequents swamps and sedge-lined edges of lakes and marshes, and areas where there are mudflats overgrown with marsh grass. Often overlooked unless flushed.

SNIPE, CURLEWS and SANDPIPERS: Scolopacidae

A numerous group of small to medium-sized wading birds, with long legs, slender bills and pointed and angular wings. In many species summer (breeding) and winter plumages differ greatly. Most of the members of this Family occurring in East and Central Africa are non-breeding visitors only, their chief breeding grounds being in Arctic or sub-Arctic regions. Many species highly gregarious in winter quarters in Africa.

AFRICAN SNIPE *Capella nigripennis* p. 97

Identification: 11". This species is difficult to distinguish from the visiting European Snipe, but upperparts are darker and tail feathers are whitish: it also has a much slower flight than the European Common Snipe. The Great Snipe is a heavier-looking bird with a relatively short bill and whitish spots on wings which are conspicuous in flight. In the hand the African Snipe may be recognised by its white belly and tail of sixteen feathers, the outer ones being narrow and mainly white.

Voice: Usually a silent bird, sometimes uttering a rasping "tsp" when flushed. In the breeding season a constantly repeated "chok, chok, chok, chok." In diving flight during courtship display produces a vibrating, drumming sound.

Distribution and Habitat: Resident, local and to some extent confined to higher altitudes, from Ethiopia southwards through Kenya and Uganda to South Africa. Occurs in swamps, marshy alpine moorlands, edges of lakes and flooded areas.

Allied Species: The European Common Snipe (*Capella gallinago*) is a winter visitor in varying numbers to East Africa, rare in Central Africa. Like the African Snipe it has a white belly: tail feathers 14-16, wide and mainly rufous and pale grey. The Great Snipe (*Capella media*) is a winter visitor and passage migrant to East Africa. In Central Africa it is less uncommon than the Common Snipe, especially in Northern Rhodesia and Nyasaland. The Great Snipe is larger in body than the African and Common Snipe but has a shorter bill. Its underparts are barred, not pure white. The Jack Snipe (*Lymnocrytes minima*) occurs spasmodically in East Africa, usually in small numbers. It is small (8 inches) and may be recognised by the absence of buff centre-stripe on crown. Usually solitary and flushes silently: flight rather slow and usually direct and of short duration.

CURLEW SANDPIPER *Calidris testacea* (M) p. 112

Identification: 7½″. In summer plumage, which is acquired from mid-April onwards, colour mainly chestnut-red with whitish rump. In some lights at a distance birds look almost blackish chestnut. In winter dress pale grey above, white below with distinct white rump when it flies. Usually in flocks. The Little Stint is smaller (5 inches) and lacks the white rump. In summer plumage belly white, not russet.

Voice: A single, liquid "tssssp."

Distribution and Habitat: A common winter visitor and passage migrant to East Africa, less frequent in the Rhodesias and Nyasaland. Occurs both on inland lakes and on the coastal mud-flats. During late April and early May vast flocks of red Curlew Sandpipers and many other waders in summer plumage may be seen at Mida Creek on the Kenya coast.

LITTLE STINT *Calidris minuta* (M) p. 112

Identification: 5-5½″. The smallest of our visiting waders. Resembles a miniature Dunlin in general appearance. In summer plumage upperparts and chest mainly rufous; breast and abdomen white; rump blackish, edged on each side by white. In winter plumage pale grey above with usually darker bases of the feathers showing, giving a slightly mottled effect: Temminck's Stint has uniform dark upperparts. The underparts of winter-plumaged Little Stint white except for a greyish patch on each side of the breast; Temminck's Stint has a greyish band across the chest. Outer tail feathers grey, not contrasting with remainder: Temminck's Stint's outer tail feathers white.

Voice: A sharp, liquid "tsss."

Distribution and Habitat: A common winter visitor and passage migrant to East and Central Africa. Occurs both on inland waters, where there are expanses of mud exposed, and on coastal mud-flats and tidal sands. Often in very large flocks, and may be associated with Curlew Sandpipers or other waders.

Allied Species: Temminck's Stint (*Calidris temminckii*) is darker and more uniform above; its outer tail feathers are white and are conspicuous in flight and at close quarters its legs are yellowish-olive, not black. In general appearance it resembles a minute Common Sandpiper, whilst the Little Stint looks like a small Dunlin. The Sanderling (*Crocethia alba*) is a winter visitor and passage migrant to the East African coast, rare inland. Occurs in small numbers Northern Rhodesia and Nyasaland. This is a thickset rather short-legged wader with very pale grey upperparts, blackish shoulders and white below. In summer plumage upperparts and throat mottled rufous and black.

RUFF *Philomachus pugnax* (M) p. 112

Identification: Male 11½″; female (Reeve) 10″. The male does not acquire full breeding plumage (the enormous erectile ruff and ear-tufts which give it its name) in East Africa, only some feathers of the upperparts and belly being moulted. In winter plumage the upperparts, head and chest are grey more or less mottled by darker feather bases and pale feather edgings: leg colour varies from orange and yellow to olive green: orange-legged examples may be mistaken for redshanks but are distinguished by generally thicker-set appearance, rather rounded head and whitish at base of bill, dark tail and rump with a conspicuous oval white patch on each side, lack of white wing patch and more erect stance. Females, called Reeves, are easily recognised in the field by their smaller size; they often form separate flocks from the males during winter. In spring both ruffs and reeves moult some of the winter plumage and acquire dark feathers edged and mottled rufous or buff.

Voice: In winter quarters a silent bird, sometimes utters a short liquid "tsss."

Distribution and Habitat: A common winter visitor and passage migrant in East and Central Africa. Frequents marshes, edges of swamps and lakes, mudflats and flooded grassy areas: equally common on both fresh and brackish water but uncommon on coast. Often swims like a phalarope, especially when attracted into deep water by hatches of aquatic flies.

Allied Species: The Redshank (*Tringa totanus*) is an uncommon winter visitor to East Africa. It may be recognised by white wing patch in flight, orange-red legs and white rump. The Terek Sandpiper (*Xenus cinereus*) has rather short orange-yellow legs and looks like a large edition of a Common Sandpiper with a long, slightly up-curved bill. Upperparts brownish-grey with some blackish streaks; underparts white with faint streaks on breast. This species is found mainly on the coast, favouring extensive mud and sand flats where it mingles with other waders such as Curlew Sandpipers and Mongolian Sand Plovers.

TURNSTONE *Arenaria interpres* (M) p. 112

Identification: 8½″. A thickset wader with short orange legs and tortoiseshell plumaged upperparts. In spring upperparts are rich chestnut and black, underparts white with broad black chest-band. In winter plumage tortoiseshell plumage replaced by dusky brown with pale edgings. Bill black, short, stout and pointed. Has characteristic method of feeding, turning over shells, stones and seaweed when seeking food.

Voice: A sharp "tuk, a, tuk."

Distribution and Habitat: Winter visitor and passage migrant to the East African coast, rare inland. It has been recorded a few times in Northern Rhodesia and Nyasaland. It frequents rocky seashores and places where large piles of seaweed have been washed up by the waves. It is usually encountered in small parties, often associated with Curlew Sandpipers, Sand Plovers and Sanderlings.

COMMON SANDPIPER *Tringa hypoleucos* (M) p. 112

Identification: 7-7½″. A small, dark-rumped sandpiper with rather short legs; associated with the margins of lakes, rivers and high-water mark on the coast. Upperparts olive-brown, mottled with black in summer plumage, and white underparts slightly streaked on throat and chest. Has characteristic flight over the surface of water with rapid, shallow wing beats and glides on down-curved wings: white wing-bar conspicuous in flight. On the ground bobs head and tail frequently.

Voice: A shrill, piping call "twee, tee tee tee tee" when flushed; also a rapid titter.

Distribution and Habitat: A common winter visitor and passage migrant throughout East and Central Africa. Many non-breeding birds oversummer in their African winter quarters. Frequents the sea coast, and the margins of dams, swamps, lakes, streams and rivers. Records of the species' breeding in East Africa not confirmed.

GREEN SANDPIPER *Tringa ochropus* (M) p. 112

Identification: 9″. Considerably larger than Common Sandpiper, and with relatively longer legs. Frequents margins of streams and rivers; very uncommon edges of lakes and swamps where Wood Sandpiper is abundant. General plumage blackish, including under wings with a brilliant white rump which contrasts strongly with rest of plumage. Wood Sandpiper much greyer, often mottled above, with whitish under wings and white rump which does not contrast strongly with remainder of upperparts. In summer plumage upperparts speckled with pale buff and throat heavily streaked dark olive-grey. Species usually shy and solitary; bobs head and tail frequently; flight direct with jerky wing beats.

Voice: A liquid, three-note whistle "teleet, pleet pleet."

Distribution and Habitat: A common but relatively local winter visitor to East Africa, Northern Rhodesia and Nyasaland. Uncommon in Southern Rhodesia. Frequents streams and rivers and small pools: very uncommon around the margins of larger swamps and lakes where Wood Sandpipers are abundant.

WOOD SANDPIPER *Tringa glareola* (M) p. 112

Identification: 8″. In spring plumage mottled above grey and silvery white; head, neck and breast finely streaked; distinct pale eye-stripe. In flight white rump and whitish underparts of wings distinct; no wing-bar. In winter whitish marking to upperparts less distinct and plumage more uniform. Much paler than Green Sandpiper which looks black and white in field. Common Sandpiper has shorter legs and dark, not white, rump.

Voice: A liquid whistle, "tluee" or a series of liquid trilling notes. When in flocks, especially when on the wing, noisier than most other sandpipers, keeping up a high-pitched trilling.

Distribution and Habitat: A common winter visitor and passage migrant to East and Central Africa, but uncommon on the coast. Favours the grassy edges of lakes and swamps, both brackish and fresh, and dams and flooded areas. It is seldom found along the margins of streams and rivers which form the main habitat of the Green Sandpiper.

MARSH SANDPIPER *Tringa stagnatilis* (M) p. 112

Identification: 9″. In winter and summer plumage this sandpiper looks very like a small, graceful Greenshank. At a distance, when size is not a very good field character, it may be distinguished by its very fine straight bill, white forehead and proportionately longer, more delicate greenish legs. Winter plumage pale grey above, white below: in summer dress, which is acquired by early March, upperparts are marked with black and throat and chest finely spotted with black. In flight white of tail and rump extends right up back, like Greenshank, but toes project further beyond tail. The Wood Sandpiper is a shorter-legged wader with a square-looking white patch on the rump.

Voice: Quite unlike that of the greenshank. Usual call one or two notes "tee-oo" or "teea, teea": also utters a liquid trill, not unlike that of the Wood Sandpiper.

Distribution and Habitat: Winter visitor and passage migrant in suitable areas throughout Ethiopian Region: immature and non-breeding birds remain in Africa during northern summer months. Common in East and Central Africa. Frequents fresh and brackish inland waters, especially where there are areas of mudflat: rarely observed on coast.

In Kenya it is abundant on lakes in the Rift Valley, especially Lake Naivasha and Lake Rudolf.

GREENSHANK *Tringa nebularia* (M) p. 112

Identification: 12″. A graceful, long-legged, long-necked wader, pale grey above, white below: in flight white of tail and rump extends up back. In summer plumage some black markings on upperparts and throat and chest spotted blackish. The Marsh Sandpiper is a small edition of this species but has a proportionately finer bill, longer green legs, and a conspicuous white forehead. Ruffs are thicker-set birds with dark rumps with a white patch on each side. The Common Redshank, an uncommon bird in East Africa, has orange, not green legs and a white patch in the wings in flight.

Voice: The greenshank has one of the most easily recognised calls, a ringing two or three-note "chew, chew, chew"; sometimes a single "tuu" or a series of the "chew" notes.

Distribution and Habitat: A widespread and often common winter visitor and passage migrant throughout the Ethiopian Region in suitable areas. Non-breeding birds summer in Africa. Frequents both inland waters (fresh and brackish) and the coast. On spring migration common along the East African coast and on lakes in the Rift Valley.

CURLEW *Numenius arquata* (M) p. 97

Identification: 20-24″. The largest of the African shore birds, easily recognised by its very long, down-curved bill, buffish-brown upperparts and throat and conspicuous white rump. Distinctive call not always diagnostic as in East Africa whimbrels often imitate the well-known "curl-ee, curl-ee." Whimbrel distinguished by smaller size and bold pale stripe down centre of crown.

Voice: A loud, far-carrying "cur-lee, cur-lee," frequently repeated and often followed by a series of bubbling calls. On East African coast the whimbrel often imitates this call, but the curlew does not imitate the whimbrel's characteristic seven-note whistle "te,ee,ee,ee,ee,ee,ee."

Distribution and Habitat: Winter visitor and passage migrant, more frequent in East than in Central Africa: non-breeding birds summer in Africa. Frequents coastal areas, especially sand and mud-flats: less common inland but some recorded most years Rift Valley lakes in East Africa.

Allied Species: The Whimbrel (*Numenius phaeopus*) occurs commonly as a winter visitor and passage migrant on the East African coast but is uncommon inland. In Central Africa it has been recorded in Nyasaland.

This species is much smaller than the Curlew (16 inches) and at close quarters buff streak down centre of crown is conspicuous: seven-note call is distinctive.

COURSERS and PRATINCOLES: Glareolidae

The Coursers and Pratincoles are small or medium-sized birds allied to the Plovers with a relatively short arched bill. In the coursers the hind toe is absent and the birds resemble small, long-legged plovers. Pratincoles have short legs and possess the hind toe: their field appearance is somewhat tern-like and like terns they are found near water, while coursers inhabit arid areas.

TEMMINCK'S COURSER *Cursorius temminckii* p. 97

Identification: 8″. A small rufous-buff, plover-like bird with a conspicuous black patch on the abdomen: often occurs on grass areas which have been recently burned. The Cream-coloured Courser is slightly larger and has white underparts without the black patch. The Two-banded Courser has two black bands across the breast: Heuglin's Courser has a chestnut V at the base of the throat, followed by chestnut breast band. The much larger Violet-tipped (Bronze-winged) Courser resembles a Crowned Plover but may be recognised by the blackish-brown patches on the throat and below the eyes.

Voice: A metallic, piping call usually uttered when the bird takes wing: otherwise silent.

Distribution and Habitat: Resident locally throughout most of the Ethiopian Region from Gambia and the Sudan, south to eastern Cape Province, South Africa. Common in East and Central Africa, but subject to local movements. It frequents short grass areas, such as open plains and aerodromes, and is much attracted to such areas after a grass fire.

Allied Species: The Cream-coloured Courser (*Cursorius cursor*) is a resident in Ethiopia, the Somalilands, south to central Kenya Colony. It is slightly larger than Temminck's Courser and has the underparts white: it occurs in arid, semi-desert country. Heuglin's Courser (*Hemerodromus cinctus*), 10 inches, resembles a miniature edition of a Stone Curlew and like that bird is partly nocturnal in its habits and is often seen on roads at night. It has a V-shaped chestnut bar at the base of the neck; chest buff with blackish streaks and a black band followed by a chestnut band across breast. It occurs as a local resident in dry bush or in Rhodesia in mopane woodland from the Sudan, Ethiopia and the Somalilands, south to the Rhodesias, Angola and Damaraland. The Two-banded Courser (*Hemerodromus africanus*) is a local resident on open plains in Somaliland, central Kenya and Tanganyika. It occurs also in Angola and South Africa, but not in Central Africa. It is a small species (8 inches) mottled buff and black above with two conspicuous black bands across the chest. The Violet-tipped Courser (*Rhinoptilus chalcopterus*) is a much larger bird (12 inches) and is very Crowned Plover-like in appearance: it has a more upright stance and the blackish patches on the throat and below the eyes distinguish it. It is mainly nocturnal in its habits and is often seen on roads at night. It is a very local resident in East and Central Africa. In many places it is spasmodic in its appearances. It is most frequent in Northern Rhodesia where it is sometimes common on roads passing through brachystegia and mopane woodland.

PRATINCOLE *Glareola pratincola* (M & R) p. 97

Identification: 9″. A tern-like brown bird with a long forked tail, white rump and sealing-wax red base to the bill. Legs black and short; throat buff with narrow black border. Immature has breast band of black streaks. Flight erratic and tern-like: chestnut under wing conspicuous in flight. The Madagascar Pratincole lacks the black collar round throat. The White-collared Pratincole is a smaller bird with a white collar round back of neck. Pratincoles are usually found in flocks and may often be seen hawking insects like huge swallows over or near water.

Voice: Noisy in flight, birds in flocks producing a harsh, rather tern-like "keeyak" or a rapid chattering call.

Distribution and Habitat: Widely distributed and resident in Ethiopian Region and locally common in East and Central Africa. Frequents lakes and other inland waters but very uncommon on coast. Much subject to local movements and in the Sudan and Ethiopia, and perhaps southwards, numbers augmented during winter months by visitors from Europe. Nearly always encountered in flocks.

Allied Species: The shorter-tailed Madagascar Pratincole (*Glareola ocularis*) occurs as a non-breeding visitor to East Africa, mainly the Kenya coast between Mombasa and Lamu where in some years it may be observed in large flocks. It may be distinguished from the Common Pratincole by its lack of a thin black collar round the throat. The White-collared Pratincole (*Galachrysia nuchalis*) also lacks the black throat collar, but may be recognised by a white collar round back of neck. It is a very local little bird associated with rocks in rivers and

SANDPIPERS and ALLIES

1. GREEN SANDPIPER page 107
Very dark above with sharply contrasting white rump; under-sides of wings appear black in flight.

2. WOOD SANDPIPER 108
Paler and more mottled than Green Sandpiper; white rump does not contrast sharply with upperparts; under-sides of wings appear pale grey in flight.

3. COMMON SANDPIPER 107
Short legs; dark rump; streaky chest patches; wags tail up and down whilst walking; flight characteristic, *see* text.

4. MARSH SANDPIPER 108
Suggests a small, slim Greenshank; bill very thin; mottled and spotted in summer and juvenile plumages, uniform pale grey and white in winter plumage.
a, *Winter*
b, *Summer*

5. TURNSTONE 106
a, *Winter:* Dark breast; short orange legs.
b, *Summer:* Upperparts mottled chestnut and black; distinctive black face and chest pattern.

6. CURLEW SANDPIPER 105
a, *Winter:* Grey above; white below; white rump.
b, *Summer:* Rufous above and below; white rump. Freshly moulted Spring birds have rufous plumage more or less edged with white.

7. LITTLE STINT 105
a, *Winter:* Pale grey above, feathers with darker bases giving a slightly mottled appearance; below white.
b, *Summer:* Very small; plumage of upperparts and chest edged rufous; rump dark with white patch on either side.

8. GREENSHANK 109
White back and rump; summer plumage mottled above, streaked on breast; winter plumage more uniform pale grey and white.
a, *Winter*
b, *Summer*

9. RUFF 106
Plump-looking, rather dark wader; rump dark brown with white patch on either side; male much larger than female (Reeve). Full summer plumage not acquired in Africa: *see* text.

1
2
3
5
a
b
a
b
4
a
7
b
b
6
a
8
a
b
9

1
♂
♀
2
♂
♀
3
♂
♀
4
5
6
7
8
9
10
11
♂
♀

SANDGROUSE, PIGEONS and DOVES

1. **YELLOW-THROATED SANDGROUSE** page 118
   Yellowish-buff throat.
2. **CHESTNUT-BELLIED SANDGROUSE** 117
   Long, needle-pointed central tail feathers.
3. **BLACK-FACED SANDGROUSE** 118
   Broad whitish band across chest; black face pattern in male.
4. **SPECKLED PIGEON** 119
   Vinous-chestnut back, white-spotted wings and pale grey rump.
5. **RED-EYED DOVE** 120
   Black collar on hind-neck; deep vinous-pink underparts.
6. **PINK-BREASTED DOVE** 120
   Chestnut wing patches; black patches on sides of neck.
7. **RING-NECKED DOVE** 120
   Black collar; underparts pale grey and white.
8. **LAUGHING DOVE** 121
   No black collar; foreneck mottled black.
9. **EMERALD-SPOTTED WOOD DOVE** 121
   Metallic green wing spots; much rufous in wings in flight.
10. **GREEN PIGEON** 122
    Green underparts; red feet.
11. **NAMAQUA DOVE** 121
    Very long tail; black face and throat in adult male. *Note:* the Namaqua Dove is drawn to a larger scale than the remainder of the pigeons and doves illustrated.

lakes in East Africa and the Rhodesias. It may be seen on rocks and small islets off Entebbe in Uganda and on the Zambesi in Central Africa.

GULLS AND TERNS: Laridae

The Gulls and Terns are medium-sized or large swimming birds. Gulls are more robust and wider-winged than the Terns with slightly hooked bills; tails usually square or rounded: gregarious in habits. Terns are more slender and graceful than gulls and tails usually forked: also gregarious in habits.

GREY-HEADED GULL *Larus cirrocephalus* p. 97

Identification: 16″. This is a medium-sized pale grey gull with a conspicuous grey head and red bill and legs; primaries black with white tips. Immature mottled pale brownish grey above and on head. The Lesser Black-backed Gull is a much larger species (21 inches) with blackish upperparts and yellow legs.

Voice: A loud, laughing cackling call, but usually the birds are silent.

Distribution and Habitat: Local resident throughout most of Ethiopian Region and locally common in East and Central Africa. This is mainly an inland waters gull but in East Africa it sometimes occurs on the coast in the non-breeding season.

Allied Species: The large Lesser Black-backed Gull (*Larus fuscus*) is an uncommon winter visitor to East Africa, Northern Rhodesia and Nyasaland. It is most frequent on inland waters. The adult has blackish-grey upperparts and yellow legs; immature birds are mottled brown and have pale brown legs.

SOOTY GULL *Larus hemprichii* p. 97

Identification: 18″. This is the common gull along the East African coast. It is dark grey-brown above with a blackish brown head and some white on the neck: bill yellowish-green with a black and red tip: immature paler on the head and throat whitish, and tail with black markings, not entirely white.

Voice: A ringing, mewing call, but birds usually silent.

Distribution and Habitat: Resident and visitor to coasts of East Africa and Zanzibar and Pemba Islands. A common species in harbours along the East African coast and at Aden, where the birds compete with kites for garbage thrown overboard from ships in port.

GULL-BILLED TERN *Gelochelidon nilotica* (M & R) p. 97

Identification: 15″. A rather thickset tern with pale grey upperparts and a rather stout, wholly black bill. Crown black in summer plumage; white with indistinct black streaking in winter. At a distance looks very gull-like but can always be recognised by forked tail.

Voice: A harsh "koowaak."

Distribution and Habitat: Common winter visitor and passage migrant to East Africa as far south as central Tanganyika. Occurs commonly on shores of lakes in Rift Valley and less frequently on the coast. It is probable that the species breeds in East Africa, perhaps in the Lake Rudolf area, where it is common and in full plumage in summer. Often observed hawking flies and tiger beetles over dry land in the vicinity of lakes.

Allied Species: The Caspian Tern (*Hydroprogne caspia*) is uncommon along the East African coast and on some inland waters (e.g. Lake Rudolf): rare in Central Africa where recorded from Northern Rhodesia. A very large tern the size of a Lesser Black-backed Gull with a heavy, bright orange-red bill: cap black in summer; white, streaked black in winter. The Lesser Crested Tern (*Sterna bengalensis*) occurs along the East African coast. It is about the same size as the Gull-billed Tern but may be recognised by its wholly yellow bill: in breeding dress crown black; in non-breeding plumage the forehead is white. This tern often associates with flocks of Sooty Gulls.

WHITE-WINGED BLACK TERN *Chlidonias leucoptera* (M & R) p. 97

Identification: 9½″. Distinctive in summer plumage with contrasting black body plumage and mainly white wings and tail. Whiskered Tern has white patch on cheeks and sides of neck and a black cap. In winter plumage indistinguishable from Whiskered Tern except for shorter bill. This is a fresh-water tern, often found in loose flocks. Flies backwards and forwards over water, frequently dipping to pick off insects on the surface.

Voice: Usually silent, but birds flying in flocks sometimes utter a sharp "terr."

Distribution and Habitat: Common winter visitor and passage migrant in suitable areas throughout Ethiopian Region. Common in East and Central Africa and a local resident in Kenya and Tanganyika, and perhaps Rhodesia. Usually found on inland waters (brackish and fresh) and rare, except on migration, in coastal areas.

Allied Species: The Whiskered Tern (*Chlidonias hybrida*) is very different from the White-winged Tern in summer plumage, and may be recognised easily by its white cheeks and sides of neck, contrasting with black crown and dark grey underparts. Immature and winter-plumaged birds indistinguishable for certain in the field from White-winged Black Tern. This is a local inland waters tern in East and Central Africa which breeds in Central Africa and perhaps in Kenya.

AFRICAN SKIMMER *Rynchops flavirostris* p. 97

Identification: 14″. The African Skimmer is a tern-like bird with dark brown upperparts and white below: wings very long: bill red with yellow tip and of remarkable structure; the bill is compressed to a thin vertical blade; lower mandible projects forwards nearly one inch in front of upper mandible. The Skimmer when feeding flies along the water surface ploughing the water with the projecting lower mandible. This characteristic ploughing of the water and the distinctive bill are good field characters. The species is usually gregarious.

Voice: A loud, harsh tern-like call "kreeep."

Distribution and Habitat: Local resident and partial migrant throughout Ethiopian Region south to the Zambesi River. Local in East and Central Africa. Perhaps most frequent on Lake Rudolf where colonies breed at Ferguson's Gulf and on Central Island.

BUTTON QUAILS: Turnicidae

Button Quails superficially resemble the true Quails, but differ in lacking the hind toe. They occur in areas of tall grass and when flushed rise at one's feet, dropping into the grass again a short distance away; they are very difficult to flush a second time.

BUTTON QUAIL *Turnix sylvatica* p. 85

Identification: $5\frac{1}{2}$″. In general appearance resembles a small buff-coloured quail or a round-winged lark. Rarely observed except when flushed at one's feet. The Black-rumped Button Quail has a distinct blackish rump in flight: the Common Button Quail has the upperparts uniform rufous-buff. The Quail Plover has a curious jerky flight and black and white wings.

Voice: A rather frog-like "whoo, whoo, whoo," very difficult to locate in grassy plains.

Distribution and Habitat: A local resident, sometimes common, throughout suitable areas of Ethiopian Region except western Cape Province, South Africa. Common in many parts of East Africa and Central Africa. Frequents bush country where there is abundant grass cover, found in an old neglected cultivation and savannah bush where there is long grass. In many places at least partially migratory and its numbers in any locality may vary greatly.

Allied Species: The Black-rumped Button Quail (*Turnix nana*) occurs in western Kenya, Uganda and Tanganyika, south to South Africa: locally common in parts of Northern Rhodesia where it occurs around edges of dambos where Common Button Quail is not found. In flight dark rump is conspicuous. The Quail Plover (*Ortyxelos meiffrenii*) is a tiny lark-like bird with conspicuous black and white wings. It occurs only in those areas where the silvery "Heskanit" grass grows. It is most frequent in the Sudan, but occurs very locally in northern Kenya and northern Uganda.

SANDGROUSE: Pteroclididae

Sandgrouse are a family of thickset, pigeon-like terrestrial birds: wings long and pointed, flight rapid. Legs short, feathered to base of toes. Most species are gregarious and inhabit arid regions: they come to drink at water in early morning or late evening, according to species.

CHESTNUT-BELLIED SANDGROUSE *Pterocles exustus*

p. 113

Identification: 12″. Sexes unlike; male with upperparts sandy-brown; female streaked and barred buff and brown. Both sexes have long narrow, needle-pointed central tail feathers. White tips to inner flight feathers form a conspicuous white bar when bird is in flight. Species gregarious and flights to water in early morning.

Voice: A guttural chuckling which sounds rather like "gutter, gutter, gutter, gutter, gutter, gutter."

Distribution and Habitat: Resident Senegal, eastwards through Sudan to Ethiopia and the Somalilands, south through Kenya to northern Tanganyika. This is the commonest sandgrouse in most parts of Kenya and northern Tanganyika. It inhabits semi-desert bush country, arid plains and open thornbush.

Allied Species: The Spotted Sandgrouse (*Pterocles senegallus*) occurs in the Sudan, Ethiopia and British Somaliland. It also possesses long narrow central tail feathers. Both sexes differ from the Chestnut-bellied Sandgrouse in having bright orange-buff throats.

BLACK-FACED SANDGROUSE *Eremialector decoratus* p. 113

Identification: 10″. Central tail feathers not elongated; black pattern on face and throat (male) and broad white band across chest are good field characters. This is a small stumpy-looking sandgrouse, far less gregarious than other species: it is usually met with in pairs or family parties: however it often forms small flocks when flighting to water in the early morning and is often associated with the Chestnut-bellied Sandgrouse.

Voice: A series of chuckling whistles of three notes "chucker, chucker, chuk." Also a series of short notes.

Distribution and Habitat: Resident in southern British Somaliland, southwards through Somalia to Kenya and central Tanganyika. Inhabits dry thorn-bush areas and semi-desert scrub. Common locally in the Tsavo National Park in Kenya.

Allied Species: The Double-banded Sandgrouse (*Eremialector bicinctus*) has two distinct narrow bands, white and black, across the chest in the male, and both sexes have black and white barred bellies. It occurs in open woodlands and stony, lightly wooded hillsides in the Rhodesias and Nyasaland. Lichtenstein's Sandgrouse (*Eremialector lichtensteinii*) is a semi-desert bush species found in the Sudan, Ethiopia, the Somalilands and the northern parts of Uganda and north-western Kenya. Lack of black throat patch in male, and black spotted neck distinguish this species from Black-faced Sandgrouse. The Four-banded Sandgrouse (*Eremialector quadricinctus*) resembles Lichtenstein's Sandgrouse but has the throat and neck unspotted in both sexes. It is an uncommon local resident in northern Uganda and north-western Kenya in arid bush country. Both it and Lichtenstein's Sandgrouse flight to water at dusk, even arriving after dark.

YELLOW-THROATED SANDGROUSE *Eremialector gutturalis* p. 113

Identification: 13″. Tail feathers not elongated. This is the largest of the East African sandgrouse: both sexes may be recognised by their conspicuous yellowish-buff throats and large size.

Voice: A harsh, guttural "gutter, gutter, gutter," not unlike calls of Chestnut-banded Sandgrouse but louder and harsher.

Distribution and Habitat: Local resident and partial migrant Ethiopia and Eritrea, southwards through Kenya and Tanganyika to the Rhodesias and South Africa. This species frequents open grassy plains, such as the Athi Plains of Kenya Colony, as well as open thornbush country.

In the Rhodesias occurs on dry open plains. Flights to drink in the early mornings, often in large flocks. Often spasmodic in its appearances in many localities in East Africa, in some years abundant, in others absent.

DOVES and PIGEONS: Columbidae

Medium-sized, plump birds with small rounded heads and the base of the bill swollen: flight rapid. Many species have characteristic deep cooing calls. The terms "dove" and "pigeon" are loosely used to indicate size, the smaller species being called doves, the larger pigeons.

SPECKLED PIGEON *Columba guinea* p. 113

Identification: 16″. This species is easily recognised by its vinous chestnut back, grey unspotted underparts, white spotted wings and, in flight, its conspicuous pale blue-grey rump. The Olive Pigeon has the underparts purplish-grey thickly spotted white and the bill and legs yellow.

Voice: A deep guttural series of "coos."

Distribution and Habitat: Resident and locally a partial migrant throughout much of the Ethiopian Region outside the forest areas. Not recorded Northern Rhodesia or Nyasaland. Inhabits open country, open acacia woodland, cultivated areas and rocky hillsides and cliffs. In many places breeds in human habitations like a domestic pigeon.

Allied Species: The Olive Pigeon (*Columba arquatrix*) is a forest species which occurs throughout most of the forest regions of Africa. It is the same size as the Speckled Pigeon and may be recognised by its bright yellow bill and feet and white spotted underparts. The Afep Pigeon or Grey Wood Pigeon (*Columba unicincta*) is a slightly smaller all-grey pigeon which is a forest haunter, extending from West Africa to Uganda. It is shy and its call, a deep booming "coo-oo," is usually the only indication of its presence. The Bronze-naped Pigeon (*Turturoena delegorguei*) is another shy forest species. It occurs from the southern Sudan, south through Kenya and Tanganyika to Nyasaland and Natal, South Africa. It is the size of an English Stock Dove (13 inches), dark grey in colour; the male has a broad white patch on the base of the hindneck; the female lacks this white patch but has a pale rufous head. It is a species which is easy to overlook unless one is listening for the call, a distinctive "coo-co-coo, coo, coo, coo, coo, coo."

PINK-BREASTED DOVE *Streptopelia lugens* p. 113

Identification: 11". A medium-sized dark grey dove with a chestnut patch on the side of each wing and a blackish patch on each side of the neck.

Voice: A deep, four-note "coo,coo,coo,coo."

Distribution and Habitat: This is a high altitude species, found in or near forest areas. It occurs in the Sudan and Eritrea and Ethiopia, southwards through Kenya and Tanganyika to Nyasaland and Northern Rhodesia. In East Africa it is a common species on the South Kinangop, Aberdare Mountains and around Nairobi.

RED-EYED DOVE *Streptopelia semitorquata* p. 113

Identification: 12". This is the largest of the brownish-grey doves with a black collar on the hind-neck. It may be recognised by its size, conspicuous pale grey forehead and deep vinous-pink underparts. In the smaller Mourning Dove and Ring-necked Dove the underparts are much paler and greyer. The Pink-breasted Dove may be recognised by its chestnut wing patch, and black patch on each side of the neck—not a black collar.

Voice: Its call-notes are characteristic, a deep "coo, coo—co,co—co,co."

Distribution and Habitat: A resident, sometimes common, throughout most of the Ethiopian Region. In East and Central Africa it occurs in wooded and forested areas in the vicinity of water. In Kenya it is frequently found in gardens where it becomes very tame. It is a common bird in Nairobi.

RING-NECKED DOVE *Streptopelia capicola* p. 113

Identification: 10". A greyish-brown dove with a black collar on the hind-neck; greyish below, merging to white on the belly. This is a paler and smaller bird than the Red-eyed Dove from which it may be distinguished by its white abdomen. The closely related Mourning Dove is larger and has the basal half of the outer tail feather black. However this is not an easy character to see in the field and the Ring-necked and Mourning Doves are best recognised by size and calls.

Voice: Song a constantly repeated, purring, three-note call of rather high pitch, "koo, koo, koo—koo, koo, koo." The Mourning Dove's song is a very deep "ho, karoo, coo-coo, coo-coo."

Distribution and Habitat: A common resident over much of East, Central and South Africa, from Ethiopia and Somaliland south to Angola and Cape Province. It frequents semi-desert bush, thornbush country, various types of woodlands and cultivated areas. In Kenya it is especially abundant in the Northern Frontier Province, where it congregates in very large flocks at water-holes during the dry weather.

Allied Species: The Mourning Dove (*Streptopelia decipiens*) occurs in East and Central Africa, usually in acacia woodland or sometimes cultivated areas. In addition to the characters enumerated above it may also be distinguished from the Ring-necked Dove by its pale orange or whitish eye, not dark brown.

LAUGHING DOVE *Streptopelia senegalensis* p. 113

Identification: 9½″. A small dove with rusty-coloured upperparts, much blue-grey in the wings and no black collar on hind neck. Bases of feathers on foreneck black giving a mottled appearance. Chest pink, merging to white on abdomen; much white on tail.

Voice: A five-note call "oh—cook, cook—oou, oou." Distinctive when once heard.

Distribution and Habitat: A resident, often common, throughout most of the Ethiopian Region. Frequents thornbush country and cultivated areas, generally below 6,000 ft. In Central Africa rather local, but often common where it does occur.

NAMAQUA DOVE *Oena capensis* p. 113

Identification: 8½″. A sparrow-sized dove with a very long tail. Male with much black on face and throat. Very small size and long tail make this species unmistakable.

Voice: Usually silent, but sometimes utters a weak "koo, koo."

Distribution and Habitat: Resident in suitable localities throughout the Ethiopian Region. Frequents arid and semi-desert country and thorn-bush areas especially in sandy localities. Common in East and Central Africa.

EMERALD-SPOTTED WOOD DOVE *Turtur chalcospilos* p. 113

Identification: 7″. A small dove with a great deal of rufous in the wings when it flies. Upperparts dull brown with large metallic green wing spots; below vinous-pink, paler on belly: bill red with a black tip. The Blue-spotted Wood Dove has dark metallic blue wing spots and a red bill with a yellow tip.

Voice: A series of prolonged coos, with well-marked pauses between each note at first, gradually dropping and becoming quicker towards the end.

Distribution and Habitat: Local resident from Ethiopia, south through eastern Kenya and Tanganyika to Central Africa, Angola and South Africa. Occurs in bush country, woodland where there is thick undercover, and coastal scrub.

Allied Species: The Blue-spotted Wood Dove (*Turtur afer*) closely resembles the Emerald-spotted Dove but inhabits denser, more heavily wooded or forested areas. Its yellow tipped red bill is a good field character if clearly seen. It occurs locally in western Kenya, Uganda, Tanganyika and in Central Africa. The Tambourine Dove (*Tympanistria tympanistria*) is another forest and woodland frequenting dove widely distributed in East and Central Africa. It is rather larger than the Emerald-spotted Dove with dark brown upperparts: its forehead, eyestripe and underparts are white, washed grey in the female. Its call is a long-drawn-out series of coos, diminishing in intensity.

GREEN PIGEON *Treron australis* p. 113

Identification: 11″. A thickset, apple-green pigeon with coral-red legs and feet. Tail feathers may be green like rest of plumage or pale grey. A broad pale grey collar on hindneck. Bruce's Green Pigeon differs in having breast and belly bright yellow.

Voice: A harsh, croaking call, not at all what one would associate with a pigeon: "ah-wa, ah-wa, gitta-rik, gitta-rik, ah-wa."

Distribution and Habitat: Local resident East and Central Africa in wooded and savannah areas where there are fig trees. Presence of birds in fruiting fig trees often not suspected until unmistakable call heard, so well does their plumage blend with the foliage. Species occurs also in the Congo, West Africa and South Africa, assuming that Delalandi's Green Pigeon is conspecific with this species.

Allied Species: Bruce's Green Pigeon (*Treron waalia*) occurs from Senegal, east to Ethiopia and Somaliland, south to northern areas of Uganda and Kenya. It may be recognised by its bright yellow underparts.

CUCKOOS and COUCALS: Cuculidae

The Cuckoos are medium-sized, slim birds with long tails: one of their chief external characters is that their first and fourth toes are directed backwards. Most species are parasitic in their breeding habits, laying their eggs in the nests of foster parents. The Coucals and Green Coucals or Yellowbills (*Centropus* and *Ceuthmochares*) build their own nests and rear their own young.

COMMON CUCKOO *Cuculus canorus* (M & R) p. 49

Identification: 13″. In flight its long tail and sharply pointed wings give this a rather sparrow-hawk-like appearance, but sparrow-hawks have broad, *rounded* wings. Upperparts and throat pale grey, below whitish barred dark grey. Some immature and females are rufous strongly barred blackish. The resident African race may be distinguished from the much commoner European bird by conspicuous yellow base to bill and complete white bars across tail.

Voice: European race rarely calls in Africa. Resident African race calls "koo-kuk"—not "cuckoo"!

Distribution and Habitat: The European bird is a common winter visitor and passage migrant throughout the Ethiopian Region. In East Africa there is a very marked northwards migration during early April along the Kenya coast. The African resident race occurs locally throughout East and Central Africa, but is uncommon. It occurs in brachystegia woodland, acacia and dry upland forest and in wooded cultivated areas. A partial migrant in some areas. The European bird winters commonly in rain forest areas.

RED-CHESTED CUCKOO *Cuculus solitarius* p. 49

Identification: 12″. A dark blue-grey cuckoo with a rusty-brown patch on the throat and upper breast; chin grey. Remainder of underparts barred buff-white and black: juvenile dark with black throat. This is a bird which is far oftener heard than seen.

Voice: A very distinctive, shrill call of the three descending notes "wip, wip, weeoo." Often calls immediately before rains break and known locally as the "rain-bird"—its call being rendered "it-will-rain."

Distribution and Habitat: Resident and local partial migrant throughout most of the Ethiopian Region. Common in East and Central Africa.

It frequents open country, woodlands, forest, bush and cultivated areas.

Allied Species: The Black Cuckoo (*Cuculus cafer*) looks like a melanistic edition of the Red-chested Cuckoo, with some indistinct barring showing on the underparts. It has a very distinctive and mournful call, a descending, long-drawn-out "too, too, toooo." It occurs throughout East and Central Africa: it is partial to trees along river banks, and in East Africa coastal scrub. The Great Spotted Cuckoo (*Clamator glandarius*) is a scarce resident in East and Central Africa and also a winter visitor and passage migrant from the North. It is 16 inches long with a conspicuous crest, long graduated tail with bold white edging and greyish-brown upperparts boldly spotted with white. Much chestnut shows in wing feathers during flight.

BLACK AND WHITE CUCKOO *Clamator jacobinus* p. 49

Identification: 13″. A medium-sized, crested cuckoo with black upperparts and a short white wing bar which is very conspicuous in flight. Underparts may be white, greyish or black, or washed buff in immature bird. Levaillant's Cuckoo resembles this species and also has a white wing bar, but is larger and has underparts whitish with heavy black streaks on throat and chest.

Voice: A loud piping call, often followed by a two- or three-note cackling call "quer-qui-quik."

Distribution and Habitat: Occurs as a partial resident and migrant throughout most of the Ethiopian Region outside the West African forest region, common but local in East and Central Africa. In East Africa it may be found at all times of the year but in the Rhodesias and Nyasaland its appearances are between October and April. It is possible that Indian breeding birds spend the non-breeding season, between September and May, in Africa. Common on spring migration on the Kenya coast. Frequents thornbush and scrub country, various types of woodland and cultivated areas where there are scrub and trees.

Allied Species: Levaillant's Cuckoo (*Clamator levaillantii*) occurs in similar habitats to the Black and White Cuckoo throughout East and Central Africa. It is a larger bird (14 inches) and may be distinguished by its whitish underparts and heavy black streaking on throat and chest: a melanistic phase also occurs which can be distinguished in the field only on size: its call is a rapid "cur, cur, cur, cur, cur, cur," changing abruptly to a high-pitched "qui, qui, qui, qui, qui."

EMERALD CUCKOO *Chrysococcyx cupreus* p. 49

Identification: 8″. Although the male is one of the most brilliantly coloured birds in Africa and the species is widespread, the Emerald Cuckoo is far oftener heard than seen. The male is brilliant metallic-green all over, including wings and tail, except for the lower breast and belly which are bright canary-yellow. The female has the upperparts metallic green with rufous bars and the underparts white, barred dark metallic green. It is much darker below than the allied Didric and Klaas' Cuckoos.

Voice: A loud, clear whistle, "choo, choo—too, wee," which is often rendered as "Hello, Georgie."

Distribution and Habitat: Resident and partial migrant throughout much of the Ethiopian Region from Gambia, the Sudan and Ethiopia to South Africa. Although mainly a forest tree-top bird it also occurs in scrub, acacia woodland and coastal thickets. It is not an easy bird to observe and its presence is usually revealed only when the male is calling: at other times it is easily overlooked. It occurs locally throughout East and Central Africa, but in Rhodesia has been recorded only between October and March; in Nyasaland it is a resident throughout the year.

DIDRIC CUCKOO *Chrysococcyx caprius* p. 49

Identification: 7½″. A small metallic green cuckoo with mainly white underparts; upperparts metallic-green with coppery gloss: tail mainly blackish with some white spots on outer feathers. The female is more heavily washed rufous-copper above, and mottled rufous below. Klaas' Cuckoo is smaller and greener and has white outer tail feathers with a few black markings. The Didric Cuckoo is parasitic mainly upon weaver-birds and it is most in evidence when colonies of weavers are breeding.

Voice: A very characteristic plaintive whistle "dee, dee, dee, DEE, dric."

Distribution and Habitat: Common resident and partial migrant throughout Ethiopian Region. It occurs in East Africa during all months, but in the Rhodesias it is present mainly between October and April. It occurs in various habitats, its presence being controlled by the presence of weaver colonies. In East Africa it is most frequent in dry thornbush and highland dry woodland. In Central Africa it occurs commonly in most types of woodland and has also been recorded from papyrus swamps.

KLAAS' CUCKOO *Chrysococcyx klaas* p. 49

Identification: 6½″. A small bright green cuckoo with very white underparts and a patch of dark green on each side of the chest: outer tail feathers white with a few black markings. The Didric Cuckoo has blackish outer tail feathers with a few white spots. The female Klaas' Cuckoo is mainly bronze-brown above with some green bars and underparts washed buff with sparse dark brown barring. The immature bird is barred green above.

Voice: A series of plaintive two- or three-note whistles, repeated slowly at intervals, "twee-teu" or "hu-ee-te."

Distribution and Habitat: A common resident and partial migrant throughout the Ethiopian Region. Found in East Africa and Nyasaland throughout the year; in the Rhodesias most records are between October and April. Frequents a variety of habitats from forest areas and woodland to bush country and coastal thickets. It is often much in evidence in fruiting fig trees. Its white outer tail feathers are much in evidence when it flies and if the green colour of the plumage is not seen clearly the bird can be mistaken for a honey-guide.

WHITE-BROWED COUCAL *Centropus superciliosus* p. 49

Identification: 16″. Coucals are heavily built, rather clumsy-looking birds with an awkward, floundering flight when flushed out of thick undercover or papyrus. One's impression is of a mainly chestnut plumaged bird with a long, broad tail. The present species may be recognised by a wide whitish stripe over the eye and in having the crown and hindneck earth-brown, the latter streaked creamy-white. Eye ruby-red and conspicuous at close quarters. The Blue-headed Coucal is larger and has a blue-black crown and nape and lacks the eye-stripe. The smaller Black Coucal is oily black in breeding plumage; streaked tawny and black in non-breeding and immature plumage.

Voice: A very characteristic bubbling call, which has been likened to water being poured out of a bottle, and which has given rise to a common name for this species—"water-bottle bird."

Distribution and Habitat: A local, sometimes common resident throughout the greater part of the Ethiopian Region. Common in East and Central Africa. Frequents grassy bush country, areas of rank undergrowth, coastal scrub and similar thick cover. Uncommon in thickets of papyrus and other swamp vegetation inhabited by the Blue-headed and Black Coucals.

Allied Species: The Black Coucal (*Centropus toulou*) is confined to swamps and marshes. This is an uncommon bird over most of East Africa, being most frequent in swamps in Tanganyika. In the Rhodesias and Nyasaland it is a commoner bird and black examples are very conspicuous sitting on some reed patch in the middle of a swampy area. The Blue-headed Coucal (*Centropus monachus*) is a large bird (18 inches) with a rich dark chestnut back and navy-blue crown and nape. It also frequents thick cover over or near water. It occurs from West Africa and Ethiopia south through Uganda, Kenya and in south-western Tanganyika.

YELLOWBILL or GREEN COUCAL *Ceuthmochares aereus* p. 49

Identification: 13″. The Green Coucal is a slim greenish-grey species with a long, broad tail and a conspicuous yellow bill. Owing to its skulking habits amongst the creepers and dense foliage of forest trees it is often overlooked unless one hears its characteristic calls. Its bright yellow bill is its most distinctive field character.

Voice: A harsh series of clicking notes culminating in a devilish chuckling scream. At times it also utters a querulous long-drawn-out "OO—weee," not unlike a kite's call-note.

Distribution and Habitat: Local and uncommon resident throughout the greater part of the Ethiopian Region. Local and uncommon in East and Central Africa. Frequents rain forests, forest strips along waterways and dense scrub; favours especially the thick cover of creeper-covered trees.

TURACOS or LOURIES: Musophagidae

The Turacos, Louries or Plantain-eaters, as they are variously called, are a group of medium or large-sized arboreal birds confined to Africa. The forest species are remarkable for their brightly coloured plumage and long tails; many species possess rich crimson flight feathers. Most have loud, harsh calls.

LIVINGSTONE'S TURACO *Tauraco livingstonii* p. 128

Identification: 16″. Plumage mainly green with a long white-tipped green crest and mainly crimson flight feathers; bill dull red. Schalow's Turaco differs in having tail glossed violet and purple, not green. The Black-billed Turaco has a much shorter and rounded crest and a black, not red, bill. Fischer's Turaco also has a short crest but hindneck is bright crimson.

TURACOS

1. HARTLAUB'S TURACO page 131
Crown bluish-black with white patch above and in front of eye.

2. LIVINGSTONE'S TURACO 127
Plumage mainly green; long white-tipped crest and reddish bill.

3. FISCHER'S TURACO 130
Bright blood-red patch on nape and hind neck

4. WHITE-CRESTED TURACO 130
Conspicuous white crest.

5. VIOLET-CRESTED TURACO 131
Head with purplish-black crest but no white patches.

6. ROSS'S TURACO 131
Orange-yellow face and bill very conspicuous.

7. WHITE-BELLIED GO-AWAY-BIRD 132
Long tail, crest and white belly.

8. GREAT BLUE TURACO 132
No red in wings; pale apple-green breast and rounded black crest.

1
2
3
4
5
6
7
8

1
2
3
4
5
6
7
8
9

PARROTS and ROLLERS

1. RED-HEADED PARROT page 133
Red forehead.

2. FISCHER'S LOVEBIRD 134
Orange-red face and throat; under the wings green. The similar Red-headed Lovebird is black under the wings.

3. YELLOW-COLLARED LOVEBIRD 135
Blackish-brown head and yellow collar.

4. LILAC-BREASTED ROLLER 136
Throat and breast rich lilac; long tail streamers. In Somalia race lilac restricted to throat.

5. ORANGE-BELLIED PARROT 133
Orange belly; females and immatures less brightly orange below.

6. BROWN PARROT 134
Yellow crown band.

7. RUFOUS-CROWNED ROLLER 136
Underparts rufous with white streaks; white nape patch.

8. BROAD-BILLED ROLLER 137
Bright yellow bill.

9. EUROPEAN ROLLER 135
Greenish-blue head and breast; pale rufous back; **no long tail streamers.**

Voice: A loud, far-carrying "kaar, kaar, kaar, kaar—kaar" frequently repeated.

Distribution and Habitat: Local resident from central Tanganyika southwards to Portuguese East Africa, Nyasaland and Southern Rhodesia. Its place taken in Northern Rhodesia by Schalow's Turaco. Occurs in forested areas and woodland. This is the common turaco of southern Tanganyika and Nyasaland in the thicker forest areas: its loud calls are one of the characteristic sounds of the forests.

Allied Species: Schalow's Turaco (*Tauraco schalowi*), which may be conspecific with Livingstone's Turaco, occurs in south-western Kenya, to Northern Rhodesia and northern Nyasaland north of the Rift Valley. This bird has a longer and more attenuated crest than Livingstone's Turaco and a violet-purple not green glossed tail. It inhabits forested and woodland areas. The Black-billed Turaco (*Tauraco schuttii*) has a short rounded crest and a black bill. It is a forest species found in the Congo to Uganda and western Kenya. It is common in the Uganda forests, where it lives alongside the Great Blue Turaco.

FISCHER'S TURACO *Tauraco fischeri* p. 128

Identification: 16″. This is another mainly green plumaged species, with a short thick crest and a bright blood-red patch on the nape and hindneck: flight feathers crimson.

Voice: A far-reaching, croaking "kaw, kaw, kaw, kaw," but less vocal than other species of turacos.

Distribution and Habitat: Resident in forested and wooded areas along the Kenya and Tanganyika coast, from the Tana River to Tanga and the Usambara mountains: also resident Zanzibar Island. Locally common, especially in the south of its range, from the Shimba Hills southwards.

WHITE-CRESTED TURACO *Tauraco leucolophus* p. 128

Identification: 14″. A violet-blue species with a green breast and conspicuous pure white crest, cheeks and throat. Mainly white head distinguishes this species from all other turacos: red flight feathers conspicuous in flight.

Voice: A variety of deep, guttural croaking calls.

Distribution and Habitat: Local, uncommon resident from Cameroons, eastwards to northern Congo, the southern Sudan, Uganda and western Kenya Colony. It occurs in more open areas than most turacos, frequenting forest and scrub strips along rivers or even dry waterways, and open parkland type of country where there are scattered fig trees.

It is numerous on the lower slopes of Mt. Elgon in Kenya and around Soroti in Uganda.

HARTLAUB'S TURACO *Tauraco hartlaubi* p. 128

Identification: 16″. This is the common forest turaco of the Kenya highlands; plumage mainly violet-blue with a green belly and crimson flight feathers. Crown and nape dark bluish-black with a round white patch above and in front of the eye and a white streak below the eye. It draws attention to itself by its loud, croaking calls.

Voice: A high-pitched croaking call, "kaw, kaw, kaw, kaw," frequently repeated.

Distribution and Habitat: Local resident highland forest areas of Kenya Colony and north-eastern Tanganyika. This is a common bird in the forest areas around Nairobi.

VIOLET-CRESTED TURACO *Gallirex porphyreolophus* p. 128

Identification: 17″. Head with thick, purplish-black crest but no white patches on face. Upperparts blue-grey merging to green on the mantle; throat and breast grass green, merging to pale grey on abdomen; flight feathers crimson. This is a savannah woodlands turaco with conspicuous pale blue-grey upperparts and red flight feathers. Hartlaub's Turaco has no pale blue-grey on upperparts, possesses white head markings and frequents forested country.

Voice: A far-carrying, gobbling call, "kurru, kurru, kurru" repeated over and over again.

Distribution and Habitat: A local resident from southern Kenya, south through Tanganyika, Portuguese East Africa, Nyasaland and the Rhodesias to South Africa. Frequents a variety of habitats including rain forest fringe, savannah woodlands and wooded water-courses.

ROSS'S TURACO *Musophaga rossae* p. 128

Identification: 20″. A large, violet-black turaco with crimson flight feathers and crest and a very conspicuous orange-yellow face and bill.

Voice: A great variety of croaking and cackling calls: birds usually found in loose parties which at times are very noisy.

Distribution and Habitat: Local resident Cameroons and Sudan, Angola, the Congo, Uganda and western Kenya and western Tanganyika to northern parts of Northern Rhodesia. Frequents forest areas of different types, wooded water-courses and in Rhodesia has been recorded in deciduous thickets.

GREAT BLUE TURACO *Corythaeola cristata* p. 128

Identification: 28-30″. This is the finest and largest of the turacos. Tail very long, pale greenish-yellow with a wide black terminal band; head with rounded black crest; no red in wings; upperparts and throat verditer-blue; breast pale apple-green, abdomen chestnut. This tree-top species frequently fans and closes its tail, rendering itself most conspicuous.

Voice: A series of loud, croaking "kok, kok, kok, kok, kok" calls terminating in a series of bubbling croaks.

Distribution and Habitat: A West African species which extends from Senegal to Angola, and eastwards to southern Sudan, the Congo, Uganda and western Kenya. It is a forest species, most frequent in the great Congo forests but also found in narrow strips of forest along rivers.

WHITE-BELLIED GO-AWAY-BIRD *Corythaixoides leucogaster* p. 128

Identification: 20″. This is a grey, white and black dry-country species. It is very conspicuous with its long tail and crest, grey chest and white belly. Usually encountered in pairs or family parties.

Voice: A very loud, penetrating sheep-like bleating call, "gaarr, warrrr," which has been rendered as "go awayaaaa"—hence the bird's common name.

Distribution and Habitat: A local resident, often common, from the southern Sudan and central Ethiopia and Somalia, south through Uganda, Kenya and northern half of Tanganyika. Frequents dry bush country and belts of acacias along watercourses.

Allied Species: The Common Go-Away-Bird (*Corythaixoides concolor*) is an entirely grey bird with a pronounced crest and a long tail. It occurs from southern Tanganyika south through Nyasaland and the Rhodesias to South Africa. It is another dry bush-country bird with a penetrating "g, wayaaa" type of call. The Bare-faced Go-Away-Bird (*Gymnoschizorhis personata*) occurs in dry thornbush and open savannah bush from Ethiopia to northern parts of Nyasaland and Northern Rhodesia. It is a pale-grey species with a white neck and chest with a patch of pale green in centre of chest; face and throat unfeathered, black. The Eastern Grey Plantain-Eater (*Crinifer zonurus*) is a large brownish-grey species (20 inches) with a conspicuous greenish-yellow bill and a white wing-bar whilst in flight. It occurs from Ethiopia to Tanganyika, but is commonest locally in Uganda in savannah woodland.

PARROTS: Psittacidae

This is a group of small or medium-sized birds with powerful hooked bills with a cere at base; first and fourth toes are directed backwards: flight direct with rapid short wing-beats.

RED-HEADED PARROT *Poicephalus gulielmi* p. 129

Identification: 12″. "Red-headed" is a somewhat misleading name as the red plumage is confined to the forehead and a patch on the shoulders and edge of wings: plumage otherwise green, with a yellowish rump. In the field it appears as a large dark-green parrot with a paler rump: the red is not always conspicuous.

Voice: A series of typical parrot squawks.

Distribution and Habitat: Local resident in highland forest areas of Kenya and northern Tanganyika. This is the parrot one often sees flying over forest on Mts. Kenya and Kilimanjaro. Elsewhere the species is found in the Congo and West Africa, south to Angola.

Allied Species: The well-known Grey Parrot (*Psittacus erithacus*), grey in plumage with a contrasting scarlet tail, occurs throughout Uganda, and in western Kenya and western Tanganyika. It occurs usually in flocks in the tops of forest trees. Grey Parrots are common in the forest areas around Entebbe, Uganda and on the Sesse Islands in Lake Victoria. The Brown-necked Parrot (*Poicephalus robustus*) resembles a large edition of the Red-headed Parrot with a silvery-looking head and dull red frontal patch. It occurs in Tanganyika, Nyasaland, the Rhodesias and eastern South Africa, but is everywhere uncommon.

ORANGE-BELLIED PARROT *Poicephalus rufiventris* p. 129

Identification: 10″. A characteristic parrot of dry bush areas, especially where baobab trees are present. The bright orange breast of the adult male is very conspicuous in the field and renders identification easy. The female is less brightly coloured and may have the underparts green or green with an orange wash. She is best identified by the associated male. The species is almost always seen in pairs or family parties. Immature birds resemble the female.

Voice: A shrill screeching call in flight.

Distribution and Habitat: Resident from British Somaliland and Ethiopia southwards through Somalia and Kenya to northern Tanganyika. It frequents dry bush and thornbush country and is very partial to baobab trees.

BROWN PARROT *Poicephalus meyeri* p. 129

Identification: 10″. This is an ash-brown parrot, more or less tinged green, with a yellow band across the crown and a blue or green rump; underparts green. The Brown-headed Parrot is a green bird with a greyish-brown head and no yellow band across the crown.

Voice: A series of harsh, characteristic parrot-type squawks.

Distribution and Habitat: Local resident and partial migrant throughout most of the Ethiopian Region except the West African forest region. Occurs in a variety of habitats including dry bush country, savannah woodland, wooded belts along water-courses and acacia country. Widespread throughout East and Central Africa, but distribution patchy and birds often absent from apparently suitable localities.

Allied Species: The Brown-headed Parrot (*Poicephalus cryptoxanthus*) occurs along the Kenya coast and in southern Kenya, south to the Zambesi River. In East Africa it is extremely partial to mangrove swamps on the coast, where it often congregates in flocks. It is common in acacia woods below 3,500 ft. in Nyasaland, but has not been recorded in Northern Rhodesia and is rare and local in Southern Rhodesia.

FISCHER'S LOVEBIRD *Agapornis fischeri* p. 129

Identification: 5½″. General colour green with forehead, cheeks and throat orange, merging to dull yellowish on crown, hindneck and chest. Undersides of wings green. The Red-headed Lovebird has a redder head and undersides of wings are conspicuously black in flight. The Central African Lilian's Lovebird has throat and chest tomato red.

Voice: A high-pitched twittering call.

Distribution and Habitat: A local resident confined to northern Tanganyika. Occurs usually in flocks or small family parties. Frequents open grasslands, dry bush country especially where there are baobab trees and cultivated areas. In some localities it does some damage to grain crops.

Allied Species: The Red-headed Lovebird (*Agapornis pullaria*) is a red-headed green species with black under the wing, conspicuous in flight. It occurs in the Sudan, eastern Congo, Uganda and northern and western Tanganyika. It is not uncommon at Entebbe, Uganda. Lilian's Lovebird (*Agapornis lilianae*) also has red on the head but has the rump green, uniform with the upperparts: both Fischer's and the

Red-headed Lovebird have blue rumps. Lilian's Lovebird occurs locally in Nyasaland and the Rhodesias where it usually frequents mopane woodland. The Black-collared Lovebird (*Agapornis swinderniana*) is green with a black and orange collar on hindneck and tail feathers red at base; rump blue. It is a forest species extending from West Africa to the Bwamba forest, western Uganda. It feeds largely on small figs, but will visit native cultivation, especially millet.

YELLOW-COLLARED LOVEBIRD *Agapornis personata* p. 129

Identification: 6″. A green lovebird with a blackish-brown head and a wide yellow band across breast and extending to form a collar on mantle.

Voice: A twittering call.

Distribution and Habitat: Local resident in various parts of Tanganyika from the Arusha area and Serengeti plains to Lake Rukwa. It frequents open bush country and grasslands, open woodland where there are baobab trees and millet cultivation. Like Fischer's Lovebird it usually forms small flocks.

ROLLERS: Coraciidae

The Rollers are thickset, medium-sized birds of brilliant plumage. Most species occur singly or in pairs unless migrating, when they form loose flocks. They are usually observed perched on some vantage point, such as a telegraph pole, dead branch or termite hill from which they scan the ground for large insects and lizards which form their diet.

EUROPEAN ROLLER *Coracias garrulus* (M) p. 129

Identification: 12″. A heavy, rather crow-like build, with a powerful hooked bill. Plumage mainly pale azure-blue with a pale chestnut back. In flight vivid blue wings with black border conspicuous. Species distinguished from others by lack of long tail streamers and azure-blue head and underparts. The Abyssinian and Racquet-tailed Rollers, which also have chestnut backs, have the outer tail feathers elongated to form long streamers.

Voice: A loud, chattering, "krak, ak."

Distribution and Habitat: A common winter visitor and passage migrant throughout East and Central Africa: in East Africa often passes through Tanganyika and Kenya in large flocks during March and early April.

Frequents open woodland and bush country and cultivated areas. Often perches on telegraph posts and wires.

Allied Species: The Abyssinian Roller (*Coracias abyssinica*) is similar to the European Roller but is brighter in general colour and has the outer tail feathers elongated to form two long narrow streamers. It occurs in Turkana in Kenya and in northern Uganda: elsewhere it is distributed from Senegal, eastwards to Ethiopia and south-western Arabia. The Racquet-tailed Roller (*Coracias spatulata*) also resembles the European bird but possesses long streamers with a black racquet-shaped tip. It occurs in brachystegia and mopane woodland in southern Tanganyika, Nyasaland and the Rhodesias: elsewhere it is found in Angola and the southern Congo, and in Portuguese East Africa.

LILAC-BREASTED ROLLER *Coracias caudata* p. 129

Identification: 16″ with tail streamers. Upperparts tawny-brown or greenish; rump and wing coverts ultramarine blue; throat and breast rich lilac; remainder underparts greenish-blue. In the Somali race of this roller, which also occurs in northern Kenya, the lilac is reduced, being confined to a patch on the throat and foreneck. Species easily recognised by combination of lilac chest and long tail streamers. Often seen perched on telegraph posts and wires. In some lights wings show brilliant blue and black in flight.

Voice: A series of harsh chattering notes.

Distribution and Habitat: Local resident and partial migrant from Somaliland and Ethiopia, southwards through East Africa and Central Africa to eastern South Africa, and westwards to Angola. Locally common throughout East and Central Africa. It occurs in woodlands, open bush country, especially where there are isolated trees to serve as vantage points, and even on open plains if there are telegraph poles on which it can perch.

RUFOUS-CROWNED ROLLER *Coracias naevia* p. 129

Identification: 13″. This is a large, thickset species which lacks tail streamers: entire underparts rufous-brown with white streaks; above olive-grey, rufous on crown and a white patch on nape. Wings and tail deep purple-blue, conspicuous when the bird flies.

Voice: Call less harsh than most other rollers, a querulous "kaak, kaak."

Distribution and Habitat: Local but widespread resident and partial migrant Senegal eastwards to Ethiopia, south through Uganda and Kenya to northern Tanganyika. In southern Africa from Nyasaland and Rhodesias to Angola in west and Natal in south. It occurs in wooded areas, bush with scattered trees and in cultivated areas. Single birds are the rule, but small parties occur when food supply (grasshoppers) is unusually plentiful.

BROAD-BILLED ROLLER *Eurystomus glaucurus* p. 129

Identification: 10″. A rather small, thickset roller, bright chestnut in colour with a conspicuous wide yellow bill. Wings brilliant dark purplish-blue in flight.

Voice: A loud, cackling, chatter.

Distribution and Habitat: Local resident and migrant (the race breeding in Madagascar visits Africa) over most of the Ethiopian Region south to Transvaal, South Africa. Occurs in woodland areas, coastal forest and riverine forest. It favours trees with dead branches which afford lookout posts.

Allied Species: The Blue-throated Roller (*Eurystomus gularis*) closely resembles the Broad-billed Roller but may be distinguished by a conspicuous blue throat patch and a forked tail. It is a West African species which occurs in the forests of western Uganda.

KINGFISHERS: Alcedinidae

The Kingfishers are a distinct family of small or medium-sized birds most of which are brightly coloured. Not all species prey upon fish: some feed largely upon large insects and lizards and occur in localities far from water.

PIED KINGFISHER *Ceryle rudis* p. 144

Identification: 10″. Head crested; plumage entirely black and white: upperparts spotted and barred black and white: below white with two or one (in female) incomplete black bands.

Voice: A sharp "keek, keek."

Distribution and Habitat: Local resident, often common, throughout Ethiopian Region in suitable localities, except British Somaliland. It occurs both on inland waters and on the coast. It is especially common in Uganda where it is often seen perched on telegraph wires over water.

GIANT KINGFISHER *Megaceryle maxima* p. 144

Identification: 16″. Head crested: upperparts slate-grey finely spotted with white (the West African race lacks these white spots); below chestnut and white with black spotting. The male has the throat and breast chestnut and the abdomen white; the female has the throat and upper breast white with black spots and the lower breast and abdomen chestnut. Immature birds have the neck and chest mixed black and chestnut. The very large size of this kingfisher and chestnut on underparts make it a conspicuous and easily identified species.

Voice: A loud, raucous "y, aark," or several harsh "kee-ak, kee, ak-kee, ak" calls: also a sustained chattering call.

Distribution and Habitat: A widely distributed but very local resident throughout Ethiopian Region in small numbers. It is associated chiefly with rivers and streams where there is a fringe of trees. Occurs also on dams and lakes where these have wooded banks. In East Africa it is most frequent on mountain streams in forest. It occurs singly or in pairs. Fresh-water crabs form its main diet.

MALACHITE KINGFISHER *Corythornis cristata* p. 144

Identification: 5″. Head crested, pale cobalt-blue barred black; upperparts bright ultramarine blue; throat white, cheeks and underparts rufous. The Malachite Kingfisher may be recognised by its elongated crown feathers: the Pygmy Kingfisher lacks the prominent crest and its crown feathers are dark ultramarine blue barred black.

Voice: A sharp, but not very loud "teep, teep" when it flies.

Distribution and Habitat: A local resident throughout most of the Ethiopian Region, excluding British Somaliland. Locally common in East and Central Africa. Frequents permanent water where there is fringing vegetation: feeds mainly upon small fish and dragon-fly larvae.

Allied Species: The larger Half-collared Kingfisher (*Alcedo semitorquata*), 6½ inches, is blue above, rufous below with blue patches on foreneck almost meeting on upper breast; bill black. It is a very local and uncommon bird in East Africa, more frequent in the Rhodesias and Nyasaland. It frequents streams and rivers with thickly wooded banks. The Shining Blue Kingfisher (*Alcedo quadribrachys*) differs from the Half-collared Kingfisher in being rich ultramarine blue, tinged with violet, above, not cobalt blue; below it is entirely deep chestnut. This is a West African kingfisher which extends into western Uganda. It occurs on forested streams and pools.

PYGMY KINGFISHER *Ispidina picta* p. 144

Identification: 4″. Lacks conspicuous crest: upperparts rich ultramarine-blue, crown barred black: sides of head and hindneck orange-rufous with lilac wash; throat white, remainder underparts orange-rufous; bill red. Lack of conspicuous head crest and general darker appearance distinguishes this species from Malachite Kingfisher.

Voice: A thin, squeaky call.

Distribution and Habitat: Local resident most of Ethiopian Region excluding British Somaliland. This is essentially a forest or woodland kingfisher. It is often found far from water and its main diet consists of crickets and other insects. It does, however, also occur on wooded streams, rivers and dams where it will prey upon fish fry.

Allied Species: The Dwarf Kingfisher (*Myioceyx lecontei*) is the same size as the Pygmy Kingfisher, but differs from it in having a curious flattened bill and chestnut crown speckled with blue. It is a rare West African forest species which extends into western Uganda.

WOODLAND KINGFISHER *Halcyon senegalensis* p. 144

Identification: 8″. A medium-sized kingfisher with a very conspicuous bill with mandible black and maxilla bright red. Upperparts greenish-blue, head greyish; below whitish to pale grey on breast; wings and wing coverts black, contrasting with remainder blue plumage.

Voice: A harsh, high-pitched trilling whistle, "kee, rrrraaah," constantly repeated.

Distribution and Habitat: A local resident, in Central Africa at least a partial migrant, throughout much of the Ethiopian Region. In East Africa absent from eastern districts of Kenya and Tanganyika. It is very common and widespread in Uganda. It frequents savannah country and open woodlands and the edges of forest.

Allied Species: The Blue-breasted Kingfisher (*Halcyon malimbicus*) is larger (9 inches) and has the breast greenish-blue. It is a forest species found locally in Uganda and western Tanganyika. The Mangrove Kingfisher (*Halcyon senegaloides*) closely resembles the Woodland Kingfisher, but has the bill entirely red. It is confined to coastal regions from Kenya south to eastern Cape Province, South Africa. The Brown-hooded Kingfisher (*Halcyon albiventris*) also has an all-red bill but has the crown dusky brown and the hind neck dingy white, forming a collar; below, throat whitish, remainder underparts dull white tinged greyish-rufous. It occurs locally in wooded and savannah country in East and Central Africa, and in eastern South Africa usually near water.

GREY-HEADED KINGFISHER *Halcyon leucocephala* p. 144

Identification: 8″. Upperparts black with contrasting bright cobalt blue wing feathers, rump and tail; head and nape pale grey, to whitish on throat and breast; abdomen dark chestnut; bill red. This is a dry country kingfisher which also occurs near water. The blue of the wings and tail are very conspicuous when the bird flies.

Voice: A weak, chattering "ji, ji, ji-jeeee."

Distribution and Habitat: Local resident and partial migrant throughout most of the Ethiopian Region. Common locally in East and Central Africa. Frequents wooded areas, acacia country and dry, semi-desert bush.

Allied Species: The Chocolate-backed Kingfisher (*Halcyon badius*) is the same size as the Grey-headed Kingfisher: it may be recognised by its dark chocolate head, back and wing coverts; below white with buff tinge on chest; bill red. This is a West African forest species which occurs in some of the forests of western and central Uganda.

STRIPED KINGFISHER *Halcyon chelicuti* p. 144

Identification: 6½″. This is one of the less brightly coloured Kingfishers. It is greyish-brown on the upperparts with a pale greenish-blue rump, conspicuous only when the bird is in flight. Underparts white or pale buff, streaked dusky on breast and flanks; bill black, tinged red at base.

Voice: A very loud, shrill trill, frequently uttered especially at dusk.

Distribution and Habitat: Resident throughout most of the Ethiopian Region but not in the West African forest areas. Common and widespread in East and Central Africa. Occurs in woodland, savannah country, cultivated areas, and in the Rhodesias and Nyasaland common in brachystegia and mopane woodland.

BEE-EATERS: Meropidae

The Bee-eaters are medium-sized, slim birds of brilliant plumage; bills long and slightly decurved; legs short and wings sharply pointed.

EUROPEAN BEE-EATER *Merops apiaster* (M) p. 144

Identification: 11″. Projecting central tail feathers conspicuous; upperparts yellowish-chestnut; crown and hindneck chestnut; forehead white; below, throat bright yellow, contrasting with greenish-blue breast and abdomen.

Voice: A distinctive liquid note "pweek," heard usually from birds flying overhead.

Distribution and Habitat: Winter visitor and passage migrant from the north, throughout the Ethiopian Region. Breeds also in South Africa.

Allied Species: The Blue-cheeked Bee-eater (*Merops persicus*) also has long central tail feathers, but is green above with a chestnut throat. It also is a winter visitor and passage migrant to the Ethiopian Region: it is locally common in East and Central Africa. The Madagascar Bee-eater (*Merops superciliosus*) is a much duller and darker bird than the Blue-cheeked Bee-eater and lacks the blue on the head of that bird: the crown is dark olive-brown and the cheeks conspicuously white. It is mainly a non-breeding visitor from Madagascar to East and Central Africa, but some birds breed on the African coastline from Kenya to northern Portuguese East Africa.

CARMINE BEE-EATER *Merops nubicus* p. 144

Identification: 14″. Central tail feathers elongated: head and throat dark greenish-blue; upperparts and belly bright carmine red; wings and tail deep carmine-red; rump pale cobalt blue. This brilliant carmine-red bee-eater with a contrasting dark head is easy to recognise. It is usually found in flocks and also breeds in large colonies. The Southern Carmine Bee-eater has the throat carmine-pink like the rest of the underparts.

Voice: A rather metallic, double note-call "took, took."

Distribution and Habitat: Resident and partial migrant from Senegal, eastwards to Ethiopia and Somalia south to northern Uganda, north-western and eastern Kenya and north eastern Tanganyika. The species is common on the Kenya coast between November and April. It frequents coastal bush, savannah country and arid bush country. Numbers are frequently attracted to grass fires. This bee-eater has developed a special method of hunting its prey in some localities, especially Turkana in north-western Kenya. There it is often seen using native stock such as sheep and goats as animated perches: it also perches on the back of Kori Bustards for the same purpose.

Allied Species: The Southern Carmine Bee-eater (*Merops nubicoides*) is an even more beautiful bird than the northern species, from which it differs in having the throat as well as the rest of the underparts bright carmine pink. It is an intra-African migrant, moving between South Africa and the southern half of eastern Tanganyika and to south-western Lake Victoria. In the northern part of its range it appears in April, moving southwards in September. In Northern Rhodesia there are records of the species throughout the year: it breeds between September and November. In Nyasaland it breeds between August and November, but occurs elsewhere in the territory throughout the year.

WHITE-THROATED BEE-EATER *Aerops albicollis* p. 144

Identification: 12″. Central tail feathers extremely long and thin, projecting four inches beyond others. Upperparts pale green, merging to blue on rump; crown blackish, forehead white continued on each side of head as white streak above eyes; below, chin white, followed by a broad black band across throat; breast and flanks pale green merging to white on abdomen. In flight wings appear pale cinnamon. Its very long central tail feathers, black throat band and cinnamon wings are good field characters.

Voice: A series of soft, double twittering notes.

Distribution and Habitat: Resident and partial migrant Senegal eastwards to Ethiopia, south through Uganda and Kenya to central Tanganyika. In East Africa mainly a passage migrant October to May, but some birds breed in Uganda and probably also in Kenya and Tanganyika. Frequents a variety of habitats, from edges of West African type forests to semi-desert bush country, acacia and savannah woodland.

LITTLE BEE-EATER *Melittophagus pusillus* p. 144

Identification: 6″. Central tail feathers not elongated; tail square. A small green bee-eater with a yellow throat, a blue-black neckpatch, and a conspicuous black eye-streak. Perches on small bushes and even on grass stems. The Blue-breasted Bee-eater is larger (7½ inches); the throat patch below the yellow throat is deep blue and there is a conspicuous white patch below the black eye-streak. It has similar habits to the Little Bee-eater. The Cinnamon-chested Bee-eater is a species of the same plumage pattern but larger again (8 inches) and has the throat patch black and the rest of the underparts deep cinnamon-rufous, not pale greenish-saffron. It has completely different habits, being a forest species which perches in trees.

Voice: Usually silent, but sometimes utters a single or double rather squeaky "teeep" or "tee, tsp."

Distribution and Habitat: Occurs as a resident and partial migrant from Senegal eastwards to Ethiopia, Eritrea and Somaliland, south to South Africa. Common throughout East and Central Africa in suitable localities, such as coastal bush, light woodland and reeds at the edges of rivers and marshes, bush country and cultivation.

Allied Species: The Blue-breasted Bee-eater (*Melittophagus variegatus*) has similar habits to the Little Bee-eater but is larger, with a dark blue throat band and a conspicuous white patch below the black eye-streak and ear-coverts. In East Africa it occurs in Uganda, Tanganyika and extreme western Kenya. In Central Africa it occurs in Northern Rhodesia where it frequents wet dambos and plains. The Cinnamon-chested Bee-eater (*Melittophagus oreobates*) is a forest species found in mountains of the southern Sudan, south-western Ethiopia and north-eastern Congo, south through Kenya and Uganda to northern and western Tanganyika. It is larger than the other two species and has a black throat-band and deep cinnamon-chestnut chest and abdomen. The Somali Bee-eater (*Melittophagus revoilii*) is a small very pale green species with pale buff underparts: silvery-blue rump conspicuous when bird flies. This species occurs in eastern Ethiopia and the Somalilands, south to the northern arid areas of Kenya. It is a desert species found in arid bush.

WHITE-FRONTED BEE-EATER *Melittophagus bullockoides*

p. 144

Identification: 9″. Tail square, central feathers not elongated. Upperparts green, to cinnamon on nape, hoary white on forehead: below, throat vivid scarlet, breast and abdomen cinnamon-buff. Upper and under tail coverts vivid ultramarine blue, conspicuous in flight.

Voice: A shrill, nasal "waark, aark" or "waar."

Distribution and Habitat: A very local resident, but not uncommon where it does occur, from central Kenya to South Africa. In East Africa it is most frequent in the Rift Valley near Lakes Naivasha and Nakuru in Kenya, and in the highlands near Iringa in Tanganyika. In Central Africa it is a local resident in Nyasaland and the Rhodesias, being most plentiful in Southern Rhodesia where it is locally common in the vicinity of rivers throughout the territory. It occurs in bush country and in cultivated areas near water in Kenya, and in scrub on hills in Tanganyika.

Allied Species: The Red-throated Bee-eater (*Melittophagus bullocki*) occurs in the southern Sudan, northern Uganda and western Ethiopia. It resembles the White-fronted Bee-eater but is smaller and its crown is green like the back, not frosty white. The Blue-headed Bee-eater (*Melittophagus mulleri*) is a rare forest species which extends from West Africa through Uganda to western Kenya. It is smaller than the White-fronted Bee-eater (7 inches) with bright deep chestnut upperparts, and the crown and nape ultramarine-blue merging to cobalt-blue and white on the forehead; chin and upper throat bright scarlet, lower throat black merging to deep blue on remainder underparts and tail.

BEE-EATERS and KINGFISHERS

1. **EUROPEAN BEE-EATER** page 140
   Projecting central tail feathers; yellow throat.
2. **CARMINE BEE-EATER** 141
   Elongated central tail feathers; mainly carmine-red plumage.
3. **WHITE-THROATED BEE-EATER** 142
   Central tail feathers extremely long and thin; chin white.
4. **SWALLOW-TAILED BEE-EATER** 146
   Tail deeply forked; throat yellow.
5. **LITTLE BEE-EATER** 142
   Small size; square tail and yellow throat. *See* text.
6. **WHITE-FRONTED BEE-EATER** 143
   Tail square; throat red.
7. **PYGMY KINGFISHER** 139
   Lacks conspicuous crest.
8. **MALACHITE KINGFISHER** 138
   Conspicuous, barred blue and black crest.
9. **GREY-HEADED KINGFISHER** 140
   Belly deep chestnut-red.
10. **GIANT KINGFISHER** 138
    Male: Throat and breast chestnut, abdomen white.
    Female: Throat and upper breast white with black markings; lower breast and abdomen chestnut.
11. **STRIPED KINGFISHER** 140
    General dull plumage and greenish-blue rump.
12. **WOODLAND KINGFISHER** 139
    Black and red bill.
13. **PIED KINGFISHER** 137
    Plumage black and white; head crested.

1
2
3
4
5
6
7
8
9
10
11
♂
12
13
♂

1
2
3
4
5
6
7
8
9
10
11
12
13
14
15
16
17

BARBETS, WOODPECKERS and SPOTTED CREEPER

The Black Bee-eater (*Melittophagus gularis*) is another West African forest bee-eater which extends eastwards to western Uganda. Its upperparts and head are black; throat scarlet, abdomen and rump bright cobalt-blue.

SWALLOW-TAILED BEE-EATER *Dicrocercus hirundineus* p.144

Identification: $8\frac{1}{2}''$. Tail deeply forked; above and below golden-green with a bright orange-yellow throat and a blue band across base of throat; upper and under tail-coverts blue. Species easily recognised by conspicuous forked tail.

Voice: A shrill, far-carrying "chiree, chiree," repeated again and again.

Distribution and Habitat: Local resident north-eastern Congo, eastwards to south-western Ethiopia, south through Uganda and Tanganyika to South Africa. In Central Africa fairly common in Nyasaland; more sparsely distributed the Rhodesias. Its main habitat is acacia woodland, light dry woodland and brachystegia.

HORNBILLS: Bucerotidae

The Hornbills are a very distinct group of birds of medium or large size characterised by their large curved bills which often possess casque-like structures on the culmens. The family has remarkable breeding habits, the female in most cases being imprisoned during incubation by plastering up the nesting hole, leaving only a narrow slit through which she is fed by the male.

TRUMPETER HORNBILL *Bycanistes bucinator* p. 160

Identification: 24-26″. This is one of the large black and white hornbills with well-developed casques on their bills. It may be distinguished from the Black and White-casqued Hornbill and the Silvery-cheeked Hornbill by its white breast and abdomen. In those two species the breast is black and only the lower abdomen white.

Voice: An assortment of very loud, harsh braying cries and a grunting call.

Distribution and Habitat: Local resident from the Tana River in Kenya, south through Tanganyika to Natal and Cape Province, westwards through Central Africa to Angola. Widely distributed in Nyasaland and the Rhodesias. Frequents thickly wooded and forest country and in coastal scrub and riverine forest. It is common in the forests of the

Kenya coast and is the black and white hornbill which is so conspicuous in the mist forest at the Victoria Falls.

BLACK AND WHITE-CASQUED HORNBILL

Bycanistes subcylindricus p. 160

Identification: 27-30″. The Black and White-casqued Hornbill may be recognised by the black and white casque and by its white secondaries which form a large white wing patch, conspicuous both when the bird is settled and on the wing. The Silvery-cheeked Hornbill has an entirely yellowish-white casque and its secondaries are black. The Trumpeter Hornbill is smaller and has the breast and abdomen white; its casque is blackish like the rest of the bill.

Voice: A great variety of very raucous calls "Raaak, raak, raak, raak, raak, ark" and loud single notes, such as "rak."

Distribution and Habitat: A resident in West Africa east to Congo, southern Sudan, Uganda, western Kenya and north-western Tanganyika. This is a true forest hornbill, local, but common where it occurs. In Uganda it occurs in most of the large forest areas and it is also common in the Kakamega forests of western Kenya. It draws attention to its presence by its loud calls.

SILVERY-CHEEKED HORNBILL *Bycanistes brevis* p. 160

Identification: 26-29″. The Silvery-cheeked Hornbill may be distinguished from the Trumpeter and Black and White-casqued Hornbills by its entirely black wings and yellowish-white casque in the male. The female has a less developed casque which is horn coloured like the remainder of the bill, and is best recognised by entirely black wings.

Voice: Similar calls to Black and White-casqued Hornbill, a series of loud, raucous brayings and grunts.

Distribution and Habitat: Resident from Ethiopia and the south-eastern Sudan, south through eastern Kenya and Tanganyika to Portuguese East Africa, Nyasaland and eastern Southern Rhodesia. This is a forest species. It is common in the mountain forest of eastern Tanganyika and the Kenya coastal forests. Like its near relative it draws attention to its whereabouts by its loud calls.

GREY HORNBILL *Tockus nasutus* p. 160

Identification: 18-20″. General plumage pale tawny-brown; head pale grey with white stripe each side of crown; breast and abdomen white; wing coverts conspicuously edged whitish-buff. Bill in male black with ivory-coloured patch at base upper mandible; female has dark reddish bill with ivory-white basal half to upper mandible. The Pale-billed Hornbill is distinguished by its pale dull yellowish bill.

Voice: A two-note, piping whistle "phee-hoo," repeated rather slowly over and over again.

Distribution and Habitat: Local resident Senegal east to Eritrea, Ethiopia and Somalia, south through East and Central Africa to Zululand and Transvaal, South Africa. This is a bush country species, usually seen in pairs or small family parties. It is common in suitable areas over East Africa. It is also common in the Rhodesias and Nyasaland where it inhabits acacia woodland and the poorer, more open brachystegia woodlands.

Allied Species: The Pale-billed Hornbill (*Tockus pallidirostris*) occurs in dry bush and woodland areas of south-eastern Kenya, Tanganyika, south to Portuguese East Africa, Central Africa and the Congo and Angola. It may be distinguished from the Grey Hornbill by its pale creamy-yellow bill.

RED-BILLED HORNBILL *Tockus erythrorhynchus* p. 160

Identification: 17-18″. Upperparts brownish-black with a white line down back; wing coverts conspicuously spotted white; underparts white; bill red with black patch base lower mandible, rather slender and down-curved. The Yellow-beaked Hornbill has white-spotted wing coverts but bill rich yellow. Von der Decken's Hornbill male has a red bill with an ivory tip and wing coverts not spotted; the female has a black bill. Jackson's Hornbill is like Von der Decken's Hornbill but has white-spotted wings; bill red with terminal third ivory-white in male; bill black in female. The Crowned Hornbill has a mainly red bill but upperparts and wings are black without spots.

Voice: A continuous, "wot, wot, wot, wot, wot, wot, wot, wot, wot."

Distribution and Habitat: Resident from Senegal and Northern Nigeria, eastwards to Ethiopia and Somalilands, south through East and Central Africa to South Africa. The species frequents dry bush country, open acacia woodland, and in the Rhodesias and Nyasaland dry acacia and mopane woodland. It is one of the characteristic birds of the semi-desert districts of Kenya and its somewhat monotonous call is a common sound.

YELLOW-BILLED HORNBILL *Tockus flavirostris* p. 160

Identification: 17-20″. A medium-sized hornbill with white underparts, conspicuously white-spotted black wings and a deep orange-yellow bill.

The combination of wing and bill characters renders this species easy to identify.

Voice: A yelping, piping note, "ke, ke, ke, ke, ke, ke," repeated over and over again.

Distribution and Habitat: Local resident from Ethiopia and Somalilands, south through Kenya and north-eastern Uganda to northern Tanganyika. The species reappears again in Central Africa, being uncommon in Northern Rhodesia and Nyasaland but more frequent in Southern Rhodesia, south to South Africa. It is essentially a dry bush country bird in East Africa, being locally common in eastern and northern Kenya. In Central Africa it occurs in dry acacia and mopane woodland.

VON DER DECKEN'S HORNBILL *Tockus deckeni* p. 160

Identification: 17-20″. A white-breasted species with black wings without white spots: bill, in male, bright red with terminal third ivory-white; female is smaller than male and has an entirely black bill. The species may be recognised on the combination of wing and bill characters. Jackson's Hornbill has the same bill characters but has the wing coverts spotted with white.

Voice: A monotonous piping whistle, not unlike that of the Red-billed Hornbill, "wek, wek, wek, wek, wek, wek, wek, wek, wek."

Distribution and Habitat: Local resident central Ethiopia and southern Somalia through Kenya to northern half of Tanganyika. Frequents dry bush country and open acacia woodland.

Allied Species: Jackson's Hornbill (*Tockus jacksoni*) closely resembles Von der Decken's Hornbill but may be distinguished by its white-spotted wing coverts. Both species occur in the Lake Baringo area, Kenya. Jackson's Hornbill occurs in central Ethiopia and south-eastern Sudan to northern Uganda and Turkana in Kenya. It has also been recorded from east-central Tanganyika.

CROWNED HORNBILL *Tockus alboterminatus* p. 160

Identification: 19-20″. Upperparts, throat, wings and tail blackish-brown; white tips to tail feathers; breast and abdomen white; bill dusky red. The species may be distinguished by its dark plumage and dull red bill.

Voice: A thin, piping whistle, quite unlike the calls of related hornbills. On hearing the call for the first time one is tempted to associate it with some small warbler rather than a bird like a hornbill.

Distribution and Habitat: Local resident from the Somalilands and southern Ethiopia, southwards through Kenya, Tanganyika and Uganda to Central Africa, Portuguese East Africa and South Africa. It also occurs in the eastern Congo and Angola. It frequents dry highland forest, woodlands and wooded river banks and locally even rain forest areas.

Allied Species: The Pied Hornbill (*Tockus fasciatus*) is a West African forest species which occurs eastwards to Uganda and the southern Sudan. It resembles the Crowned Hornbill but may be distinguished immediately by its ivory-white bill with a reddish tip.

GROUND HORNBILL *Bucorvus leadbeateri* p. 92

Identification: 42″. This species and the closely related Abyssinian Ground Hornbill, are the largest of the African hornbills. General plumage black with white primaries which are conspicuous only when the bird is in flight. Skin of face and throat unfeathered, bright red; in female throat skin red or blue. Usually seen in pairs or family parties walking over the ground. In the distance they have a distinct resemblance to domestic turkeys.

Voice: A succession of deep lion-like grunts.

Distribution and Habitat: Very local resident in Kenya, Uganda, and Tanganyika, south through Congo and Central Africa to South Africa; also occurs in Angola. It frequents open country, sparse woodland and in the Rhodesias along the edges of dambos. In Kenya it is most frequent in the Rift Valley and the Mara River area.

Allied Species: The Abyssinian Ground Hornbill (*Bucorvus abyssinicus*) occurs in Eritrea and British Somaliland, south through Ethiopia and the Sudan to Uganda and northern Kenya. It may be distinguished from the Ground Hornbill by a patch of red at the base of the upper mandible (in the Ground Hornbill the bill is entirely black) and the bare skin of the face and neck being mainly blue; bill has a curious casque which is truncated and open in front.

HOOPOES: Upupidae

The Hoopoes are a small group of medium-sized birds of unmistakable appearance. Plumage boldly barred pinkish-rufous, white and black with a conspicuous crest of erectile feathers. Feeds largely on the ground: ant-lion larvae are an important item of diet.

AFRICAN HOOPOE *Upupa africana* p. 176

Identification: 11″. Plumage bright pinkish-rufous; wings and tail black barred white, except for primaries which are black. Long rufous, black-tipped erectile crest and curved bill. Flight rather butterfly-like, comparatively slow and undulating. European and Senegal Hoopoes have a conspicuous white bar across the primaries.

Voice: A low, penetrating "hoo-hoo-hoo-hoo-hoo, hoo, hoo." The call could be mistaken for that of a dove when first heard.

Distribution and Habitat: Local resident from the Congo to Ethiopia, southwards through East and Central Africa and Portuguese East Africa to South Africa. Frequents dry bush, acacia and brachystegia woodland, and cultivated areas.

Allied Species: The European and Senegal Hoopoes (*Upupa epops*) which are races of the same species may be distinguished by the white bar across the flight feathers: in the African Hoopoe the primaries are black. The European Hoopoe is a winter visitor and passage migrant south to Tanganyika with one record for Nyasaland. The Senegal Hoopoe is a resident race which occurs in northern Uganda and Kenya and north-eastern Tanganyika.

WOOD HOOPOES AND SCIMITAR-BILLS: Phoeniculidae

The Wood-hoopoes are medium-sized, slender birds with black plumage glossed green, blue or purple. Tails long and graduated; bills long and down-curved. Arboreal in habits, usually in small flocks, except the smaller Scimitar-bills; noisy birds keeping up a constant chatter.

GREEN WOOD HOOPOE or KAKELAAR

Phoeniculus purpureus p. 176

Identification: 15-16″. A slender black bird, highly glossed green above and below, with a long graduated tail and a curved red bill and red legs. A white bar across wings in flight and white tips to tail feathers except for central pair. Occurs in noisy family parties, climbing over tree branches and exploring cracks for insects in the manner of woodpeckers.

Voice: A series of harsh, chattering cries.

Distribution and Habitat: Local resident throughout most of the Ethiopian Region outside the West African forest area. Locally common in East and Central Africa. Frequents various types of woodlands, especially acacia.

WHITE-HEADED WOOD HOOPOE *Phoeniculus bollei* p. 176

Identification: 14-15″. Plumage black with bright green metallic body feathers; wings and tail glossed purplish-blue: head white. No white markings on wings and tail. Bill and feet conspicuously red. Occurs in forest in noisy family parties.

Voice: A series of high-pitched, cackling calls: very noisy.

Distribution and Habitat: Local resident West African forest region eastwards through Uganda to western and central Kenya. This is a forest species locally common in the Kenya highland forests, including the Mt. Kenya forests and the forests around Nairobi.

ABYSSINIAN SCIMITAR-BILL *Rhinopomastus minor* p. 176

Identification: 9″. This is the smallest of the Wood Hoopoes, black with metallic purplish-blue wash on upperparts, wings and tail; bill very curved and slender, bright orange-yellow; feet black. No white markings on wings and tail.

Voice: Far less noisy than the larger species, uttering a short trill at intervals.

Distribution and Habitat: Local resident from the Somalilands and Ethiopia, southwards through Uganda and Kenya to the southern half of Tanganyika. This is a bush or arid bush country bird, favouring acacia woodlands and acacia belts along dry river courses. Usually seen in pairs or small family parties.

Allied Species: The Scimitar-bill (*Rhinopomastus cyanomelas*) is a larger species (11 inches) with black bill and feet, and a white bar across the flight feathers and white tips to some of the tail feathers. It occurs in open woodland, savannah and bush country throughout East and Central Africa, south to South Africa.

OWLS: Strigidae

Mainly nocturnal birds of prey characterised by large heads, rather flattened faces and conspicuous "facial discs" and forward facing eyes. Plumage soft and downy and flight noiseless: ear-tufts present in many species; hooked bills and powerful claws.

AFRICAN BARN OWL *Tyto alba* p. 160

Identification: 13″. No ear tufts: above golden-buff profusely mottled grey and speckled white; underparts white with some dark-brown spotting on chest and flanks. Legs long and facial disc distinctive, heart-shaped.

Voice: A wavering, wild shriek. At nesting place may produce subdued snoring noise and bill snapping.

Distribution and Habitat: Local resident throughout most of Ethiopian Region and throughout East and Central Africa. Often associated with human habitations, making its home in lofts and immediately below roofs. Often breeds in disused hammerkops' nests. Nocturnal in habits, feeding almost entirely upon rats and mice.

Allied Species: The Cape Grass Owl (*Tyto capensis*) is a close relative of the Barn Owl but may be distinguished by its blackish-brown upperparts, which may or may not be peppered with white. This is a very uncommon bird from western Kenya to South Africa. It frequents open moorland type country and extensive marshes. Like the Barn Owl it is nocturnal in its habits and also preys upon small rodents. In Kenya it is most frequently encountered on the moorlands of Mt. Kenya and the Aberdare Mts., the South Kinangop plateau and on the moorlands of the western highlands of Kenya.

AFRICAN MARSH OWL *Asio capensis* p. 160

Identifications: 16″. Short ear tufts present: often starts hunting, quartering the ground in a harrier-like manner, at dusk before it is completely dark. This bird is a dark brown and buff edition of the well-known European and American Short-eared Owl. Upperparts tawny brown with slight buff mottling; below whitish, mottled dull brown and buff.

Voice: Generally a silent bird but sometimes produces a hoarse croak.

Distribution and Habitat: Local resident from the southern Sudan and Ethiopia, south through East and Central Africa to Angola and South Africa. Frequents open grasslands, moors, swamps and marshes.

Allied Species: The African Wood Owl (*Ciccaba woodfordi*) is a thickset forest and woodland species widely distributed in East and Central Africa. It has a general resemblance to the Tawny Owl of Europe but is smaller: no ear tufts.

AFRICAN SCOPS OWL *Otus scops* (M & R) p. 160

Identification: 7″. This tiny owl may be recognised by the combination of very small size and ear tufts. Plumage finely vermiculated pale grey, brown and white, with black and white streaks on breast. The Pearl-spotted Owlet is larger (8 inches) and lacks ear-tufts; below it is white with brown streaks, not vermiculated grey. The European race of Scops Owl is slightly larger (7½ inches) and has a longer, less rounded wing. It is a winter visitor to East Africa.

Voice: The call of the African Scops Owl is one of the characteristic sounds of the African night, a soft two-note "ke-oo" run together to sound as one note.

Distribution and Habitat: Resident throughout the Ethiopian Region in suitable habitats. Common in many places in East and Central Africa, frequenting bush country, acacia belts along dry river beds, savannah woodland and areas where there are baobab trees.

Allied Species: The White-faced Scops Owl (*Otus leucotis*) is a larger species (10 inches) with a conspicuous white facial disc bordered black on each side; has long black-tipped ear tufts. This is a local species in East and Central Africa, it occurs in woodland and bush and acacia country. Its call is distinctive, a rather dove-like "cuc-coo."

PEARL-SPOTTED OWLET *Glaucidium perlatum* p. 160

Identification: 8″. Distinguished by lack of ear tufts, rather small round head and relatively longer tail than most owls. Underparts white broadly streaked dark brown. This species is more frequently observed during the daytime than most owls and its whereabouts is often indicated by the presence of various small birds engaged in mobbing.

Voice: A distinctive, low but far-carrying "we-oo, we-oo."

Distribution and Habitat: Resident in West Africa, outside the forest region, eastwards to Ethiopia and the Somalilands south to the Zambesi River. Locally common in many areas in East and Central Africa. Occurs in dry bush country, savannah, acacia and other types of woodland.

Allied Species: The Barred Owlet (*Glaucidium capense*) is slightly larger than the Pearl-spotted Owlet. It differs by having the breast barred rich brown, not streaked.

SPOTTED EAGLE OWL *Bubo africanus* p. 160

Identification: 20″. A thickset owl with conspicuous ear tufts; upperparts tawny brown, vermiculated and mottled greyish-white and with rounded white spots on mantle; below whitish with irregular brown barring and heavy spotting on the breast. Verreaux's Eagle Owl is larger and finely vermiculated grey all over, not spotted.

Voice: A low, mournful hooting, "hoo, hoo, hoo."

Distribution and Habitat: Local resident throughout most of the Ethiopian Region in suitable localities. Locally common throughout East and Central Africa. Frequents rocky slopes, bush-clad ravines and savannah country. Often seen on roads after dark and many are killed by motor vehicles.

VERREAUX'S EAGLE OWL *Bubo lacteus* p. 160

Identification: 24-26″. Ear tufts present; general colour finely vermiculated brownish-grey and underparts without heavy spotting; facial disc whitish with a black band on each side. This owl is sometimes encountered in the daytime sleeping in some thickly foliaged acacia tree: its whitish face and the black edging on each side are good field characters.

Voice: A mournful, "hu; hu; hu; hu; hu; hu; hu" in ascending scale.

Distribution and Habitat: Resident in small numbers throughout the Ethiopian Region outside the forest regions. Locally common in many parts of East and Central Africa. It frequents wooded water courses, acacia and brachystegia woodlands and bush and savannah country. In Kenya it is more than usually common in the Amboseli National Reserve where it can be found in daytime sleeping in large acacia trees near water.

Allied Species: The African Fishing Owl (*Scotopelia peli*) is a large (25 inches) species which inhabits wooded and forested water-courses where there is thick cover; feeds on fish. Head very large and plumage especially lax; bright rufous buff barred and spotted with dark brown. It is a rare bird in East Africa, most frequent along the Tana River in Kenya, but is commoner and more widespread along the larger rivers of Central Africa.

NIGHTJARS: Caprimulgidae

These are nocturnal, insectivorous birds with small weak bills but huge gapes, large eyes, tiny feet and long wings. Plumage of "dead-leaf" pattern which gives excellent camouflage when bird immobile during day.

EUROPEAN NIGHTJAR *Caprimulgus europaeus* (M) p. 161

Identification: 10-10½". This species is best recognised by the combination of the following characters: black streaks in centre of back, white tips to two outer pairs tail feathers and white spots to three outer flight feathers (male) and by the absence of a rufous collar on hind neck.

Voice: Apparently silent in Africa.

Distribution and Habitat: Common winter visitor and passage migrant to East Africa; uncommon visitor to Central Africa. Frequents bush country, semi-desert areas, open woodland and cultivated areas. In East Africa it is sometimes very abundant along the Tanganyika and Kenya coast during the northwards migration in April.

DONALDSON-SMITH'S NIGHTJAR

Caprimulgus donaldsoni p. 161

Identification: 6½". This species is so much smaller than related nightjars that size is one of the best characters for field recognition. It is rich rufous in general colour with dark and cream markings; its wing coverts and breast are spotted creamy white: two outer pairs tail feathers with broad white tips and white spots on first four flight feathers.

Voice: A series of short churring calls.

Distribution and Habitat: Resident from Somalilands and eastern and southern Ethiopia, south through Kenya to north-eastern Tanganyika. A bird of bush and arid bush country, locally common in parts of eastern and northern Kenya. It is usually numerous in the Tsavo National Park, being most in evidence after rain when many insects are flying.

ABYSSINIAN NIGHTJAR *Caprimulgus poliocephalus* p. 161

Identification: 9½″. Best field characters are very dusky plumage and white two outer pairs of tail feathers. These tail feathers have dusky outer webs but when the bird is in flight the feathers appear entirely white. Rufous collar on hind neck. The Dusky Nightjar resembles this species but tail feathers have broad white tips and do not appear to be completely white. The White-tailed Nightjar has the apical half of the outer tail feathers white but is easily distinguished by its very bright orange-rufous, black-spotted general appearance.

Voice: A plaintive, drawn-out "pee, ooo, wee"; not unlike the call-note of the Grey Plover.

Distribution and Habitat: Local resident and partial migrant from Eritrea and Ethiopia and south-eastern Sudan, south through Kenya to northern Tanganyika. Mainly a bird of highlands country. It is one of the commoner nightjars in the eastern and western highlands of Kenya and is numerous around Nairobi.

Allied Species: The Freckled Nightjar (*Caprimulgus tristigma*) is a heavily built nightjar with a noticeably large head. It is associated with rocky outcrops. It is a very dark-coloured species and lacks the large cream-coloured spots and streaks to upperparts, characteristic of most nightjars: white patch on throat and tail tipped white. Its call is a rather owl-like "whow, whow." It occurs locally in suitable areas where there are rocky outcrops throughout East and Central Africa. The Plain Nightjar (*Caprimulgus inornatus*) is a smaller species (9 inches) with a rather small head and slim appearance: upperparts grey or buffish-grey without conspicuous spots: best field characters are lack of white patch on throat and narrow dark band along shoulder, bordered above creamy-buff; outer tail feathers broadly tipped white.

DUSKY NIGHTJAR *Caprimulgus fraenatus* p. 161

Identification: 10″. A dusky nightjar, boldly mottled blackish-brown and with conspicuous large orange-buff spots on back and wing coverts; rufous collar on hind neck. Species distinguished from Abyssinian Nightjar by broad white tips to two outer pairs tail feathers. In Abyssinian Nightjar these tail feathers appear wholly white. In female

Dusky Nightjar tail tips are grey, not white. The Gaboon and Long-tailed Nightjars have the white tail tips and the outer webs of the two pairs of outer tail feathers white. Otherwise with their boldly buff-spotted upperparts and wing coverts they resemble the Dusky Nightjar.

Voice: A low chuckling churr.

Distribution and Habitat: A local resident and partial migrant from Eritrea, the Somalilands and Ethiopia, south to southern Tanganyika. Occurs on open plains, bush country and highlands. Local movements probably controlled by supplies of insect food.

Allied Species: The White-tailed Nightjar (*Caprimulgus natalensis*) has the apical half of the outer two pairs of tail feathers white, and the upperparts handsomely mottled orange-buff and black. It is especially associated with water, occurring near swamps, marshes and streams: its call is a continuous "chuk, chuk, chuk, chuk, chuk, chuk, chuk." It is a local resident and partial migrant in western Kenya and Uganda, southwards to Northern Rhodesia.

GABOON NIGHTJAR *Caprimulgus fossii* p. 161

Identification: 9″. This nightjar is boldly spotted with cream on the upperparts and wing coverts and somewhat resembles a pale edition of the Dusky Nightjar. Best identified on tail characters: tail not strongly graduated and central pair of feathers not elongated; outer web of two outer pairs tail feathers white or creamy-buff. The Long-tailed Nightjar has the central tail feathers greatly lengthened.

Voice: A prolonged "tok, tok, tok, tok, tok" churring call.

Distribution and Habitat: Local resident and partial migrant from West Africa, eastwards to Kenya and Uganda, south through Tanganyika and Central Africa to South Africa. Locally common in East and Central Africa. Frequents open areas, bush country and savannah woodland.

Allied Species: The Long-tailed Nightjar (*Scotornis climacurus*) resembles the Gaboon Nightjar but may be distinguished by its elongated central tail feathers—from one to six inches beyond others—and two buff bars across wings. It occurs in bush and arid bush country and savannah woodland in the Sudan and Ethiopia, south through Uganda and Kenya to north-eastern Tanganyika, and westwards to Nigeria.

PENNANT-WINGED NIGHTJAR *Semeiophorus vexillarius* p. 161

Identification: 12″. Adult male possesses remarkable ninth primary feather which is elongated to about twice the total length of the bird: upperparts both sexes mottled and spotted dark brown and buff;

conspicuous rufous collar on hind neck; below mottled on breast but abdomen white. Combination of large size and white belly best field characters if pennant wing feathers absent.

Voice: A silent bird for a nightjar: on its breeding grounds reputed to utter a high-pitched piping call.

Distribution and Habitat: Non-breeding visitor to southern Sudan, Uganda and Kenya between February and August, migrating southwards to breeding grounds in southern Tanganyika and Central Africa in August and September. Locally common, especially in Northern Rhodesia. Frequents woodlands and stony hillsides.

STANDARD-WING NIGHTJAR *Macrodipteryx longipennis* p. 161

Identification: 9″. The adult male is remarkable in having the shaft of the ninth primary elongated about 12 inches and terminating with a very broad flag-like web. In flight the "standards" can be mistaken for two small birds flying above and behind the nightjar! The female lacks the standards. Both sexes may be distinguished by having no white spots on the flight feathers.

Voice: A shrill, continuous churring.

Distribution and Habitat: Occurs as a breeding visitor to southern Sudan, Eritrea, Ethiopia, Uganda and north-western Kenya: in non-breeding season birds move northwards to northern Ethiopia and the Central Sudan. They occur in open areas and bush country: they appear to favour the near vicinity of water. It is locally a common bird in north-western Uganda from February to May.

MOUSEBIRDS or COLIES: Coliidae

The Mousebirds are peculiar to Africa; they have the ability to move the outer toes backwards or forwards; claws strong and hooked, adapted for climbing branches; plumage hair-like and lax; tail long and graduated, composed of ten stiff feathers; bill thick and rather finch-like; usually occurs in small flocks or family parties: their habit of climbing and running about amongst branches with their long tails usually pointed downwards gives them a very rat or mouse-like appearance.

SPECKLED MOUSEBIRD *Colius striatus* p.p. 161

Identification: 14″. Upperparts brown; head slightly crested; sides of face greyish-white; chin and throat dusky, feathers with pale tips giving

HORNBILLS and OWLS

1. **BLACK AND WHITE-CASQUED HORNBILL** page 147
White wing patch; parti-coloured casque.
2. **SILVERY-CHEEKED HORNBILL** 147
Wings black; casque pale.
3. **TRUMPETER HORNBILL** 146
White breast and abdomen.
4. **CROWNED HORNBILL** 149
Dull red bill; white tips to outer tail feathers.
5. **GREY HORNBILL** 147
Ivory-white patch on sides of bill; pale plumage.
6. **YELLOW-BILLED HORNBILL** 148
Orange-yellow bill; white spots on wing coverts.
7. **RED-BILLED HORNBILL** 148
Red bill; white spots on wing coverts.
8. **VON DER DECKEN'S HORNBILL** 149
Wing coverts black, unspotted; male's bill red with ivory tip; female's bill black.
9. **AFRICAN SCOPS OWL** 154
Very small size; ear tufts.
10. **AFRICAN BARN OWL** 153
Golden-buff upperparts; heart-shaped facial disc.
11. **PEARL-SPOTTED OWLET** 155
No ear tufts; relatively long, white-spotted tail
12. **VERREAUX'S EAGLE OWL** 155
Black band on each side of facial disc; underparts finely vermiculated without heavy spots.
13. **SPOTTED EAGLE OWL** 155
Underparts with heavy spotting; eyes yellow or brown, not orange.
14. **AFRICAN MARSH OWL** 153
Short ear tufts; frequents open country and quarters ground for prey like a harrier.

1
2
3
4
♂
5
6
7
8
♀
9
10
11
12
13
14

♂
1
♀
2
3
4
5
6
7
8
9
10
11
12

HONEY-GUIDES, MOUSEBIRDS and NIGHTJARS

1. **GREATER HONEY-GUIDE** page 170
White outer tail feathers; pink or greyish-pink bill. Male with black throat. Immature resembles female but has orange-buff wash on chest and throat.

2. **WAHLBERG'S HONEY-GUIDE** 171
Resembles small grey flycatcher except for white on outer tail feathers.

3. **SPECKLED MOUSEBIRD** 159
Gregarious; long tail; speckled chest; crested.

4. **LESSER HONEY-GUIDE** 171
White outer tail feathers; stumpy bill.

5. **BLUE-NAPED MOUSEBIRD** 162
Gregarious; blue nape patch; long, slender tail.

6. **STANDARD-WING NIGHTJAR** 159
Male: Wing " standards "; no white spots on flight feathers.
Female: No " standards "; no white spots on flight feathers or tail.

7. **GABOON NIGHTJAR** 158
Outer webs of two outer pairs tail feathers white or creamy-buff: central tail feathers not elongated.

8. **DUSKY NIGHTJAR** 157
Broad white or pale grey tips to outer tail feathers; rufous collar; wings conspicuously spotted.

9. **ABYSSINIAN NIGHTJAR** 157
Two outer pairs tail feathers white on inner webs; rufous collar.

10. **DONALDSON-SMITH'S NIGHTJAR** 156
Small size; rich rufous and orange-buff markings on upperparts; white tips outer pairs tail feathers.

11. **EUROPEAN NIGHTJAR** 156
Black streaks on upperparts; no rufous collar.

12. **PENNANT-WINGED NIGHTJAR** 158
Remarkable elongated 9th primary, the pennant. Female lacks " pennants." In both sexes breast mottled but abdomen white.

a speckled appearance; remainder underparts tawny with brown barring on breast. In flight the bird reminds one of a tiny cock pheasant with a long brown tail.

Voice: A series of short twittering call-notes and a harsher single or double "tsssk."

Distribution and Habitat: Resident, often abundant, throughout most of the Ethiopian Region including East and Central Africa. Inhabits forested and wooded areas, dense scrub, and cultivated areas. Occurs in small flocks. At times destructive to growing vegetables and fruit trees.

Allied Species: The White-headed Mousebird (*Colius leucocephalus*) is a dry country species found in southern Somaliland, Kenya and northern Tanganyika. It may be distinguished from the Speckled Mousebird by its barred upperparts and white crown and crest.

BLUE-NAPED MOUSEBIRD *Colius macrourus* p. 161

Identification: 14″. General plumage greenish ash-grey; tail feathers very long and slender; head crested; turquoise-blue patch on nape. Base of bill and face deep red. Uniform colour and blue nape patch distinguish this species.

Voice: A loud, clear whistle "peeeeee, peeeeeee."

Distribution and Habitat: Resident from Senegal eastwards through the Sudan to Ethiopia and Somaliland, south through Uganda and Kenya to Tanganyika. This is a bird of bush and arid bush country, usually encountered in small flocks.

Allied Species: The Red-faced Mousebird (*Colius indicus*) differs from the Blue-naped Mousebird in being more greenish-grey above and in lacking the blue nape patch. It occurs in bush and dry bush from southern Tanganyika, south through the Rhodesias and Nyasaland to the Zambesi River.

TROGONS: Trogonidae

The Trogons are medium-sized forest birds with soft plumage, brilliantly green above, vivid red on the belly; their first and second toes turned backwards. Although so brilliantly coloured they are easily overlooked as they remain motionless when settled.

NARINA'S TROGON *Apaloderma narina* p. 176

Identification: 12″. Upperparts, head, throat and upper breast brilliant, shining green; remainder underparts crimson; tail dark blue-green, outer three pairs of tail feathers whitish. The female has the throat and upper breast brown, merging to greyish-pink on chest; belly crimson. One's first indication of a trogon is a flash of vivid green and scarlet as the bird moves from perch to perch, but when motionless, in spite of its bright colours, it is not easy to see against a background of green foliage. Birds usually single or in pairs: sometimes they are members of mixed arboreal bird parties. The Bar-tailed Trogon is smaller and has the outer tail feathers barred black and white.

Voice: A rather dove-like, soft, "coo, coo" repeated over and over again. The male raises and lowers the tail as it calls and this movement often gives away the bird's whereabouts.

Distribution and Habitat: Locally distributed in forested or thickly wooded areas throughout most of the Ethiopian Region in suitable localities. In East Africa occurs in rain forest, riverine forest, coastal bush and woodland and dry highland forest. In Central Africa occurs in most suitable areas, sometimes found in brachystegia and mopane woodland.

Allied Species: The Bar-tailed Trogon (*Heterotrogon vittatum*) is smaller, has the outer pairs of tail feathers white, barred with black and the throat, sides of face and top of head black washed with bronzy green. It occurs in mountain forests of East Africa and Northern Rhodesia and Nyasaland.

BARBETS: Capitonidae

The Barbets are related to the woodpeckers and like those birds have the first and fourth toes directed backwards; birds thickset with short, heavy bills: extremely variable plumage characters. Barbets are mainly fruit eaters, and are often numerous in fruiting fig and other fruit-bearing trees.

DOUBLE-TOOTHED BARBET *Lybius bidentatus* p. 145

Identification: 9″. A large barbet, blackish above, with a deep crimson breast and a conspicuous, large ivory-coloured bill. Attracted to fig trees. The larger Black-breasted Barbet also has an ivory-white bill but has the throat and upper breast black, not crimson.

Voice: A rather wood-hoopoe-like "cheks, cheeks," but often a silent bird for a barbet.

Distribution and Habitat: Local resident and probably partial migrant in search of fruiting trees West Africa, eastwards to Ethiopia, south to Uganda and western Kenya. Occurs in lightly forested areas, savannah woodlands and open park-type country where there are isolated fig trees. In Kenya not uncommon in the Kitale—Mount Elgon area, and in Uganda widespread where there are fig trees.

Allied Species: The Black-breasted Barbet (*Lybius rolleti*) occurs in northern and north-western Uganda. It is a very large barbet (11 inches) with an ivory coloured bill, black throat and breast and a crimson belly; a tuft of hair-like feathers is present on the chin. Like the Double-toothed Barbet it is usually found where there are fruiting fig trees. The Black-billed Barbet (*Lybius guifsobalito*) is a medium-sized (6 inches) species, glossy black in colour with forehead, face and throat scarlet; bill black. It is a local resident in Eritrea, Ethiopia, the southern Sudan and central and western Uganda. The Red-faced Barbet (*Lybius rubrifacies*) is also medium sized, black and with the forehead and face red; the throat however is black like the remainder of the upperparts. It occurs in south-western Uganda and north-western Tanganyika in open savannah woodland.

BLACK-COLLARED BARBET *Lybius torquatus* p. 145

Identification: 6″. Upperparts finely vermiculated brown and grey; crown, face and foreneck scarlet; a black band across breast; belly pale yellow. The combination of red face, black chest band and yellow belly renders this species easy to identify. Often seen in pairs on the topmost branches of dead or leafless trees.

Voice: A loud, three- or four-note whistle, repeated several times, "kor, kooroo—kor, kooroo."

Distribution and Habitat: Local resident, at times common, Belgian Congo, eastwards to Kenya, south to South Africa. In Kenya most frequent coastal forests, including brachystegia woodlands. In Central Africa, where it is widespread, it does not normally occur in virgin brachystegia or mopane woodlands. Occurs normally in savannah woodlands and park-like country where there are fig and other fruit-bearing trees.

Allied Species: The White-headed Barbet (*Lybius leucocephalus*) is a black and white species with a white head. It occurs from the southern Sudan, Belgian Congo, Uganda and Kenya, south to Tanganyika. It is a bird of savannah woodlands or cultivated areas where there are fig trees.

BROWN-BREASTED BARBET *Lybius melanopterus* p. 145

Identification: $6\frac{1}{2}''$. A red-headed barbet with a wide pale brown band across the chest; belly white; wings and tail black. Its red throat, brown chest and white belly are characteristic. The bill is pale grey.

Voice: A harsh, nasal "aark, aark."

Distribution and Habitat: A local species which ranges from southern Somaliland, south through eastern Kenya and Tanganyika to Nyasaland and Mozambique. It frequents open savannah woodlands, riverine forest and thick coastal scrub. It is most frequent in the forests of the Shimba Hills, south-eastern Kenya and parts of eastern Tanganyika.

Allied Species: The Hairy-breasted Barbet (*Tricholaema flavipunctatum*) is a medium-sized (6 inches) species, very thickset, with dark upperparts thickly spotted with yellow and two conspicuous white stripes on the face, above and below the eye; underparts yellowish-green, streaked and spotted black and with the terminations of the breast feathers long and hair-like. It is a forest species which occurs from West Africa to Uganda, where it is common in the Bwamba forest, western Uganda. Like many other barbets it is most in evidence around fruiting fig trees. The Red-fronted Barbet (*Tricholaema diadematum*) is a bush country species which is commonest in acacia woodland along streams. It is 5 inches in length, blackish above with yellow streaks; frontal half of the crown bright red; eye-stripe pale yellow; below yellowish-white more or less spotted brown. It occurs from the southern Sudan and central Ethiopia south through Kenya and Uganda to Tanganyika and

Nyasaland. The Brown-throated Barbet (*Tricholaema melanocephalum*) is another dry country species inhabiting Kenya and Tanganyika. It is smaller than the Red-fronted Barbet (4½ inches) with brown upperparts streaked yellow on back and rump; throat brown; rest underparts white with a few brown and red-tipped feathers in the centre of the breast. The Spotted-flanked Barbet (*Tricholaema lacrymosum*) is yet another small (5 inches) bush and savannah country barbet. It has the mantle, crown and throat blue-black with a white stripe above the eye and another from the bill running along side of neck; belly yellowish-white with drop-like black spots along flanks. It occurs locally in Uganda, Kenya and Tanganyika.

p. 145

GREY-THROATED BARBET *Gymnobucco bonapartei*

Identification: 7″. General colour dusky brown except head and neck which are ashy-grey; two bristle tufts, like tufts from a toothbrush, at base of bill around nostrils. These bristle tufts are conspicuous in the field and render this species easy to identify.

Voice: A long-drawn-out "hoooo" or "choooo," difficult to locate unless bird is perched in some dead tree. When feeding often completely silent, its presence being indicated by falling figs.

Distribution and Habitat: Local resident in forest areas from West Africa across to Uganda and western Kenya. It is locally common in most of the Uganda forests and in the Kakamega and Cherengani forests of western Kenya.

Allied Species: Whyte's Barbet (*Buccanodon whytii*) occurs locally in wooded areas in southern Tanganyika and Central Africa. It is a medium-sized species (6 inches) dark brown in colour, blackish on hind crown and chest: forehead and curved band below eye pale greenish-yellow or whitish. Flight feathers edged white. This is a species found mainly in evergreen forest and tall brachystegia woodland in southern Tanganyika and Central Africa.

WHITE-EARED BARBET *Buccanodon leucotis* p. 145

Identification: 6″. This is a blackish-looking barbet with a white belly and a conspicuous white streak down each side of neck: rump conspicuously white when bird flies away from observer.

Voice: A three-note "ko, ko, ko" and a short, shrill trill.

Distribution and Habitat: Evergreen forest species, found locally in Kenya, Tanganyika, Nyasaland, Southern Rhodesia and Angola. In East Africa the species is most common in the forest on the Chyulu Hills, south-eastern Kenya and on Mt. Kilimanjaro in Tanganyika.

Allied Species: The Green Barbet (*Buccanodon olivaceum*) is a medium-sized (6 inches) dark olive-green species. It occurs in coastal forests of Kenya and in northern and southern Tanganyika to mountain forest in Nyasaland. The Yellow-spotted Barbet (*Buccanodon duchaillui*) is a forest species which extends from West Africa to the forests of Uganda and western Kenya. It is another medium-sized bird (6 inches) with yellow-spotted black upperparts and a bright crimson crown; throat blue-black, rest of underparts mottled yellow and black. This very handsome species is often overlooked owing to its favouring the tops of forest fig trees.

MOUSTACHED GREEN TINKER-BIRD

Viridibucco leucomystax p. 145

Identification: 3½″. General plumage olive, more greyish on underparts; a whitish stripe from base of bill down sides of neck. This tiny barbet is a tree-top haunter and is difficult to observe, but they are sometimes seen at clumps of the parasitic *Loranthus*, the berries of which form an important item of diet. The whitish moustache stripe is fairly conspicuous through glasses.

Voice: A monotonous "tink, tink, tink, tink" repeated over and over again: also reputed to utter a shrill trill.

Distribution and Habitat: Local, but sometimes common, resident in mountain forest from central Kenya to Nyasaland. In East Africa it is most numerous in the forests of the western highlands around Molo and Elburgon, Kenya.

Allied Species: The Green Tinker-bird (*Viridibucco simplex*) occurs from the coastal forests of Kenya, south through Tanganyika to southern Nyasaland. It is slightly smaller than the Moustached Green Tinker-bird (3 inches) and lacks the whitish moustache stripe. The Western Green Tinker-bird (*Viridibucco coryphaea*) is a West African forest species which occurs in western Uganda. It is black above with a broad yellow streak from crown to rump.

RED-FRONTED TINKER-BIRD *Pogoniulus pusillus* p. 145

Identification: 3½″. Upperparts blackish, heavily streaked pale yellow or white; rump lemon yellow; forehead bright scarlet; underparts pale greenish-buff. This is a common bird in bush country: its red forehead is conspicuous in the field. The Red-fronted Barbet which occurs alongside this species is a much larger bird with a heavy bill.

Voice: A shrill, slow trill.

Distribution and Habitat: Local resident, often common, from Eritrea and Somalilands south to northern half of Tanganyika. Place taken in Central Africa by Yellow-fronted Tinker-bird which has a yellow forehead. This is a bush and acacia country species: it is often common in acacia woodland along river and wadis.

Allied Species: The Yellow-fronted Tinker-bird (*Pogoniulus chrysoconus*) closely resembles the Red-fronted Tinker-bird, but has the forehead yellow. It occurs in the southern Sudan, south through Uganda and western and southern Tanganyika to the Rhodesias and Nyasaland, where it is common and widespread.

GOLDEN-RUMPED TINKER-BIRD *Pogoniulus bilineatus* p. 145

Identification: 4″. Upperparts glossy black with a bright golden-yellow rump; conspicuous white stripe above and below eye; black moustache stripe: underparts pale grey, pale greenish-yellow on belly. The Lemon-rumped Tinker-bird has the rump patch pale lemon-yellow; the Yellow-throated Tinker-bird has yellow stripes above and below eye and the throat greenish-yellow.

Voice: A monotonous "tink" uttered again and again with a few seconds' interval between notes.

Distribution and Habitat: A local resident in forests from Uganda and Kenya, south to Natal, South Africa. It occurs in rain forest, highland dry forest, coastal woodland and scrub and evergreen forest. It is locally common in Northern Rhodesia and Nyasaland, although absent from some apparently suitable localities, but in Southern Rhodesia it is confined to the Eastern Districts above 1,000 feet.

Allied Species: The Lemon-rumped Tinker-bird (*Pogoniulus leucolaima*) is a West African species which extends to Uganda, western Kenya and northern and western Tanganyika. It is very similar to the Golden-rumped Tinker-bird, the main distinction being the colour of the rump patch, pale lemon-yellow, not golden-chrome-yellow. It is a forest species; it is especially common around Entebbe, Uganda. The Yellow-throated Tinker-bird (*Pogoniulus subsulphureus*) is another forest species which extends from West Africa to central Uganda. Its facial stripes are pale yellow, not white and it has a yellow chin. The Speckled Tinker-bird (*Pogoniulus scolopaceus*) has the upperparts dark brown, speckled with yellow; below greenish-yellow, mottled brown. This is yet another West African forest species which occurs in Uganda and western Kenya. It creeps about branches of high forest trees in the manner of a woodpecker.

LEVAILLANT'S BARBET *Trachyphonus vaillantii* p. 145

Identification: 8½". This is one of the several brightly coloured "ground barbets" which occur in bush country and woodland and which are associated with termite hills into which they burrow to nest. The present species has a black nape and mantle and a short black crest; head and throat bright yellow heavily mottled with crimson; a white spotted black band across chest; remainder underparts bright yellow with scarlet streaks on breast. The Red and Yellow Barbet has white spotted upperparts and no red streaks on the breast.

Voice: A curious churring, trilling song which has been likened to that of a nightjar; also utters an up-and-down clinking call.

Distribution and Habitat: Local resident Tanganyika, south through the Rhodesias and Nyasaland to South Africa. It is a bird of bush country and dry woodlands where there are thickets, dead trees and ant-hills.

RED AND YELLOW BARBET *Trachyphonus erythrocephalus* p. 145

Identification: 9". Another brightly plumaged "ground barbet." A striking yellowish and red bird with upperparts, wings and tail heavily spotted with round white spots. At first sight it may give the impression of a gaudily coloured woodpecker and like a woodpecker it has an undulating flight. The underparts are bright pale yellow, washed with orange on the chest with a narrow white-spotted black band across the chest; the male has a black streak down the centre of the throat.

Voice: A loud and unmistakable "toogel-de-doogle" repeated over and over again, often by several birds in chorus.

Distribution and Habitat: A local resident from Somaliland and Kenya to north-eastern Tanganyika. Frequents semi-arid bush country and open thornbush areas, favouring localities where there are termite hills in which it breeds. It is widely distributed and common in many parts of the Northern Frontier Province of Kenya.

D'ARNAUD'S BARBET *Trachyphonus darnaudii* p. 145

Identification: 6". Upperparts brown with whitish spots on back, wings and tail; crown black spotted with yellow; sides of face yellow, spotted black; underparts pale sulphur yellow spotted with black on the throat and breast. Some races have the crown completely black and extensive black on the throat and chest.

Voice: Birds call in chorus, two or more facing one another and uttering a loud four-note song "doo, do, dee, dok" over and over again.

Distribution and Habitat: Local resident from the southern Sudan, southern Ethiopia and Somalia, southwards through Kenya and Uganda to south-western Tanganyika. This is mainly a bird of dry bush country and open thornbush areas. It is common in the Tsavo National Park in Kenya.

Allied Species: The Yellow-billed Barbet (*Trachylaemus purpuratus*) is a West African forest species which extends to Uganda and the forests of western Kenya. It is about the size of a Red and Yellow Barbet (9 inches) shiny black above with a yellow belly, and a bright yellow unfeathered face and bill. It is usually seen while feeding in fruiting forest trees.

HONEY-GUIDES: Indicatoridae

A Family of rather small birds, 4½-8 inches long, of sombre brown, olive, grey and white plumage. All species have a considerable amount of white in their three outer pairs of tail feathers, a conspicuous field character when the bird is in flight. They are parasitic in their nesting habits, laying their eggs in the nests of birds such as bee-eaters, barbets and woodpeckers. Honey-Guides feed largely upon bees' wax and bee larvae and are often encountered near native beehives hung in trees. They can be attracted by nailing lumps of bees' comb to tree trunks. The Greater Honey-guide has developed a most remarkable habit of guiding human beings to the nests of wild bees in order to feed upon the honeycomb and grubs when the nest is chopped out.

GREATER or BLACK-THROATED HONEY-GUIDE

Indicator indicator p. 161

Identification: 8″. Upperparts greyish-brown, below dusky white; throat black in adult male; yellow patch on shoulders not usually observed in field; bill of adult bright pink; outer three pairs of tail feathers mainly white, conspicuous in flight. Species remarkable in having a distinct immature plumage in which white underparts are washed with orange-buff on neck and chest. Best identified by size, pink bill of adult and black throat of adult male.

Voice: A very distinct two-note call "weet—eer" repeated every few seconds. Birds have special calling places where they sit at intervals for weeks on end. When trying to draw attention to a bees' nest they have an excited chattering cry "ke, ke, ke, ke, ke, ke, ke, ke, ke."

Distribution and Habitat: A widespread resident, but not common, throughout most of the Ethiopian Region including East and Central Africa. Occurs in a variety of habitats, including the edges of rain forest and in highland dry forest, cultivated areas where there are trees, woodland of all kinds, arid thornbush areas and acacia country.

Allied Species: The Scaly-throated Honey-guide (*Indicator variegatus*) is slightly smaller than the Greater Honey-Guide, 7½ inches. It may be distinguished by the dusky bases to the feathers of the throat and chest, which show through to create a scaly appearance; its bill is grey. This is a species which is found largely in acacia woodland and in riverine woodland. It occurs throughout East and Central Africa, but is rare in Southern Rhodesia where it is known only from the Sabi River and Mt. Selinda.

LESSER HONEY-GUIDE *Indicator minor* p. 161

Identification: 5½″. Upperparts dull olive, below pale grey to whitish on abdomen; bill short and stumpy; three outer pairs of tail feathers mainly white. Its most distinctive character is its white outer tail feathers which are very conspicuous when the bird flies.

Voice: A continuous, monotonous "pew, pew, pew," with an occasional interval.

Distribution and Habitat: A common and widespread species throughout most of the Ethiopian Region, including East and Central Africa. Occurs in a variety of habitats, from forest, savannah woodland and cultivated areas to bush and arid bush country. Often overlooked as it is conspicuous only in flight when attention is aroused by its white outer tail feathers.

WAHLBERG'S HONEY-GUIDE *Prodotiscus regulus* p. 161

Identification: 4½″. Bill slender and pointed; general colour greyish-brown, paler on abdomen; three pairs outer tail feathers mainly white; a tuft of white feathers on each side of rump but these are not usually conspicuous in the field. The appearance of this bird is very like that of one of the small grey or brown flycatchers, and it has the same habit as those birds of sitting motionless on some acacia branch. It is readily distinguished by its white outer tail feathers. Cassin's Honey-guide is olive above and usually frequents a different habitat.

Voice: Usually silent but sometimes utters a sunbird-like "zeet, zeet."

Distribution and Habitat: An uncommon and very local resident over most of the Ethiopian Region, including East and Central Africa. It occurs in savannah woodland and bush and acacia country. In East Africa it specially favours large yellow-barked acacia trees near water.

It is perhaps commoner than is thought as it is a species that is easily overlooked.

Allied Species: Cassin's Honey-Guide (*Prodotiscus insignis*) closely resembles Wahlberg's Honey-guide but is darker above with a deep olive wash. It inhabits forests and rain forest throughout East and Central Africa, but is everywhere uncommon.

WOODPECKERS: Picidae

This is a family of chisel-billed, wood-boring birds with powerful feet (two toes directed forwards, two backwards) and stiff tails which act as props in climbing tree trunks and branches: flight undulating. Woodpeckers nest in holes which they excavate in trees.

FINE-BANDED WOODPECKER *Campethera taeniolaema* p. 145

Identification: 7″. Upperparts bright olive-green; crown and nape crimson (crown white-spotted in female); underparts closely barred olive-green and pale yellow. It may be distinguished by unbarred green upperparts and closely barred underparts.

Voice: Usually a silent bird, but sometimes utters a series of typical woodpecker "yaffling" notes.

Distribution and Habitat: A bird of highland forest, this species occurs in the eastern Congo, Uganda, north-western and central Kenya, and northern Tanganyika. It is usually seen on dead trees on the edge of forest and in forest clearings. It is most frequent in the forests of the western Highlands of Kenya around Molo.

NUBIAN WOODPECKER *Campethera nubica* p. 145

Identification: 7″. Upperparts olive-grey, spotted and indistinctly banded yellowish; crown and nape scarlet, the female with the crown black with white spots; below creamy white with round black spots on breast and flanks; shafts of tail feathers yellowish. The red nape and golden tail are conspicuous in field; the distinctive round black spots on the breast are to be seen only with glasses when the bird is settled. The Golden-tailed Woodpecker is greener above and has black streaks on the underparts, not round spots.

Voice: A loud and far-carrying "cing, cing, cing, cing," almost a metallic, yaffling call, difficult to describe in words but not easily forgotten when once heard.

Distribution and Habitat: Local resident from Sudan and Somalilands, south through Uganda and Kenya to northern half of Tanganyika. A bird of open bush and acacia woodland, often common and conspicuous.

Allied Species: The Golden-tailed Woodpecker (*Campethera abingoni*) differs from the Nubian Woodpecker in having black streaks, not spots, on the underparts. It is mainly a woodlands species, found in East and Central Africa and in South Africa, but everywhere uncommon except in the eastern districts of Southern Rhodesia where it is locally common.

CARDINAL WOODPECKER *Dendropicos fuscescens* p. 145

Identification: 5″. A small woodpecker with the upperparts conspicuously barred blackish-brown and yellowish; forehead brown; crown and nape scarlet in male, dark brown in female: below dusky-white, streaked black on breast and flanks. This is the commonest and most widespread of the small woodpeckers, distinguished by its "laddered" back and streaked underparts.

Voice: A rather brief trilling call.

Distribution and Habitat: Resident, often common, throughout East and Central Africa: occurs also in West and South Africa. Frequents a great variety of country from arid bush to woodlands and forests. Often found in pairs and as members of mixed bird parties.

Allied Species: The uncommon Brown-backed Woodpecker (*Ipophilus obsoletus*) occurs locally in East Africa, south to northern Tanganyika. It is slightly smaller than the Cardinal Woodpecker and may be recognised by its plain ash-brown back. The Uganda Spotted Woodpecker (*Dendropicos poecilolaemus*) resembles the Cardinal Woodpecker and like that species has barred upperparts: it may be distinguished by having the neck and chest finely spotted black, not streaked.

BEARDED WOODPECKER *Thripias namaquus* p. 145

Identification: 9″. A large, dusky-looking woodpecker with a conspicuous red nape patch in male, black in female. Upperparts dusky olive-brown, barred and spotted white; black streak on each side of throat; centre of throat white; rest of underparts finely barred and mottled olive-grey or blackish and white.

Voice: A series of loud, harsh "yaffling" calls.

Distribution and Habitat: Widely distributed from French Equatorial Africa, Ethiopia and the Somalilands, south to South Africa. Locally common in East and Central Africa. Frequents highland forested areas, woodlands and especially acacia woodlands. In Southern Rhodesia occurs chiefly in acacia country and mopane, uncommon in brachystegia woodland.

GREY WOODPECKER *Mesopicos goertae* p. 145

Identification: 7″. Head and underparts grey, sometimes with a red streak down centre of belly; crown red in male. Back golden-green with a contrasting red rump. Lack of barring and streaking and combination of grey head and belly, and golden-green back and red rump render this species easy to identify.

Voice: A three-note, metallic "yaffle."

Distribution and Habitat: Occurs from West Africa eastwards to Ethiopia, southwards through Kenya and Uganda to northern Tanganyika. Frequents open woodlands, cultivated areas where there are trees and acacia woodland. It is a common bird in the Kenya Highlands.

Allied Species: The Red-breasted Wryneck (*Jynx ruficollis*) is a woodpecker-like bird but lacks the stiff tail feathers of the true woodpeckers, its rectrices being soft and rounded. General plumage "nightjar-like," rufous-brown, marbled, speckled and vermiculated with white and dark brown; throat and upper breast deep chestnut brown. It frequents dead timber and acacia woodland and in silhouette looks remarkably like a weaver-bird. It occurs locally throughout East Africa but is everywhere most uncommon: in Central Africa it has been recorded from Nyasaland. Elsewhere it occurs in West and South Africa.

SWIFTS: Apodidae

In general appearance swallow-like but may be distinguished by the formation of their wings which are more slender and scythe-like, their short tails and their manner of flight which is rapid and direct, often gliding considerable distances without flapping wings. Structurally quite distinct from Swallows with flat skulls and a foot structure in which all four toes point forwards.

NYANZA SWIFT *Apus niansae* p. 209

Identification: 6″. Plumage sooty black with whitish throat; tail rather short, forked. Rough-winged Swallows are black in plumage but have very long forked tails and a characteristic swallow flight. Horus and White-rumped Swifts have white rumps. The European Common Swift is slightly larger; it is not distinguishable for certain in field.

Voice: A typical swift-type screech at nesting sites.

Distribution and Habitat: Resident and perhaps local partial migrant Eritrea, Ethiopia, Kenya and northern Tanganyika. Aerial, may occur anywhere but especially over high ground. Swifts, including this species, are often in evidence in the vicinity of storm clouds. Breeds in high cliffs, in Kenya there are colonies in the cliffs at Hell's Gate, Naivasha, where they nest alongside the Mottled Swift.

Allied Species: The very large Mottled Swift (*Apus aequatorialis*) is a resident and partial migrant from Eritrea and Ethiopia southwards through Kenya and Uganda to the Rhodesias, Nyasaland and South Africa. Length 8½ inches, brown in colour, with pale edgings to the feathers of the underparts giving a mottled appearance; ill-defined pale chin patch. The Alpine Swift (*Apus melba*) is slightly smaller, 8 inches, white below with a brown breast band. In East Africa the Alpine Swift breeds on cliffs on Mt. Kenya and the Ruwenzori Mts. of Uganda. It has been recorded in Northern Rhodesia. In the Kenya Highlands it is sometimes seen in the wake of thunderstorms.

LITTLE SWIFT *Apus affinis* p. 209

Identification: 5″. A black swift with a square, not forked tail, a white patch on the rump and a whitish chin patch. The Horus Swift and the White-rumped Swift have forked tails in addition to white rumps.

Voice: A sharp, shrill twittering call, usually when flying in flocks around nesting sites.

Distribution and Habitat: Local resident and partial migrant throughout the Ethiopian Region in suitable localities. Aerial, associated with buildings in towns and country, bridges and cliffs. Gregarious, often in large flocks; breeds in colonies.

Allied Species: The Mottled-throated Spinetail (*Telacanthura ussheri*) is an uncommon species associated with baobab trees in which it nests. It occurs very locally in East Africa and the Rhodesias, but is everywhere scarce. It resembles a Little Swift but has a longer tail, a white mottled throat and upper breast and a small white patch on the abdomen. Boehm's Spinetail (*Neafrapus boehmi*) is a very small species (3 inches) with a very short tail. It may be recognised by its white breast and abdomen. Like the Mottled-throated Spinetail it also is associated with baobab trees. It occurs rarely in Kenya, Tanganyika, and the Rhodesias.

WHITE-RUMPED SWIFT *Apus caffer* p. 209

Identification: 5½″. A slimly built swift, black with a sharply contrasting white rump and white throat patch. Tail deeply forked and the outer

WOOD HOOPOES, HOOPOE, TROGON and CROWS

NOTE: *The Piapiac, Pied Crow and Cape Rook are drawn to a smaller scale than the remainder of species illustrated.*

1
2
3
4
5
6
7
8

1 ♂
2
3
4
5
6
♀
7 ♂
8 ♂
9 ♂
10 ♂
11 ♂
12 ♂
13 ♂
14
15
16

BROADBILL, PITTA, LARKS, PIPITS, WAGTAILS and LONGCLAW

1. **AFRICAN BROADBILL** page 179
   Large broad bill; white feathers on back; crown black in male, grey in female.
2. **AFRICAN PITTA** 179
   Rump and spots on wing coverts brilliant pale blue; abdomen deep carmine-red.
3. **RUFOUS-NAPED LARK** 180
   Conspicuous rufous wings and relatively short tail.
4. **FLAPPET LARK** 181
   Tawny-rufous underparts. Skulking species usually noticed during display flight when it produces a far-carrying " brrrrr, brrrrr " sound.
5. **RED-CAPPED LARK** 182
   Chestnut cap and patches each side of the chest.
6. **CRESTED LARK** 181
   Pale sandy plumage and distinctive crest.
7. **FISCHER'S SPARROW LARK** 182
   Small, stumpy lark with heavy bill; often in flocks; crown tinged rufous; black face mask in male.

8-12. **YELLOW and BLUE-HEADED WAGTAILS** 184
   Underparts yellow in all races. **EASTERN YELLOW WAGTAIL** (8) has crown yellow; **BLACK-HEADED WAGTAIL** (9), black without eyestripe; **DARK-HEADED WAGTAIL** (10), grey without eyestripe; **BLUE-HEADED WAGTAIL** (11), grey with white eyestripe; **EASTERN BLUE-HEADED WAGTAIL** (12), very pale grey with white eyestripe.

13. **GOLDEN PIPIT** 185
   Wings conspicuously bright canary-yellow *in flight;* underparts bright yellow with black chest band. Female duller.
14. **RICHARD'S PIPIT** 184
   Upperparts with dark centres to feathers; much white in outer tail feathers.
15. **AFRICAN PIED WAGTAIL** 183
   Black and white; black breast band.
16. **YELLOW-THROATED LONGCLAW** 185
   Large, robust pipit with yellow underparts and black breast band; often perches on bushes.

pairs of tail feathers long and slender. The Horus Swift also has a white rump and a white throat but has the tail much less deeply forked and with the outer tail feathers broad, not attenuated.

Voice: A low twittering call.

Distribution and Habitat: Occurs locally over much of the Ethiopian Region in suitable localities. Common in East and Central Africa: certainly a partial migrant in some areas. When breeding it takes over the mud nests of swallows, unlike the Horus Swift which breeds in tunnels and the Little Swift which builds its own nest of airborne debris. Occurs in the vicinity of nesting swallows and often over inland lakes and swamps.

HORUS SWIFT *Apus horus* p. 209

Identification: 5½″. A thickset, black swift with a white rump, forked tail and extensive white on the throat extending on to the upper breast. Tail not deeply forked like White-rumped Swift and outer pairs of tail feathers not attenuated.

Voice: A shrill, twittering scream, usually when in flocks at nesting colony.

Distribution and Habitat: Local resident and partial migrant from Sudan and Ethiopia, south through East and Central Africa to South Africa, west to Angola. Breeds in colonies in holes which it digs out in sandy banks of rivers and cliff areas. Aerial, but often seen over water and in the wake of thunderstorms.

PALM SWIFT *Cypsiurus parvus* p. 209

Identification: 5″. A very slimly built swift with a deeply forked tail and outer tail feathers attenuated. Pale greyish-brown all over, indistinctly whitish on throat. Associated with various types of palm trees, such as Coconut, Borassus and Dom palms, in which it nests. Slim build and greyish-brown plumage render it easy to identify.

Voice: A very high-pitched twittering call uttered on the wing.

Distribution and Habitat: Locally distributed over much of the Ethiopian Region in suitable habitats where palms exist. It occurs throughout East and Central Africa, being especially common on the Kenya coast and in Nyasaland.

BROADBILLS: Eurylaimidae

This is mainly an Asiatic Family with a few species in Africa. They are flycatcher-like in their general appearance and may be recognised by their large and very broad bills.

AFRICAN BROADBILL *Smithornis capensis* p. 177

Identification: 5″. Upperparts brown or olive-brown, streaked black; crown black, grey in female; feathers of lower back and rump mainly white; bird sometimes puffs these feathers out, when they are its most important field character; at other times they are hidden by the scapular feathers. Bill very large and broad, black above, pink below; underparts whitish, streaked black on chest and flanks. Large bill and streaked breast usually conspicuous in field. Bird usually sits on a horizontal branch, from which it takes remarkable circular flights around its perch, displaying as it does so the white feathers of its back.

Voice: A most remarkable and un-bird-like sound, a high-pitched vibrating sound like a klaxon horn—"rrrrrrrrrrrrrrrrrrrrrrrr" produced either during the bird's circular flight or while it is at rest.

Distribution and Habitat: Locally distributed in small numbers from West Africa eastwards to Uganda and Kenya, south through Tanganyika to Central Africa and South Africa. Frequents forest areas, bamboo forest and dense forest and scrub along rivers.

Allied Species: The Red-sided Broadbill (*Smithornis rufolateralis*) may be recognised by rufous patches on each side of the chest. It is a West African forest species which extends eastwards to western Uganda.

PITTAS: Pittidae

A group of brilliantly coloured forest birds of thrush size; legs long, tails very short. Very shy and seldom observed alive in the wild state.

AFRICAN PITTA *Pitta angolensis* p. 177

Identification: 7″. A plump, thrush-sized bird with dark green upperparts; crown black with a broad olive-buff stripe on each side; rump and spots on wing coverts brilliant pale verditer blue; throat pale pink, breast buff; abdomen and under tail coverts deep carmine-red. Owing to its retiring habits this is a species which is not often seen. Usually the most one sees is a fleeting glimpse as a bird is disturbed from the forest undergrowth when the impression is a dark bird with a great deal of bright pale blue and carmine-red.

Voice: A deep, short trill, followed by a sharp flap of the wings.

Distribution and Habitat: Occurs as a breeding bird in central Tanganyika south to the Zambesi River and Transvaal: birds in breeding quarters from September to March. In non-breeding season migrates by night to Congo, northern Tanganyika, Kenya and Uganda. Migrating birds sometimes attracted by lights and consequently picked up in various unlikely places. Frequents forest areas and very dense scrub. In Southern Rhodesia most frequent in Eastern District.

Allied Species: The Green-breasted Pitta (*Pitta reichenowi*) differs in having a green breast and a black patch on the throat. It is a West African species which extends into Uganda, where it is most frequent in the Budongo Forest.

LARKS: Alaudidae

A group of ground-loving song birds: often gregarious in non-breeding season. Hind claw often elongated and more or less straight. Build usually heavier and bills more robust than pipits and wagtails which are also terrestrial in their habits.

RUFOUS-NAPED LARK *Mirafra africana* p. 177

Identification: 6-7″. Rufous or greyish-brown above with very distinct black centres to the feathers: nape more or less rufous; wings mainly rufous, conspicuous in flight; below buff or rufous-buff with black markings on chest; tail relatively short for size of bird. The Red-winged Bush Lark is larger and has a long tail, and habitually perches on the tops of small bushes.

Voice: Song uttered from post, termite hill or small bush: a clear whistle of four or five notes, "cee-wee-wee, chee, wee" repeated over and over again.

Distribution and Habitat: Local resident Nigeria eastwards to the Sudan, south through East and Central Africa to South Africa. Common in many parts of Kenya and Uganda. Occurs in open plains and grassy bush country.

Allied Species: The Red-winged Bush Lark (*Mirafra hypermetra*) is larger

(9 inches) with a comparatively long tail: in general plumage it closely resembles the Rufous-naped Lark, but has contrasting black patches on each side of foreneck. It perches on small bushes much more often than that species. It occurs locally from the Somalilands and Ethiopia south through northern Uganda, Kenya and Tanganyika. It is locally common in the Northern Frontier Province of Kenya, especially at Isiolo and at Marsabit.

FLAPPET LARK *Mirafra rufocinnamomea* p. 177

Identification: 5″. This is a lark which varies greatly in general colour: it may be dark reddish-brown, earth-brown or bright cinnamon, the feathers mottled black and edged whitish; outer tail feathers pale rufous buff; below tawny rufous, spotted black on chest. The species attracts attention during its mating display flights when it produces a loud "brrrr, brrrr, brrrrr, brrrrr" sound high in the air.

Voice: A soft, two-note "tooee, toee."

Distribution and Habitat: Local resident from the Sudan and southern Ethiopia, south throughout East and Central Africa to the Zambesi valley. Frequents open bush country and plains where there is some bush cover. Locally common in the Tsavo National Park in Kenya, and the Queen Elizabeth National Park in Uganda. In the Rhodesias and Nyasaland frequents brachystegia scrub and secondary growth on old cultivation.

CRESTED LARK *Galerida cristata* p. 177

Identification: $6\frac{1}{2}$″. A rather plump lark, sandy in colour with streaks on back and chest; most distinctive feature long upstanding crest. Short-crested Lark very similar but underparts more heavily marked blackish-brown on chest, and crest shorter: very difficult to distinguish in the field. As a general rule, there are exceptions, the Crested Lark prefers sandy areas, whilst the Short-crested Lark is associated with rocks.

Voice: A liquid three-note whistle, "chee, chee, choo," delivered from a perch, the ground and rarely in flight.

Distribution and Habitat: Occurs locally from West Africa to the Somalilands, south to northern Uganda and northern Kenya. Frequents sandy semi-desert areas, open desert country and in Somaliland coastal sand-dunes.

Allied Species: The Short-crested Lark (*Galerida malabarica*) occurs in rocky desert country in Somaliland, Ethiopia and northern Kenya. It closely resembles the Crested Lark but the crest is shorter and the blackish breast spotting more distinct.

FISCHER'S SPARROW LARK *Eremopterix leucopareia* p. 177

Identification: 4½″. The sparrow-larks are characterised by their heavy, finch-like bills and blackish patch on belly: usually gregarious. The present species has a rufous tinged crown edged dark brown; remainder upperparts greyish-brown; below, throat and broad stripe down centre of belly blackish-brown, remainder underparts buffish-white.

Voice: A low "tweet-ees" flock call. A brief warbling song when nesting, uttered from the ground.

Distribution and Habitat: Local resident Kenya Colony, Tanganyika and Nyasaland. Frequents short grass plains, open bush country and semi-desert country. In East Africa it occurs up to an altitude of 6,000 ft.; in Nyasaland it occurs commonly only below 3,000 ft. Found usually in flocks, even in the breeding season.

Allied Species: The Chestnut-headed Sparrow Lark (*Eremopterix signata*) occurs in the Somalilands, Ethiopia and northern Kenya and the south-eastern Sudan. It has the crown chestnut with a white patch in the centre. It is a bird of semi-desert and desert areas. It is abundant locally in northern Kenya. The Chestnut-backed Sparrow Lark (*Eremopterix leucotis*) has the upperparts chestnut, feathers edged white: the head and neck black with ear coverts and band across hind-neck white; female lacks black on head and neck. This is a plains and open thornbush country species found in Kenya, Tanganyika and Central Africa, south to South Africa. It is locally common in the Isiolo district, northern Kenya, in thorn scrub on black cotton soil.

RED-CAPPED LARK *Calandrella cinerea* p. 177

Identification: 5½″. A warm brown lark with white underparts and conspicuous chestnut crown and chestnut patch each side of the chest. Occurs in pairs or in loose flocks.

Voice: A short twittering flock call or a two-note "tee, twee" when the bird rises.

Distribution and Habitat: Local resident and partial migrant, especially in the south of its range, throughout East and Central Africa, south to Cape Province, South Africa. Locally common in many parts of Kenya, Uganda and the Rhodesias. Frequents ploughed fields, cultivated areas, short grass plains, airfields and localities where grass fires have burned.

WAGTAILS and PIPITS: Motacillidae

This is a group of graceful, slender terrestrial birds which run and walk. The pipits are generally brown above, usually streaked: they resemble larks but are more slender and have a different and more upright carriage, and their bills are very slender. Wagtails have long tails and strongly marked patterns, often with much yellow: they fall into two groups, those which occur singly or in pairs on or near water, and those which occur in flocks and are associated with cattle and herds of other domestic animals which disturb insects upon which the wagtails feed.

AFRICAN PIED WAGTAIL *Motacilla aguimp* p. 177

Identification: 8″. A large black and white wagtail associated with human habitations. Upperparts black with a white band over eye and a triangular white patch on each side of the neck. Below white with a black breast band: much white in wings and tail.

Voice: Typical wagtail "tssssp": song very similar to that of a canary.

Distribution and Habitat: Widely distributed throughout the greater part of the Ethiopian Region; common in East and Central Africa. Closely associated with human dwellings but also occurs on sandbanks in rivers and sometimes along rocky streams. A very tame and confiding bird.

Allied Species: The European White Wagtail (*Motacilla alba*) is smaller (6 inches) has pale grey upperparts and a black throat in spring plumage. It is an abundant winter visitor to the Sudan and Ethiopia, uncommon in Kenya and northern Uganda. It occurs in flocks and is sometimes associated with yellow wagtails, especially on migration. The Mountain Wagtail (*Motacilla clara*) is a pale grey species, very slim and with a long tail, and with a narrow black chest band, which frequents smaller rivers and streams especially where there is running water and rocks. It occurs throughout East and Central Africa. It can be confused with the European Grey Wagtail (*Motacilla cinerea*) which is a winter visitor to East Africa, and a bird of similar habits, but the Grey Wagtail always has some yellow on the belly, while the Mountain Wagtail is entirely white on the belly. Wells' or Cape Wagtail (*Motacilla capensis*) has smokey-brown upperparts and whitish underparts: narrow black bar across chest. Frequents the edges of swamps, lakes and marshes in pairs or family parties. It is an uncommon resident in East and Central Africa, except Nyasaland. Elsewhere it occurs in the eastern Congo and in South Africa.

YELLOW and BLUE-HEADED WAGTAILS

Budytes flavus (M) p. 177

Identification: 6½″. Slender, long-legged wagtail with yellow underparts: crown may be yellow, blue-grey or black, depending on geographical race. Race with yellow crown is Eastern Yellow Wagtail (*Budytes flavus luteus*); grey crown with well-marked white eye-stripe, Blue-headed Wagtail (*Budytes flavus flavus*); very pale grey cap with white eye-stripe, Eastern Blue-headed Wagtail (*Budytes flavus beema*); cap grey with no white eye-stripe, Dark-headed Wagtail (*Budytes flavus thunbergi*); crown black, Black-headed Wagtail (*Budytes flavus feldegg*). Females and immature birds are duller and browner than males and apart from the female of the Black-headed Wagtail, which has a blackish crown, they are not racially identifiable in the field. Species occurs in flocks (on migration in loose flocks of several hundreds) and often associates with herds of cattle, sheep and goats for the insects which the animals flush.

Voice: A musical whistle, "tsoopee," or a harsher "tsrrr."

Distribution and Habitat: Common winter visitor and passage migrant East and Central Africa. The Eastern Yellow, Blue-headed and Dark-headed Wagtails winter south to South Africa; the Eastern Blue-headed and Black-headed Wagtails occur south to Tanganyika in East Africa. The Black-headed Wagtail is most frequent in Uganda and western Kenya. Very large mixed flocks of these wagtails occur in Uganda (for example at Entebbe) and western Kenya on spring migration. Species frequents grazing areas of short grass, especially in the vicinity of water, and newly ploughed fields. In the Kenya Highlands these wagtails flock with numbers of Red-throated Pipits on the spring migration.

RICHARD'S PIPIT *Anthus richardi*

p. 177

Identification: 6″. A slim, long-legged Pipit with much white on two outer pairs tail feathers: upperparts boldly streaked blackish; whitish stripe over eye; below pale buff with dark brown streaks on the breast. Hind claw long, longer than hind toe. This is the commonest of the open country pipits in East and Central Africa.

Voice: A sharp "tweep" or "tsseep, tsseep." A brief, often repeated song when breeding.

Distribution and Habitat: Common resident and partial migrant throughout the greater part of the Ethiopian Region in suitable localities. Locally common or abundant in many parts of East and Central Africa. Occurs on open plains, grazing land, and semi-desert country, and in the vicinity of inland waters. Occurs in pairs, single birds or family parties, not flocks.

Allied Species: The Long-billed Pipit (*Anthus similis*) is found throughout East and Central Africa, being most frequent in the brachystegia woodlands of southern Tanganyika and the Rhodesias. Farther north it occurs on grassy slopes, especially where there are rocky or gravel outcrops. It is a larger bird than Richard's Pipit with indistinctly streaked upperparts, lacks white in the outer tail feathers and has the hind claw shorter than the hind toe; flanks unstreaked. The Tree Pipit (*Anthus trivialis*) is a common winter visitor and passage migrant to East and Central Africa from Europe and western Asia. It is best identified in its winter quarters by the habitat it chooses, woodlands and even forest areas: it perches readily in trees and bushes. It has black streaked upperparts; below creamy-buff boldly streaked black on breast and flanks. It is slightly smaller than Richard's Pipit. The Red-throated Pipit (*Anthus cervinus*) is another winter visitor and passage migrant from the North. It is an open country pipit, usually found in loose flocks, and is often associated with flocks of yellow wagtails. It occurs throughout East Africa, being common in the highlands of Kenya Colony, but has not been recorded in the Rhodesias and Nyasaland. It has streaked upperparts and a rufous-buff or rusty-red throat: heavily streaked black on underparts.

GOLDEN PIPIT *Tmetothylacus tenellus* p. 177

Identification: 6″. Upperparts pale olive-green with dusky centres to feathers giving slightly mottled appearance: below bright canary-yellow with a black chest band; wings and tail bright canary-yellow. When seen perched this bird appears as a rather yellowish-green pipit with no conspicuous field character, but immediately it takes wing its entire appearance changes, when it looks as brightly yellow as a canary. The female is duller than the male. This bird is remarkable among the passerine birds in having the lower third of the tibia bare, as if it were a wading bird, in spite of the fact that it is an arid bush country species.

Voice: Utters a series of weak whistles, but otherwise silent.

Distribution and Habitat: Local resident from Somalilands and Ethiopia, south through Kenya to north-eastern Tanganyika. Occurs in dry bush country. It is fairly common in parts of the Tsavo National Park in Kenya and in the dry country north of the Tana River it is sometimes abundant. Usually seen singly or in family parties.

YELLOW-THROATED LONGCLAW *Macronyx croceus* p. 177

Identification: 8″. The longclaws are a group of robust pipits with yellow or red on underparts. The present species has the underparts bright yellow with a black chest band; above brown, feathers with dark centres giving broadly streaked appearance. The Pangani Longclaw has the throat bright orange-yellow, a streaked throat band and the yellow of the underparts confined to the centre of the breast.

Voice: A rather drawn-out whistle "tuewhee," uttered over and over again.

Distribution and Habitat: Local resident throughout East and Central Africa. Elsewhere occurs from Senegal and Angola to Natal. Frequents open woodland, grass country where there are bushes, cultivated areas and in Central Africa dambos in brachystegia woodland.

Allied Species: Fulleborn's Longclaw (*Macronyx fulleborni*) differs from the Yellow-throated Longclaw in having the yellow of the breast suffused with buff and the flanks brownish-buff. It occurs in the highlands of southern Tanganyika, Northern Rhodesia and Angola. Sharpe's Longclaw (*Macronyx sharpei*) is a small species (7 inches) with pale yellow underparts and a band of black streaks across the chest. It occurs in the highlands of Kenya, over 7,000 ft. The Pangani Longclaw (*Macronyx aurantiigula*) is the same size as the Yellow-throated Longclaw but has the throat orange-yellow and the yellow of the underparts confined to the centre of the belly. It is a local resident in central and eastern Kenya and north-eastern Tanganyika. It frequents bush country. The Rosy-breasted Longclaw (*Macronyx ameliae*) is a grassy plains species, often found at the edges of marshes. It has the underparts bright salmon-red. It occurs in western Kenya and Tanganyika, south through Central Africa, where it is more widely distributed and frequent than in East Africa, to Natal.

BABBLERS and CHATTERERS: Turdoididae

The Babblers and Chatterers are a group of thrush-like and -sized birds which occur in noisy parties in bush and thorn-bush country. They have scaly legs and rounded wings: plumage usually dull grey, brown or rufous.

ARROW-MARKED BABBLER *Turdoides jardinei* p. 192

Identification: 9″. Stocky birds which occur in noisy parties: general colour greyish-brown; paler below, with white arrowhead-shaped tips to feathers of throat and breast: eye conspicuously yellow or orange-yellow. The Black-lored Babbler is similar but has bluish-white eyes.

Voice: A succession of chattering, babbling call-notes which draws attention to the birds.

Distribution and Habitat: Local resident Uganda and south-western Kenya, south through Tanganyika and Central Africa to South Africa. Inhabits rank bush, the edges of papyrus swamps, rank grass and bush, sugar cultivation and wherever there is sufficient undergrowth in woodland and riverine forest. Babblers have a typical "follow my leader" method of progression, one leaving cover for the next patch of bush with low, direct flight, followed in rapid succession by remainder of party.

Allied Species: The Black-lored Babbler (*Turdoides melanops*) has a black spot in front of eye and bluish-white eyes. It frequents acacia bush, usually near water, and papyrus and reed beds. It occurs locally in Kenya and Uganda, south to central Tanganyika. The Northern Pied Babbler (*Turdoides hypoleuca*) occurs locally in acacia country in southern Kenya and northern and north-eastern Tanganyika. It has the underparts white with a dark patch on each side of the chest.

RUFOUS CHATTERER *Argya rubiginosa* p. 192

Identification: 8″. A gregarious bird seen in small flocks in thick undergrowth and thorn thickets: cinnamon rufous in colour, slightly darker and browner on upperparts; bill yellow, eyes pale yellow. Like the true babblers it draws attention to itself by its noisy chattering.

Voice: A variety of chattering and bubbling calls and a plaintive whistle, not unlike that of the Blue-naped Mousebird.

Distribution and Habitat: Local resident southern Sudan, central and southern Ethiopia, south through eastern Uganda and Kenya to Tanganyika. Frequents thick bush and tangled cover in arid or semi-arid areas: locally common in coastal bush in Kenya and Tanganyika.

BULBULS: Pycnonotidae

The Bulbuls are a group of thrush-like birds of plain green, yellow, grey and brown plumage: tarsus very short; arboreal in habits and most species are inhabitants of forest and woodland; food mainly fruits with some insects; many species are outstanding songsters.

DARK-CAPPED or YELLOW-VENTED BULBUL
Pycnonotus xanthopygos p. 192

Identification: 7″. A common garden bird throughout much of East and Central Africa. Upperparts greyish-brown, blackish or dark brown on head and chin, merging to pale brown on chest; belly white; under tail-coverts pale yellow. The head appears slightly crested at times: the yellow under tail-coverts are conspicuous. Upon alighting the bird often half raises its wings and utters a short warbling song.

Voice: A rapid, short song "too, de de, de, che che," and a scolding alarm call.

Distribution and Habitat: A common and widely distributed bird found throughout the greater part of the Ethiopian Region, including East and Central Africa. Occurs as a garden bird, in old cultivation, woodland, coastal scrub, open forest and in secondary growth especially Lantana thickets: one of the commonest African birds.

RED-TAILED GREENBUL *Tricophorus calurus* p. 192

Identification: 7″. A rather thickset, stocky species. Dark olive-green above, reddish tail, yellow belly and very conspicuous white throat, which is often puffed out and which is the bird's most distinctive field character. Another greenbul, *Phyllastrephus albigularis,* is called the White-throated Greenbul, but it does not have a conspicuous white throat in the field.

Voice: A loud, drawn-out "teeeeeep" and a brief warbling song.

Distribution and Habitat: A West African species which extends eastwards to Uganda. It is a forest bird, locally common, and on account of its white throat readily identifiable in the field, which is more than can be said of most greenbuls. It is especially common in the Bwamba forest, western Uganda.

FISCHER'S GREENBUL *Phyllastrephus fischeri* p. 192

Identification: 6½″. A uniform coloured species, greyish-olive above, wings and tail slightly tinged rufous, paler yellowish-olive below, whitish on the throat.

Voice: A series of short notes "trip, trip, trip, trip, trip, tee, tee, tee, tee"; song a series of flute-like whistles.

Distribution and Habitat: Local resident from southern Sudan and southern Somalia, south through Kenya, Uganda and Tanganyika to Mozambique, Nyasaland and Northern Rhodesia. A bird of forest, heavy woodlands, dense scrub and riverine forest. Common in the forests around Nairobi.

YELLOW-WHISKERED GREENBUL *Stelgidocichla latirostris* p. 192

Identification: 7″. Upperparts dark olive; below paler olive to yellowish in centre of belly; two conspicuous bright yellow streaks from base of bill on each side of throat. In life this bird appears very dark, sometimes even blackish in forest undergrowth, but may be identified always at close quarters by the yellow stripes on each side of the throat.

Voice: A series of high and low whistles; song a series of from 8 to 10 notes, repeated over and over again.

Distribution and Habitat: Common resident southern Sudan and eastern Congo, eastwards through Uganda to eastern Kenya Highlands; southwards to northern and western Tanganyika. Inhabits lowland and mountain forest, dense scrub and riverine forest. One of the commonest forest birds in Uganda and western Kenya.

FLYCATCHERS: Muscicapidae

This is a large family of small or medium-sized birds, usually with flattened bills and well-developed bristles at gape: immature plumages spotted. Many species perch upright on some vantage point, such as a dead branch or wire fence, from which short erratic flights are made after their insect prey. Some other species hunt insect food amongst foliage in manner of warblers.

DUSKY FLYCATCHER *Alseonax adustus* p. 192

Identification: 4½″. A small, plump flycatcher with a rather short tail, dark sepia or greyish-brown with a pale chin and abdomen. Immature heavily spotted buff-white above and on chest. Usually seen perched on a dead twig from which it makes short flights: very tame and confiding.

Voice: Usually silent, but sometimes utters a soft two-note call, or when nest approached a weak chatter.

Distribution and Habitat: A widely distributed and common resident in East and Central Africa. Also in West Africa and South Africa. In East Africa occurs in wooded and forest areas, also common in tree-shaded gardens. In the Rhodesias and Nyasaland it occurs both in evergreen forest and in brachystegia woodland.

Allied Species: The European Spotted Flycatcher (*Muscicapa striata*) is a winter visitor and passage migrant in East and Central Africa. It is larger (5½ inches) and slimmer than the Dusky Flycatcher with a longer tail and lightly streaked whitish breast. The Swamp Flycatcher (*Alseonax aquaticus*) is the same size as the Spotted Flycatcher but is plump in appearance. It is dark sepia-brown with a conspicuous white throat and belly. It has a restricted habitat, being confined mainly to the margins of papyrus and reed beds in or near water. It occurs locally in the southern Sudan, southwards through Uganda, western Kenya and Tanganyika to north-eastern Northern Rhodesia.

PALE FLYCATCHER *Bradornis pallidus* p. 192

Identification: 6-7″. Upperparts, wings and tail greyish-brown; below pale brown merging to white on throat and centre of abdomen: immature with buff-spotted upperparts. Generally resembles a large Spotted Flycatcher, but plumper and lacks breast streaks. Usually found in pairs. The smaller Grey Flycatcher is greyer with narrow dusky streaks on crown.

Voice: Usually silent: sometimes utters weak chirping call.

Distribution and Habitat: A locally common and widespread resident in East and Central Africa: found throughout the greater part of the Ethiopian Region. Inhabits savannah woodland and acacia country, coastal scrub and cultivated areas.

Allied Species: The Grey Flycatcher (*Bradornis microrhynchus*), 5 inches, occurs in dry bush and savannah country from Ethiopia and Somaliland, south through Uganda, Kenya and Tanganyika. It often frequents drier bush country than the Pale Flycatcher from which it differs in being greyer and having dusky crown streaks.

WHITE-EYED SLATY FLYCATCHER *Dioptrornis fischeri*

p. 192

Identification: 6½″. Upperparts slate-grey, paler below; a conspicuous white ring around eye. Immature has whitish spots on upperparts. A plump-looking flycatcher recognised by its slaty-blue plumage and white eye-ring. Often alights on the ground to pick up insects; very active at dusk, often observed on paths in wooded or forest areas in the manner of a robin-chat.

Voice: Usually silent: most vocal in evening when utters a sharp, sunbird-like "tsssk" and a short descending trill.

Distribution and Habitat: Resident, locally common, in wooded areas of East Africa and the Nyika plateau in Nyasaland and Northern Rhodesia. Occurs in highland forest, forest margins and scrub, and in cultivated areas where there are trees. A common bird in the highlands of Kenya where it is well-known in gardens.

Allied Species: The Ashy Flycatcher (*Alseonax cinereus*) occurs locally in wooded areas in East and Central Africa. It is a small (5 inches) rather slim species, pale blue-grey above, whitish below with a wash of blue-grey on breast and flanks; a white streak above and below eye.

SOUTH AFRICAN BLACK FLYCATCHER

Melaenornis pammelaina p. 192

Identification: 8″. Plumage entirely black with a bluish gloss: immature bird spotted tawny. Behaves in manner of a puff-backed shrike, searching foliage for insects. The Drongo is also all black but has a long forked, not rounded tail and ruby-red, not dark brown eyes. The male Black Cuckoo-Shrike also resembles a Black Flycatcher but may be distinguished by its conspicuous yellow gape wattles.

Voice: A low, piping "twee, twee, twee, eeee."

BABBLERS, BULBULS and FLYCATCHERS

1
2
3
4
5
♀
8
♂
6
7
9
10
11
12
♀
13
♂
14
15

2
♀
1
♂
3
♂
4
♂
♀
5
6
8
7
9
♀
10
♂
11
12
13
14

THRUSHES and ALLIES

1. **EUROPEAN ROCK THRUSH** page 197
Thickset, wheatear-like bird with rufous tail; male has blue-grey head, neck and mantle and rufous belly; female duller and more mottled.

2. **CAPPED WHEATEAR** 198
White rump; black chest band.

3. **EUROPEAN COMMON WHEATEAR** 198
White rump; black wings contrast with colour of mantle; female duller.

4. **STONECHAT** 200
Conspicuous white neck, wing and rump patches; female browner and duller; lacks eyestripe.

5. **RED-TAILED or FAMILIAR CHAT** 199
Dull greyish-brown chat with rufous rump and tail.

6. **SPOTTED MORNING WARBLER** 202
Spotted underparts; rufous tail.

7. **RED-BACKED SCRUB ROBIN** 202
Rufous back and tail, white eye streak and dusky breast streaks. A skulker in bush country.

8. **ROBIN CHAT** 201
White eye stripe; orange-rufous throat and chest contrast with pale grey belly.

9. **WHITE-BROWED ROBIN CHAT** 200
White eye stripe; underparts and tail rufous; central tail feathers olive-brown.

10. **WHITE-HEADED BLACK CHAT** 199
White wing patch; male has white cap, female white throat. Inhabits brachystegia/mopane woodlands.

11. **WHITE-STARRED BUSH ROBIN** 203
Brilliant yellow belly; slate blue head with white spot in front of eye.

12. **OLIVE THRUSH** 196
Belly rufous; bill and feet orange-yellow.

13. **GROUND-SCRAPER THRUSH** 197
Heavily spotted underparts; orange-buff wing patch conspicuous in flight.

14. **ANTEATER CHAT** 199
Blackish, starling-like bird often seen along roads; whitish wing patch conspicuous in flight.

Distribution and Habitat: Sparsely distributed resident, locally common in Kenya, Tanganyika, Nyasaland and the Rhodesias; also in South Africa. Inhabits woodland, acacia and bush country. In Kenya not uncommon in the Tsavo National Park.

Allied Species: The Black Flycatcher (*Melaenornis edolioides*) is a West African species which occurs in woodlands and cultivated areas in Uganda, western Kenya and north-western Tanganyika. Its plumage is completely blackish-slate; it lacks the metallic blue gloss of the South African Black Flycatcher.

SILVERBIRD *Empidornis semipartitus* p. 192

Identification: 8″. A slim, rather long-tailed flycatcher, pale silvery-grey above and bright rufous below. Immature spotted pale buff on upperparts and mottled black below. Usually occurs in pairs; very shy and difficult to approach but even at a distance the silvery back and rufous underparts render identification easy.

Voice: Usually silent, but male has soft warbling song.

Distribution and Habitat: An uncommon and very local resident in dry bush and acacia woodland in Ethiopia, Uganda, western Kenya and northern Tanganyika. In Kenya it is locally common in the Lake Baringo area.

CHIN-SPOT FLYCATCHER *Batis molitor* p. 192

Identification: 4½″. A small, rather stumpy black, grey and white flycatcher: male has black band across chest, female a chestnut band and a chestnut patch on the throat. Immature resembles female but has buff speckling above and on chest. Species differs from the Wattle-eyed Flycatchers in lacking red eye wattles. Occurs in pairs usually in acacia trees. In flight produces a sharp "brrrrrp" with wings. Chestnut throat patch of female conspicuous in field.

Voice: A clear squeaky "chrr—chrr" and a louder double alarm call.

Distribution and Habitat: A common and widespread resident in East and Central Africa: also in Portuguese East Africa and South Africa. Inhabits bush country and woodland, especially acacia, and also forest edges, cultivation and in gardens.

Allied Species: The Cape Puff-back Flycatcher (*Batis capensis*) is a forest and woodland species which occurs locally in southern Kenya, Tanganyika, Portuguese East Africa, Nyasaland and the Rhodesias, south to South Africa. The male has a much wider black chest band than the Chin-spot Flycatcher: the female has the throat and chest rufous-brown.

WATTLE-EYE FLYCATCHER *Platysteira cyanea* p. 192

Identification: 5″. A conspicuous black and white flycatcher with bright scarlet eye-wattles and a white wing-bar. Male white below with a narrow black band across chest; female with throat and chest dark chestnut. Scarlet eye wattles prominent in field and distinguish wattle-eyes from puff-back flycatchers. Occurs in pairs; habits tit-like, obtaining much of its food from foliage of trees and shrubs.

Voice: A series of short, clear whistles and various churring notes.

Distribution and Habitat: Local resident in woodland and forests Uganda, western Kenya and north-western Tanganyika.

Allied Species: The Black-throated Wattle-eye (*Platysteira peltata*) differs in lacking the white wing-stripe and female has the throat and chest glossy black, not chestnut. It occurs in wooded areas eastern Kenya, Tanganyika and Central Africa. The Chestnut Wattle-eye (*Dyaphorophyia castanea*) is a thickset forest undergrowth flycatcher (4 inches) which appears almost tailless in the field. The male has blackish upperparts, rump and underparts white with a broad black breast band: the female has the crown and rump slate-grey; remainder upperparts, throat and breast chestnut; belly white: eye-wattles purplish-grey. The species occurs locally in forests of western Kenya, Uganda and north-western Tanganyika.

BLUE FLYCATCHER *Erannornis longicauda* p. 192

Identification: 5½″. A very beautiful small blue flycatcher with a long graduated tail. Plumage caerulean blue, paler on throat and belly. Immature spotted buff on upperparts. Tame and confiding, readily identified by colour and habit of constantly fanning its tail.

Voice: A brief, sunbird-like twittering song.

Distribution and Habitat: A local resident in woodland and forest areas, in cultivation where there are trees and in gardens in western Kenya, Uganda, western and north-eastern Tanganyika, Nyasaland and northern Northern Rhodesia.

PARADISE FLYCATCHER *Terpsiphone viridis* p. 192

Identification: Male 12-14″; female 8″. Unmistakable: combination of very long tail and chestnut, black, grey and white plumage render species easy to identify. In some parts of its distribution, especially in eastern Kenya, a white phase of plumage in the adult male is commoner than the normal chestnut plumage. In this phase the back, wings and tail are white, not chestnut. The female, which is much shorter-tailed than the male, does not acquire a white plumage. Immature plumage resembles that of female but is duller.

Voice: Call-note a sharp and loud two- or three-note whistle ; song a loud and distinct warble.

Distribution and Habitat: Widespread, locally common resident throughout East Africa. In Central Africa mainly a summer migrant from September to March, but some birds resident throughout year. Also in West Africa and Congo. Inhabits wooded areas, forests, thick scrub, thornbush and acacia country, cultivated areas and gardens; white phase common in Tsavo National Park, Kenya.

Allied Species: The Black-headed Paradise Flycatcher (*Terpsiphone rufiventris*) 8 inches, has a much shorter tail than the Paradise Flycatcher and its underparts are bright rufous. It occurs in forests of western Kenya, Uganda, north-western Tanganyika and northern Northern Rhodesia.

THRUSHES, WHEATEARS, CHATS, and Allies: Turdidae

A group of rather long-legged birds of upright stance: eyes inclined to be large and bills usually pointed and slender: juvenile plumages spotted. Most species spend much time on the ground and feed mainly upon insects.

OLIVE THRUSH *Turdus olivaceus* p. 193

Identification: 9″. Upperparts dark olive-brown, paler on throat and breast with dusky streaks on throat: belly contrasting bright rufous; bill and feet orange. Immature bird has black-spotted underparts.

Voice: Typical scolding thrush-type call-notes and a loud, usually brief warbling song.

Distribution and Habitat: Local resident in East and Central Africa, south to Cape Province, South Africa. Inhabits forests and well-wooded areas, dense scrub, cultivation where there are trees and bush and well-treed gardens. A very common garden bird of the Kenya Highlands.

Allied Species: The Kurrichane Thrush (*Turdus libonyanus*) is a pale edition of the Olive Thrush with a white throat, streaked only on the sides, and a white abdomen. It occurs in cultivated and woodland areas, often in drier localities than those favoured by Olive Thrush. It is a locally common resident in Tanganyika and Central Africa. The Bare-eyed Thrush (*Turdus tephronotus*) is a pale, ashy-grey thrush with an orange-rufous belly and a patch of bare yellow skin around the eyes. It favours arid bush country and coastal scrub from Somaliland and eastern Ethiopia south through central and eastern Kenya to eastern Tanganyika.

GROUND-SCRAPER THRUSH *Turdus litsipsirupa* p. 193

Identification: 8½″. A rather thickset thrush with a short tail, and bearing a marked resemblance to a European mistle thrush. Above brownish-grey, below pale buff with heavy black spots. An orange-buff patch in the wings, conspicuous when the bird is flying.

Voice: A rather harsh thrush-type alarm call, "cheeer, cheeer" and a loud, clear song of four or five liquid whistles repeated over and over again.

Distribution and Habitat: A locally common resident in open brachystegia woodland and open scrub in Tanganyika and Central Africa, Angola and South Africa. It also occurs on the high plateau of Ethiopia where it frequents cultivated areas.

EUROPEAN ROCK THRUSH *Monticola saxatilis* (M) p. 193

Identification: 7½″. A thickset, wheatear-like bird recognised in all plumages by its short chestnut tail and ill-defined white patch on back. In spring male has pale blue-grey head, neck and mantle and distinct white lower back; breast and abdomen rich orange-rufous. Female, winter-plumaged male and immature are dull mottled brown above with speckled-buff or rufous underparts. Shy and difficult to approach. Usually solitary although loose flocks occur on spring migration. Perches on bare rocks, fence posts and small bushes.

Voice: Usually silent; sometimes utters a sharp "chak, chak."

Distribution and Habitat: Widespread winter visitor and passage migrant to East Africa, as far south as central Tanganyika. In winter quarters frequents rocky, bush country and rocky outcrops.

Allied Species: The Little Rock Thrush (*Monticola rufocinerea*) is a bird of forested or wooded ravines from Somaliland and Ethiopia, south through eastern Uganda and western and central Kenya to northern Tanganyika. It is smaller than the European Rock Thrush, 6 inches, with a rufous tail and rump but lacks the white back patch. Its general appearance, and its habit of constantly flicking its tail, resemble a large redstart rather than a rock thrush. The Angola Rock Thrush (*Monticola angolensis*) is a typical bird of open brachystegia woodland, found locally in southern and western Tanganyika, Nyasaland, the Rhodesias and Angola. It also lacks the white back patch. In general it resembles the European Rock Thrush but is conspicuously mottled blue-grey and black on head and mantle in all plumages.

EUROPEAN COMMON WHEATEAR *Oenanthe oenanthe* (M)

p. 193

Identification: 6″. In all plumages white rump conspicuous and wings blacker than body plumage: adult male has mantle blue-grey, a broad white eye-stripe, black ear coverts and black wings; below pinkish buff merging to white on throat and belly. Female and immature are deeper buff below with brownish upperparts.

Voice: A rather harsh "chack" or "chack-weet," but comparatively silent in winter quarters.

Distribution and Habitat: Common winter visitor and passage migrant in East Africa, becoming less frequent in Nyasaland and rare in the Rhodesias. Inhabits all types of open country, but favouring hillsides and rocky outcrops.

Allied Species: The Isabelline Wheatear (*Oenanthe isabellina*) resembles a pale, sandy grey edition of a female Common Wheatear, but wings not conspicuously darker than rest of plumage. It is a common winter visitor and passage migrant to Kenya, eastern Uganda and northern Tanganyika. In the hand it may always be identified by its creamy-white under wing coverts: the female Common Wheatear has black under wing coverts with white tips. The Pied Wheatear (*Oenanthe leucomela*) is a winter visitor to Kenya and northern Tanganyika. It is smaller than the Common Wheatear with a longer patch of white on the rump and tail. Male very distinct with whitish or cream-coloured crown contrasting with black mantle and chest; female dusky-brown with greyish-brown throat and breast; abdomen white. Schalow's Wheatear (*Oenanthe lugubris*) is a resident in the Rift Valley in Kenya and northern Tanganyika. It resembles a thickset Pied Wheatear but may be identified in all plumages by its cinnamon-buff, not white rump.

CAPPED WHEATEAR *Oenanthe pileata*

p. 193

Identification: 7″. Upperparts dark russet-brown with white rump; crown, sides of neck and ear-coverts black; forehead and stripe over eye white; underparts white, a broad black band across chest; flanks rufous. Upright stance more marked than in most wheatears; broad black breast-band best field character. Immature has buff-spotted upperparts.

Voice: One of the best African bird mimics, imitating the calls and songs of many other species of birds and other sounds. It has its own brief warbling song which is repeated over and over again, and which is often uttered during display flight.

Distribution and Habitat: Widely distributed but not common in Kenya, eastern Uganda, Tanganyika and Central Africa, to Angola and South Africa. In some areas a partial migrant. Frequents open country from alpine moorlands and short-cropped grasslands to coastal flats. It is most attracted to grassland areas which have been burnt.

RED-TAILED or FAMILIAR CHAT *Cercomela familiaris* p. 193

Identification: 6″. A slimly built grey-brown chat with a rich rufous rump and rufous lateral tail feathers. An active and confiding species, often alighting on the ground. European bird-watchers, seeing it for the first time, are reminded of a female black redstart.

Voice: A loud series of whistles "tweep, tweep, tweep, tweep" and a three-note alarm call.

Distribution and Habitat: Very local and uncommon resident in Kenya and Uganda, becoming common in Tanganyika and Central Africa. Also in West and South Africa. Frequents many types of country from arid bush and rocky hillsides to lowland cultivated areas, but most frequent on rocky outcrops in open brachystegia woodland.

WHITE-HEADED BLACK CHAT *Thamnolaea arnotti* p. 193

Identification: 7″. Also called Arnott's Chat. A thickset black and white chat inhabiting brachystegia and mopane woodlands. Adult male glossy black with white crown and white wing patch: female also has white wing patch but is black above; throat and chest white, belly black. Immature resembles female but throat usually black. Very conspicuous birds in open woodland, found in pairs or family parties. Feeds largely on the ground but perches freely.

Voice: A loud whistling song, interspersed with harsher notes: call a double, loud "tweeep, tweeep."

Distribution and Habitat: A widespread resident, locally common, in Tanganyika, Nyasaland and the Rhodesias: also Angola and South Africa. Typically a bird of brachystegia woodland, but also occurs in dense mopane woodland and at the edges of cultivation.

ANTEATER CHAT *Myrmecocichla aethiops* p. 193

Identification: 8″. A thickset blackish-brown bird having something of the appearance of a starling, with a white patch in the wings, formed by the white bases of the flight feathers and seen only when the bird is flying. Often common at roadsides; tame and confiding.

Voice: Various piping and whistling calls and an attractive whistling song. Some birds are mimics of other birds' calls.

Distribution and Habitat: Local resident western and central Kenya and northern Tanganyika. Also in Senegal and Nigeria, West Africa and locally in Sudan. A common bird in the highlands and Rift Valley of Kenya. Inhabits open country with scattered bush and trees, also open acacia woodland.

Allied Species: The Sooty Chat (*Myrmecocichla nigra*) has the flight feathers entirely black and is smaller, 7 inches, than the Anteater Chat. Male glossy black with a white shoulder patch; female and immature dark brown throughout. Locally resident western Kenya, Uganda, western Tanganyika and northern Northern Rhodesia. Frequents open country with scattered scrub and termite hills.

STONECHAT *Saxicola torquata* p. 193

Identification: 5″. The stonechats resident in Africa are races of the well-known British bird. Male has distinctive black head and throat, a conspicuous white half collar, a white rump and a small white wing patch: a patch of deep chestnut on chest. Female tawny brown with small white wing patch; cinnamon brown below. Immature mottled buff above. Flight jerky, perches on tops of bushes, fences and on telegraph wires.

Voice: A scolding, "tsk, tsk, tsk" and a softer clicking note: song a rapid warble.

Distribution and Habitat: Local resident, often common, in areas above 3,000 feet in Uganda, Kenya, Tanganyika and Nyasaland. Also occurs at lower levels in Rhodesias. Also in West Africa, Angola, Portuguese East Africa and South Africa. Frequents mountain moorlands, cultivated areas, scattered bush in grassland and lush marshy areas.

Allied Species: The European Whinchat (*Saxicola rubetra*) resembles a female stonechat but is easily distinguished by its prominent creamy-white eye-stripe. It is an uncommon winter visitor and passage migrant to East Africa, Nyasaland and Northern Rhodesia.

WHITE-BROWED ROBIN CHAT *Cossypha heuglini* p. 193

Identification: 8″. Thrush-like but with relatively longer tail. Above olive-grey; crown and sides of face black with conspicuous white eye-stripe; below bright orange-rufous; tail rufous except central pair feathers which are olive-brown. Immature spotted and mottled tawny-buff on upperparts. A bird of thick undergrowth, feeding mainly on ground; usually shy; occurs in gardens. The Common Robin Chat also has a white eye-stripe but is smaller and only throat and chest rufous; belly pale grey.

Voice: A loud, purring "pip, ir, eee"; song a series of sustained flute-like whistles of great beauty; sings especially at dusk and at dawn. Singing birds very difficult to locate: may be ventriloquial. Often mimics other birds' calls, such as Red-chested and Black Cuckoos.

Distribution and Habitat: A locally common resident over much of East and Central Africa, but apparently absent from the eastern Kenya Highlands, including Nairobi, where its place is taken by Ruppell's Robin Chat. Also in Sudan, south-western Ethiopia, Angola, Portuguese East Africa and South Africa. Frequents forests, woodlands where there is thick undergrowth, wooded gardens, scrub and dense coastal bush.

Allied Species: Ruppell's Robin Chat (*Cossypha semirufa*) closely resembles White-browed Robin Chat but is smaller (7 inches) with greyer mantle and black central tail feathers. It occurs in Ethiopia and in highland forest in southern Kenya and northern Tanganyika. The Red-capped Robin Chat (*Cossypha natalensis*) is a shy, skulking species which would be overlooked were it not for its loud warbling song, sometimes interspersed with mimicry of other birds' songs. It has the centre of back and wings blue-grey, central tail feathers dark-brown, remainder of plumage rich orange-rufous. It is widely distributed in East and Central Africa, south to South Africa, frequenting dense forest and scrub undergrowth. The Snowy-headed Robin Chat (*Cossypha niveicapilla*) is a West African forest species found in Uganda, western Kenya and north-western Tanganyika. It has a snowy white cap, a black mantle and orange-rufous underparts. Like most of the Robin Chats it is an outstanding songster and mimic.

ROBIN CHAT *Cossypha caffra* p. 193

Identification: 6½". A rather small robin chat with the habits of an English robin: often seen in gardens. Has well-marked white eye-stripe; may be recognised by orange-rufous throat and chest and contrasting grey belly. The White-browed Robin Chat also has a white eye-stripe but its underparts are entirely rufous. Usually shy and retiring, but becomes tame and confiding in gardens where it is protected. Feeds largely on ground, where it progresses by hopping with much fluting of tail.

Voice: An outstanding warbling song: also a mimic of other birds' calls and songs.

Distribution and Habitat: A widespread resident in East Africa in forests, wooded and scrub areas. In Northern Rhodesia it occurs on the Nyika plateau in scrub outside forest; in Nyasaland it is a common bird above 5,000 feet in undergrowth and scrub. In Southern Rhodesia it is common in eastern districts at high levels. Elsewhere it occurs in Portuguese East Africa and South Africa.

SPOTTED MORNING WARBLER *Cichladusa guttata* p. 193

Identification: 6½″. A lightly built thrush-like bird, dull rufous-brown with a conspicuous cinnamon-red tail; below buff-white heavily spotted with black. Shy and skulking, disappearing into thick cover when disturbed, when its red tail suggests a robin chat.

Voice: An extremely variable, clear whistling song: bird most vocal in early morning and at dusk: also mimics the calls and songs of many other birds. Alarm notes harsh and scolding.

Distribution and Habitat: Local resident southern Sudan, south-western Ethiopia and Somalia, south through Uganda and Kenya to central Tanganyika. Inhabits dry bush country, especially thickets of Salvadora bushes along dry river beds, palm tree scrub and dense coastal bush. Relatively shy and retiring: usually seen as it disappears into thick scrub, when its red tail is conspicuous. Feeds largely on ground, often in shade of bushes and palm scrub. It is a common bird of the semi-desert areas of northern Kenya.

Allied Species: The Morning Warbler (*Cichladusa arquata*) is a little larger, unspotted buff below with a narrow black neck band. It occurs in scrub in vicinity of borassus and other palms. A local resident, usually below 2,500 feet, in south-western Uganda, southern Kenya, Tanganyika, Nyasaland and the Rhodesias. Species has a fine clear song.

RED-BACKED SCRUB ROBIN *Erythropygia leucophrys* p. 193

Identification: 6″. Of slim build, often with drooping wings. Rufous-brown above, paler on rump; distinct white eye streak; tail bright rufous with black subterminal bands and narrow white tips to all but central pair of feathers; below white to tawny on flanks and heavy dark streaking on throat and breast. Immature mottled black and tawny above. This is a skulking bush country bird with conspicuous red tail and streaked throat.

Voice: Alarm call of several harsh scolding notes: a clear warbling song, variable and apparently ventriloquial.

Distribution and Habitat: Locally common resident Uganda, western and southern Kenya, Tanganyika, Portuguese East Africa, Nyasaland and the Rhodesias, south to South Africa: also Angola and Congo. Inhabits bush country, open woodlands with undergrowth, and dense scrub.

Allied Species: The White-winged Scrub Robin (*Erythropygia leucoptera*) occurs in Kenya, north-eastern Uganda and northern Tanganyika. It differs from the Red-backed Scrub Robin in having much white on the wings, the white tail tips wider than black subterminal bars and breast streaking pale greyish and indistinct.

WHITE-STARRED BUSH ROBIN *Pogonocichla stellata* p. 193

Identification: 6″. A robin-like forest bird, brilliantly golden-yellow below with a slate-blue head and an olive-green mantle; a small white spot in front of each eye and a silvery white spot bordered with black at the base of the throat; tail yellow and black. Juvenilc olive-green spotted dull yellow; immature green above with few yellow spots, below pale mottled green. In East Africa typically a bird of bamboo forest. Often perches on ground to feed on ants: much in evidence when safari ants are present.

Voice: A rather harsh "tssst" or "tsssp" and a two-note call. Song a high-pitched flute-like warble.

Distribution and Habitat: A local resident Kenya, Uganda, Tanganyika, Nyasaland and Northern Rhodesia: in Southern Rhodesia confined to forests of eastern border. Also in the Kivu district of the Congo and in South Africa. Inhabits forest areas, often favouring bamboo and mixed bamboo and mountain forest.

WARBLERS: Sylviidae

A large family of small, active insectivorous birds of slim build: related to thrushes and flycatchers but bills slender and juvenile plumages unspotted. Many species, especially among the "leaf warblers," *Phylloscopus*, and the Fan-tailed Warblers, *Cisticola*, lack distinctive markings and may appear confusingly alike. Voice, behaviour, habitat and distribution are important in their identification.

BLACKCAP WARBLER *Sylvia atricapilla* (M) p. 208

Identification: 5½″. Male recognised by sharply defined black crown; upperparts greyish-brown; sides of head and below ash-grey. Female and immature have red-brown crowns.

Voice: Usually silent in winter quarters except for harsh churring note usually uttered from cover. Migrating males sometimes utter a brief warbling song.

Distribution and Habitat: A very common winter visitor and passage migrant in East Africa: also recorded from Nyasaland. Frequents forest and wooded areas, scrub and gardens. Much attracted to fruiting fig trees, where it feeds upon both insects and fruit.

Allied Species: The Garden Warbler (*Sylvia borin*) resembles the Blackcap Warbler but is uniformly coloured, without a black or rufous cap. It is a common winter visitor to East Africa, less frequent in Nyasaland and the Rhodesias.

CINNAMON BRACKEN WARBLER *Sathrocercus cinnamomeus* p. 208

Identification: 5½″. A skulking forest undergrowth warbler, bright rufous with short rounded wings and a broad tail; paler below. Presence usually detected by bird's loud call-notes or when it flushes from undergrowth when disturbed.

Voice: Usual call a harsh, rasping "cheee, cheee": song a loud clear warble uttered from dense herbage near ground.

Distribution and Habitat: Local resident highland areas East Africa, Nyasaland and Northern Rhodesia. Occurs in or near mountain forest in thick tangled undergrowth, bush, bracken and bamboo. In East Africa found on mountains up to 12,500 feet and higher.

Allied Species: The Evergreen Forest Warbler (*Sathrocercus mariae*) also frequents dense mountain forest undergrowth. Its general appearance is dull and dingy brown, paler on throat. It occurs locally in central and southern Kenya Highlands, Tanganyika, Nyasaland and the Nyika plateau in Northern Rhodesia.

BROWN WOODLAND WARBLER *Seicercus umbrovirens* p. 208

Identification: 4″. The Woodland Warblers are closely related to the Willow Warblers which they resemble in habits and appearance. Upperparts tawny-brown with wings and tail edged bright green; below white with a tawny wash on throat and flanks. Immature yellowish below. Arboreal, hunting its food among branches and foliage of trees and bushes.

Voice: A tinkling, warbling song, not unlike that of the Willow Warbler but clearer. Also utters a series of short trills and a two-note call "tee, teewe."

Distribution and Habitat: Local resident highlands of Ethiopia, Eritrea and Somaliland, south through highlands of Uganda, eastern Congo, Kenya and northern Tanganyika to the Uluguru Mts. Inhabits forested and woodland country.

Allied Species: The European Willow Warbler (*Phylloscopus trochilus*) is an abundant winter visitor and passage migrant throughout East and Central Africa. It is slim and dainty in appearance: above greenish with a yellow eye-stripe; below pale yellowish to white on belly.

GREY WREN WARBLER *Calamonastes simplex* p. 208

Identification: 5″. A dark grey bush country warbler with a rather long tail which is constantly cocked up and down. Underparts have trace of whitish bars across belly. Immature slightly paler than adult.

Voice: A loud, metallic clicking or bleating call "tk, tk" repeated over and over again.

Distribution and Habitat: Common local resident Ethiopia and Somaliland south through Uganda, Kenya and Tanganyika to northern Northern Rhodesia. Inhabits dry bush and acacia country and in south of range thickets in brachystegia woodland.

BLACK-COLLARED APALIS *Apalis pulchra* p. 208

Identification: 5″. The Apalis Warblers which are well represented in East and Central Africa are of slim build with long, narrow, strongly graduated tails; plumage may be brown, grey or green. Many species have black bar or collar across neck. Most are forest dwellers, either in undergrowth or in tree-tops. The Black-collared Apalis has grey upperparts; below white with a black chest band and rufous flanks and belly. Tail frequently raised over back and wagged from side to side. Usually frequents forest undergrowth and bush.

Voice: A brief, loud warbling song: call a double "cheewe, cheewe."

Distribution and Habitat: Local resident mountain and highland forests of Kenya and Uganda. A common species in the forests of the western highlands of Kenya and in the Mpanga forest in western Uganda.

BLACK-BREASTED APALIS *Apalis flavida* p. 208

Identification: 4½″. The widely accepted name "black-breasted" is unfortunate as species only has a black patch in centre of chest and in the Somaliland race there is no black on the underparts at all. Above green, merging to grey on the forehead; below white with broad yellowish band across chest with black patch or spot in centre. Immature paler and greener.

Voice: A two-note soft churr and a brief warbling song.

Distribution and Habitat: A widely distributed resident in East and Central Africa, south to South Africa. Frequents a variety of habitats from forests and woodland to bush, thorn scrub and acacia woodland.

BLACK-THROATED APALIS *Apalis jacksoni* p. 208

Identification: 4½″. Black throat and contrasting yellow breast and white neck-streak render identification easy; crown grey, mantle bright green. Immature paler and duller.

Voice: A loud, distinct churring call.

Distribution and Habitat: A local resident highland forests of Uganda, western and central Kenya and north-western Tanganyika. Also in eastern Congo, Angola and Cameroons. Frequents both the forest undergrowth and tree-tops: seen usually in pairs.

GREY-CAPPED WARBLER *Eminia lepida* p. 208

Identification: 6″. A thickset warbler: appearance suggestive of a small greenbul. Upperparts bright green, including wings and tail; crown grey encircled by a black band; underparts pale grey with conspicuous dark chestnut patch in centre of throat. Immature duller. A skulking bird keeping to thickets and dense undergrowth.

Voice: Extremely variable: various loud trills and clear whistles: often mimics other birds.

Distribution and Habitat: Widely distributed but uncommon resident Uganda, western and central Kenya and northern Tanganyika; also southern Sudan. Inhabits thick scrub and forest undergrowth, and dense vegetation along streams and rivers: not uncommon in gardens in Entebbe, Uganda.

BUFF-BELLIED WARBLER *Phyllolais pulchella* p. 208

Identification: 3½″. A tiny Apalis-like warbler: above pale greyish-brown; below pale yellowish-buff with no distinctive markings. Usually in pairs in acacias.

Voice: A series of soft trilling notes, not unlike the flock call of the Yellow White-eye.

Distribution and Habitat: Local, sometimes common resident in Uganda, western and central Kenya and northern Tanganyika: also in Sudan, Ethiopia, Eritrea and the eastern Congo. Frequents acacia woodland and open bush country. Usually in family parties or pairs: sometimes associated with penduline tits.

CROMBEC *Sylvietta brachyura* p. 208

Identification: 3½″. Plump little warbler with an extremely short tail; silvery grey above with a pale eye-stripe; dusky streak through eye; rufous below merging to white on throat and abdomen. Usually in pairs, climbing amongst branches of thorn trees and bushes in a manner reminiscent of a nuthatch.

Voice: A sharp two-note "tic, tic" and a brief warbling song.

Distribution and Habitat: Local resident, often common, Senegal and Cameroons eastwards to Ethiopia, Eritrea and Somaliland, south through Uganda and Kenya to north-eastern Tanganyika. Inhabits dry bush and coastal scrub and acacia woodland.

Allied Species: The Red-faced Crombec (*Sylvietta whytii*) is larger (4½ inches), lacks the dusky eye streak and has more extensive rufous underparts. It is found in bush and acacia country and in brachystegia scrub and woodland. It occurs locally in Uganda, Kenya, Tanganyika, Nyasaland and the Zambesi valley and eastern districts of Southern Rhodesia.

YELLOW-BELLIED EREMOMELA *Eremomela icteropygialis* p. 208

Identification: 3½″. A short-tailed warbler with pale grey upperparts, throat and breast and contrasting pale yellow belly. Penduline Tits resemble the Yellow-bellied Eremomela but lack contrasting yellow belly.

Voice: A weak, plaintive, "tsee, tsee."

WHITE-EYES, TITS and WARBLERS

1. **KIKUYU WHITE-EYE** page 238
   Large white eye-ring; broad yellow forehead band.
2. **YELLOW WHITE-EYE** 238
   Narrow white eye-ring; narrow yellow forehead band.
3. **BLACKCAP WARBLER** 204
   Sharply defined dark crown, black in male, red-brown in female.
4. **BROWN WOODLAND WARBLER** 205
   Tawny-brown upperparts; wings and tail edged green: arboreal in habits.
5. **GREY WREN WARBLER** 205
   Dark grey plumage; long tail constantly raised and lowered.
6. **CINNAMON BRACKEN WARBLER** 204
   Bright rufous upperparts; broad tail: undergrowth skulker.
7. **GREY-CAPPED WARBLER** 206
   Black crown band; chestnut throat patch.
8. **CROMBEC** 207
   Very short tail; grey upperparts; rufous belly.
9. **GREY-BACKED CAMAROPTERA** 210
   Short tail; grey back contrasting with green wings.
10. **YELLOW-BELLIED EREMOMELA** 207
    Very short tail; pale yellow belly.
11. **PECTORAL-PATCH CISTICOLA** 210
    Small; stumpy-tailed; streaked upperparts; dusky patch each side chest.
12. **BLACK-THROATED APALIS** 206
    White neck streak; black throat.
13. **RATTLING CISTICOLA** 211
    Mantle streaked; *see* text.
14. **BLACK-BREASTED APALIS** 206
    Small black patch in centre of chest; back green.
15. **AFRICAN PENDULINE TIT** 226
    Short tail; whitish belly; bill short, tapering and sharp.
16. **SINGING CISTICOLA** 211
    Upperparts uniform, not streaked; *see* text.
17. **GREY TIT** 225
    White cheek and neck patch; black cap and throat.
18. **BUFF-BELLIED WARBLER** 207
    Greyish-brown above; pale buff below: arboreal in acacia trees.
19. **WHITE-BREASTED TIT** 226
    White belly; wing feathers edged white.
20. **TAWNY-FLANKED PRINIA** 211
    Long graduated tail; pale eye-stripe.
21. **BLACK-COLLARED APALIS** 205
    Black chest band; rufous flanks.

1
2
3
♂
4
5
6
7
8
9
10
11
12
13
14
15
16
17
18
19
20
21

1
2
3
4
5
6
7
8
9
10
11
12

SWALLOWS and SWIFTS

1. **EUROPEAN SWALLOW** page 212
   Deeply forked tail; rump blue-black, uniform with mantle.
2. **MOSQUE SWALLOW** 213
   Large size; rufous rump and under tail coverts.
3. **STRIPED SWALLOW** 213
   Striped underparts; rufous rump and cap.
4. **AFRICAN SAND MARTIN** 214
   Slightly forked tail; brownish grey throat and chest.
5. **BANDED MARTIN** 214
   Unforked tail; dark chest band.
6. **WIRE-TAILED SWALLOW** 212
   Very slender and long outer tail feathers; rufous cap.
7. **BLACK ROUGHWING SWALLOW** 214
   Entirely black plumage; long and deeply forked tail.
8. **NYANZA SWIFT** 174
   Rump dark; tail forked.
9. **WHITE-RUMPED SWIFT** 175
   Rump white; tail deeply forked and outer feathers strongly attenuated.
10. **HORUS SWIFT** 178
    Rump white; tail forked; outer feathers slightly attenuated; throat appears very white.
11. **LITTLE SWIFT** 175
    Rump white; tail square.
12. **PALM SWIFT** 178
    Slim build; uniform greyish-brown plumage; tail deeply forked and attenuated.

Distribution and Habitat: Widespread resident, often common, from Sudan, Ethiopia and Somaliland south through Kenya and Tanganyika to Nyasaland and the Rhodesias. Much attracted to flowering acacia trees. Usually in pairs or family parties.

Allied Species: The very similar Yellow-vented Eremomela (*Eremomela flavicrissalis*) is smaller (3 inches) with a white breast, the pale yellow confined to lower belly. It occurs in Somaliland and northern and eastern Kenya in semi-desert bush. The Green-cap Eremomela (*Eremomela scotops*) has grey upperparts and a green cap; below yellow, white on chin. A bird of open bush and brachystegia woodland. It occurs locally in Uganda and in western and central Kenya, becoming common in brachystegia woodland in Tanganyika, Nyasaland and the Rhodesias.

GREY-BACKED CAMAROPTERA *Camaroptera brevicaudata* p. 208

Identification: 4″. A rather short-tailed warbler with head, mantle and underparts grey, contrasting with green wings. A skulking species inhabiting thick cover.

Voice: A drawn-out, plaintive bleating call "squeeeee" frequently repeated, which draws attention to the bird in spite of its skulking habits.

Distribution and Habitat: Common and widespread resident East and Central Africa: also West and South Africa. Inhabits thick undergrowth and bush of all descriptions, from mountain forest to semi-desert thorn-scrub.

Allied Species: The Green-backed Camaroptera (*Camaroptera brachyura*) differs in having the mantle green, not grey. It occurs in coastal districts of Kenya, southwards through Tanganyika to Nyasaland and the Rhodesias. It inhabits thick cover in bush and woodlands.

PECTORAL-PATCH CISTICOLA *Cisticola brunnescens* p. 208

Note: The Cisticolas are a large group of brown-plumaged warblers with either streaked or unmarked upperparts: in most species tail feathers have black subterminal patch and white tip. The identification of the many species of Cisticolas found in East and Central Africa does not come within the scope of this field guide. Anyone wishing to study this group is advised to consult H. Lynes' "Review of the Genus Cisticola," Ibis Supplement, 1930.

Identification: 3½″. Stumpy-tailed species with upperparts streaked black; top of head buff; dusky patches on each side of chest. Frequents open grasslands where conspicuous when indulging in jerky display flights during breeding season.

Voice: High-pitched "zeet zeet zeet," call uttered in flight.

Distribution and Habitat: Locally common resident Ethiopia and Somaliland, south through Kenya and Tanganyika to the Rhodesias and South Africa. Frequents open grasslands, with or without scattered bush.

RATTLING CISTICOLA *Cisticola chiniana* p. 208

Identification: 5″. Mantle streaked dusky on brown or greyish-brown; crown dark rufous-brown, more or less streaked dusky-brown. A characteristic bird of thorn-bush and brachystegia scrub. In pairs or family parties; draws attention to itself by its scolding call-notes.

Voice: A loud, scolding "chaaaaaa, chaaaaaa."

Distribution and Habitat: Common resident locally in suitable areas East and Central Africa, south to South Africa. In East Africa it is a common and typical bird of thornbush country: farther south it is common in brachystegia and open woodland.

SINGING CISTICOLA *Cisticola cantans* p. 208

dentification: 5½″. Upperparts and crown not streaked. Mantle greyish-brown, crown rufous; below white with buff wash on breast.

Voice: A loud "tsss, wip, tsss, wip" repeated over and over again: also a brief, clear warbling song of four or five notes.

Distribution and Habitat: Common resident throughout East and Central Africa. Frequents rank grass and other herbage, favours rank secondary vegetation in neglected cultivation and forest plantations.

TAWNY-FLANKED PRINIA *Prinia subflava* p. 208

Identification: 5″. A uniform tawny-brown, cisticola-like warbler with a long graduated tail and a conspicuous pale eye-stripe. Actions jerky, frequently raising and lowering tail.

Voice: A loud churring "chee, cheer" often repeated, and a short piping song.

Distribution and Habitat: Common and widespread resident throughout East and Central Africa and also in most of the Ethiopian Region except western Cape Province. Frequents rank grass and other herbage, scrub along streams, edges of forest, regenerating bush and scrub in old cultivated areas, forest plantations and gardens.

SWALLOWS and MARTINS: Hirundinidae

Swallows and their allies are a well-marked group of birds which capture their insect food on the wing. They bear a superficial resemblance to swifts, but wing formation differs in being less slender and scythe-like. Build slim and flight graceful, less direct and rapid than swifts. Many species possess long and slender outer tail feathers: feet very small: bill short with wide gape.

EUROPEAN SWALLOW *Hirundo rustica* (M) p. 209

Identification: 7½″. Long slender outer tail feathers; above including rump glossy blue-black; forehead and throat chestnut; blue-black band across chest, remainder underparts creamy-white.

Voice: A high-pitched, rapid twitter, or a single high "tstwee." Warbling song rarely heard in winter quarters.

Distribution and Habitat: An abundant winter visitor and passage migrant throughout East and Central Africa. Occurs in any type of open country, but especially vicinity of lakes, cattle pastures and open grasslands. Frequently perches on telegraph wires: gregarious, usually seen in flocks.

Allied Species: The Angola or Uganda Swallow (*Hirundo angolensis*) lacks the long tail streamers of the European Swallow and has belly ashy-grey. It is a common resident, locally migratory, in Uganda, western and central Kenya and western Tanganyika. In Central Africa it has been recorded from Nyasaland and Northern Rhodesia. The Ethiopian Swallow (*Hirundo aethiopica*) occurs locally from Ethiopia, south through Uganda and Kenya to north-eastern Tanganyika, most frequent along the Kenya coast. Its best field character is its white, not chestnut throat.

WIRE-TAILED SWALLOW *Hirundo smithii* p. 209

Identification: 6″. Outer tail feathers long and wire thin; upperparts glossy purplish-black with a rufous crown; below white. Easily distinguished from other black-backed swallows by its chestnut crown and very slender tail streamers.

Voice: A soft twittering warble.

Distribution and Habitat: Widely but locally distributed throughout East and Central Africa: partial migrant in some areas. Not usually gregarious, normally occurs in pairs. Occurs near water and often associated with human habitations and bridges.

Allied Species: The Grey-rumped Swallow (*Hirundo griseopyga*) is a slimly built species, white below with a pale grey rump and crown. It occurs locally in East and Central Africa and is migratory in many areas. Usually in small flocks, often associated with sand martins. Frequently perches on ground.

MOSQUE SWALLOW *Hirundo senegalensis* p. 209

Identification: 9″. A large heavy-looking swallow with developed tail streamers; upperparts blue-black with contrasting rufous rump; underparts, including under tail coverts, pale rufous. Occurs in pairs. In lowland areas associated with baobab trees; in highland areas of East Africa found in vicinity isolated cedar (juniper) trees.

Voice: A distinct, metallic "peeeep": often calls on the wing. Song a low, slow twitter.

Distribution and Habitat: Local resident and partial migrant East and Central Africa: also in Congo and West Africa and in Portuguese East Africa. Occurs from sea level to localities over 8,000 feet in Kenya. Inhabits open park-type country, cultivated areas where there are large isolated trees and bush and coastal scrub where there are baobab trees.

Allied Species: The Red-rumped Swallow (*Hirundo daurica*) is smaller, 7 inches, with black under tail coverts. Local resident and partial migrant East Africa, Nyasaland and Northern Rhodesia. The Rufous-chested Swallow (*Hirundo semirufa*) differs from both the Mosque and Red-rumped Swallows in having the lores, a streak under the eye and the ear coverts blue-black, not rufous. It occurs locally in Uganda, western Kenya, Nyasaland and the Rhodesias.

STRIPED SWALLOW *Hirundo abyssinica* p. 209

Identification: 7″. Easily recognised by black-streaked underparts and chestnut crown and rump: outer tail feathers thin and elongated.

Voice: Squeaky, metallic notes, not unlike a violin being tuned: also a brief warbling song.

Distribution and Habitat: Widely distributed throughout the Ethiopian Region in suitable localities. Common resident and local migrant in East and Central Africa. May be encountered anywhere outside forest areas and often associated with human habitations and bridges.

AFRICAN SAND MARTIN *Riparia paludicola* p. 209

Identification: 4½″. Tail very slightly forked: upperparts, throat and breast earth-brown; belly white.

Voice: Weak twittering notes.

Distribution and Habitat: Widely distributed resident and partial migrant East and Central Africa, south to South Africa. Gregarious, sometimes in large loose flocks. Most numerous in vicinity of rivers, lakes and swamps.

Allied Species: The European Sand Martin (*Riparia riparia*) has earth-brown upperparts; below white with a brown chest band; tail slightly forked. Common winter visitor and passage migrant East Africa, less common in Nyasaland and Rhodesias. The African Rock Martin (*Ptyonoprogne fuligula*) is uniform tawny-brown with an ill-defined rufous throat: tail slightly forked, conspicuously spotted with white when spread in flight. Frequents human habitations, cliffs and rocky outcrops: widely distributed but local throughout East and Central Africa.

BANDED MARTIN *Riparia cincta* p. 209

Identification: 6½″. Tail square or very slightly forked; upperparts dark brown with white streak on each side of the forehead; underparts white with dark brown band across chest. The European Sand Martin is smaller, has a forked tail and lacks the white forehead streaks.

Voice: A silent species; sometimes utters a brief twitter.

Distribution and Habitat: Widespread resident and local migrant throughout Ethiopian Region, including East and Central Africa. Usually in pairs or small parties; favours open grasslands with scattered bushes and the vicinity of water.

BLACK ROUGHWING SWALLOW *Psalidoprocne holomelaena* p. 209

Identification: 7″. Entire plumage black with an oily greenish tinge; tail very long and deeply forked; under wing coverts and axillaries ash-brown. Occurs in small, loose flocks, perching in dead trees and hawking backwards and forwards along forest roads and glades.

Voice: Usually silent, but sometimes utters a weak twittering call.

Distribution and Habitat: Widespread local resident and partial migrant East Africa, and in South Africa. Usually seen in small parties. Most frequent in highland areas where it inhabits forests and wooded areas.

Allied Species: Eastern Roughwing Swallow (*Psalidoprocne orientalis*) is also entirely black with oily green tinge, but has under wing-coverts and axillaries white. It occurs locally in forested and wooded country in Tanganyika, Nyasaland and the Rhodesias. The White-headed Roughwing Swallow (*Psalidoprocne albiceps*) is black with a conspicuous white head in male; female has dark head but some white on chin. Local resident and partial migrant Uganda, western and central Kenya, Tanganyika, Nyasaland and Northern Rhodesia.

CUCKOO SHRIKES: Campephagidae

The Cuckoo Shrikes are a group of medium-sized, shrike-like birds inhabiting forests and woodland. In some species sexes very dissimilar, the males being black and the females yellow, white and olive-grey. In the hand cuckoo shrikes may always be identified by stiff pointed feather shafts of lower back and rump: these give the impression of spines when brushed upwards.

BLACK CUCKOO SHRIKE *Campephaga sulphurata* p. 228

Identification: 8″. Male entirely black with bluish-green gloss; conspicuous yellow gape wattles. These yellow gape wattles distinguish the Black Cuckoo Shrike from other black-plumaged birds such as Square-tailed Drongo and Black Flycatcher. Some males possess yellow shoulders. Female olive-brown above, barred dusky; wings and tail edged yellow and white; underparts white, barred black and yellow. Rather inconspicuous birds, usually in pairs, and often members of mixed bird parties. Restless and always on move, feeding on caterpillars from foliage of trees and bushes.

Voice: Usually silent, but sometimes utters a soft low trill.

Distribution and Habitat: Widely distributed resident East and Central Africa, south to Angola, Portuguese East Africa and South Africa. Inhabits forests, woodlands, bush country and coastal scrub.

Allied Species: The Purple-throated Cuckoo Shrike (*Campephaga quiscalina*) is glossy blue-black with a purple throat and yellow gape. The female is olive-green above with an ashy-grey head; throat greyish-white; remainder underparts bright yellow with indistinct dusky barring. This is a widely distributed bird in forests in Uganda, western and central Kenya and in northern Tanganyika. Also in Congo, Angola and West Africa.

WHITE-BREASTED CUCKOO SHRIKE *Coracina pectoralis* p. 228

Identification: 10″. A pale blue-grey bird with a white belly. Often a member of mixed bird parties in open woodland. Rather oriole-like in general behaviour, but not in colour.

Voice: A soft double whistle and a drawn-out trill.

Distribution and Habitat: Widely distributed but very uncommon Kenya and Uganda, becoming more frequent southern Tanganyika and common locally in Northern Rhodesia. Elsewhere in West Africa, the Congo and the Transvaal, South Africa. Inhabits open woodlands, especially brachystegia.

GREY CUCKOO SHRIKE *Coracina caesia* p. 228

Identification: 9″. A rather pale bluish-grey bird with darker wings and tail: male has blackish patch in front of eye. Immature barred black above and below. A forest tree-tops bird, often a member of mixed bird parties: usually in pairs.

Voice: Usually silent, but sometimes utters an oriole-like whistle.

Distribution and Habitat: Local resident throughout most of the Ethiopian Region in forested areas. Widely distributed but uncommon eastern Uganda, Kenya, Tanganyika, Nyasaland and the eastern border of Southern Rhodesia. Inhabits evergreen and mountain forests.

DRONGOS: Dicruridae

Medium-sized black, shrike-like birds with hooked bills and more or less forked tails, the outer feathers curving outwards towards the tip, "fish-tail" fashion. Feeding habits resemble those of some species of flycatchers —catching insects in flight and returning to same perch.

DRONGO *Dicrurus adsimilis* p. 228

Identification: $9\frac{1}{2}$″. Plumage black; tail forked and "fish-tailed"; inner webs of flight feathers ashy imparting a pale wash to the wings when bird flies; iris red. Immature has greyish tips to feathers of mantle and underparts. The male Black Cuckoo Shrike is black, but lacks the forked tail, has a yellow gape and dark brown eyes. The Black Flycatcher is of slim build with an unforked tail and dark brown eyes.

Voice: A great variety of harsh, metallic call-notes and clear whistles.

Distribution and Habitat: Common resident thoughout most of the Ethiopian Region. Widespread and often abundant in East and Central Africa. Inhabits all types of woodland, acacia and thorn bush country and semi-wooded scrub.

Allied Species: The Square-tailed Drongo (*Dicrurus ludwigii*) is smaller, 7 inches, with a slightly forked tail. It frequents forest areas and dense woodland. It is locally but widely distributed in East Africa, but more frequent in Nyasaland and the Rhodesias.

HELMET SHRIKES: Prionopidae

A group of medium-sized, shrike-like birds with hooked bills. One of their main characteristics is their extreme sociability, being found always in small flocks, even during the nesting season. Flight graceful and butterfly-like. Calls also distinctive, a loud communal chattering and bill-snapping. In most species feathers of forehead project forwards and there is a fleshy wattle around eye.

STRAIGHT-CRESTED HELMET SHRIKE *Prionops plumata*

p. 228

Identification: 8″. A distinctively patterned black and white bird with lemon-yellow eye wattles: crown blue-grey with bristly feathers of forehead directed forwards. Always in small compact flocks which draw attention to themselves by their chattering and bill-snapping. Usually very tame and fearless of humans.

Voice: A loud chattering call, interspersed with occasional flute-like notes and bill snapping.

Distribution and Habitat: Widely distributed and locally common resident East and Central Africa, south to South Africa: also in West Africa. Inhabits bush country, acacia woodlands, and open brachystegia woodland.

Allied Species: The Curly-crested Helmet Shrike (*Prionops cristata*) differs in having a striking crest of long curly white feathers. It occurs in northern districts of Uganda and in northern and western Kenya. The Grey-crested Helmet Shrike (*Prionops poliolopha*) lacks yellow eye wattles and is larger, 10 inches, with a lax, grey occipital crest and a black patch on each side of the chest. It is an uncommon bush country bird in central districts of southern Kenya and northern Tanganyika. It is not uncommon in the Loliondo district of northern Tanganyika where mixed flocks of Grey-crested and Straight-crested Helmet Shrikes occur.

RETZ'S RED-BILLED SHRIKE *Sigmodus retzii* p. 228

Identification: 8″. A rather thickset dark brown helmet-shrike with sharply contrasting dark breast and white abdomen, and white-tipped tail; bill, eye-wattles and feet red: crest of erect feathers on forehead. Always in small flocks and often associated with parties of wood hoopoes.

Voice: Noisy chattering interspersed with soft whistles; also a sharp double alarm call.

Distribution and Habitat: Local resident, generally uncommon, from southern Somaliland, south through Kenya and Tanganyika to Nyasaland and the Rhodesias: also in South Africa and Angola. Inhabits open forest and woodland areas, especially brachystegia, and coastal scrub.

Allied Species: The Chestnut-fronted Shrike (*Sigmodus scopifrons*) is a smaller bird, 7 inches, grey above with a curious pad of velvet-like chestnut bristles on forehead; tail tipped white; below slate-grey to white on abdomen. An uncommon local resident in woodland, especially brachystegia, in eastern districts Kenya and Tanganyika, south to Mozambique.

WHITE-CROWNED SHRIKE *Eurocephalus anguitimens* p. 228

Identification: 9″. Dry thornbush country species. Mantle dusky-brown with contrasting white crown and rump; a wide black patch behind eye; below white with a brown patch on each side of breast. Immature has crown brown and upperparts barred. Found always in small parties; field appearance distinctive, white crown and rump being very conspicuous; remarkable for stiff, gliding flight between trees on rigid wings. Has a slight resemblance to a White-headed Buffalo Weaver but lacks the red rump characteristic of that species.

Voice: A harsh "kaa, kaa, kaa" and various other chattering and whistling calls.

Distribution and Habitat: Local resident Ethiopia, Eritrea, Somaliland and Sudan, south through northern Uganda, Kenya, and Tanganyika, and in Southern Rhodesia. Also occurs in Angola and South Africa. Typical bird of bush country, common in the dry thornbush country of Kenya.

SHRIKES: Laniidae

Conspicuously coloured medium-sized birds with strong hooked bills. Some species perch on vantage points from which they can pounce on their prey: others, more skulking, feed among foliage of trees and bushes. Call-notes usually harsh but songs sometimes surprisingly musical.

NORTHERN BRUBRU *Nilaus afer* p. 228

Identification: 5″. A striking black and white bird with chestnut flanks: white stripe over eye extending to nape; active and always on the move in trees and bush, searching foliage for insect food. Calls frequently.

Voice: A loud, prolonged "keeeeeeeerr" and a three- to five-note loud clear whistle.

Distribution and Habitat: Widely distributed resident West Africa, eastwards through Sudan to Ethiopia, Eritrea and Somaliland, south through Uganda and Kenya to northern Tanganyika. Place taken in southern Tanganyika and Central Africa by closely allied Black-browed Brubru, which may be conspecific. Frequents bush, scrub and woodland country. In East Africa much attracted to flowering acacia trees where it feeds on the many insects which visit the flowers.

Allied Species: The Black-browed Brubru (*Nilaus nigritemporalis*) lacks the white stripe over the eye in the male and the female has a short eye-stripe which does not extend to the nape, and black streaking and barring on throat and breast. It occurs in woodland and bush areas in Tanganyika and Central Africa.

FISCAL SHRIKE *Lanius collaris* p. 229

Identification: 9″. Above black with a conspicuous white V-shaped patch on back; rump grey; below white; tail long and graduated, black, broadly tipped white. Immature barred black and tawny above. One of the commonest and best-known East African birds, being common even in townships: often seen perched on telegraph wires.

Voice: A rather sharp, drawn-out "cheeeeeeeee": alarm call a clear whistle.

Distribution and Habitat: Widespread but local resident, often common, throughout most of the Ethiopian Region including East and Central

Africa. Inhabits cultivated areas, the vicinity of human habitations, lightly wooded country and edges of dambos.

Allied Species: The Uhehe Fiscal (*Lanius marwitzi*) differs only in having a white eye-stripe and a much darker immature plumage. It has a restricted distribution in the Uhehe and Njombe highlands of Tanganyika. Mackinnon's Grey Shrike (*Lanius mackinnoni*) is very like the Fiscal Shrike but has upperparts grey instead of black and a white stripe over eye. Local resident open woodlands, cultivation and forest margins in Uganda, western Kenya and north-western and central Tanganyika.

LONG-TAILED FISCAL *Lanius cabanisi* p. 229

Identification: 12″. Upperparts black, merging to grey on rump; white wing-bar; underparts white; tail very long, black. Commonly seen in small parties, birds perched close together in single bush, raising, lowering and swinging tails in pendulum fashion.

Voice: A variety of harsh scolding calls and a clear whistle.

Distribution and Habitat: Local resident from southern Somaliland south through central and eastern Kenya to eastern Tanganyika. Inhabits coastal open low scrub and grasslands with scattered bushes. Common in coastal district and on the Athi Plains, central Kenya.

Allied Species: The Grey-backed Fiscal (*Lanius excubitorius*), 10 inches, has upperparts pale grey, forehead and broad streak through eye black; below white; tail white with broad black tip. Also occurs in small parties and much given to tail waving and noisy chattering. It occurs locally in Uganda, western Kenya to Rift Valley and south to central and western Tanganyika in bush and acacia woodland. The Lesser Grey Shrike (*Lanius minor*), 8 inches, has blue-grey upperparts and pale pink underparts; forehead and broad streak through eye black; black wings and tail with very prominent white wing-bar and white outer tail feathers. It is a common passage migrant in East Africa, Nyasaland and Northern Rhodesia and a winter visitor to Southern Rhodesia and farther south. The Somali Fiscal (*Lanius somalicus*), 9 inches, has a blue-grey mantle and a black cap and nape; white wing-bar and secondaries tipped white. It occurs in Somaliland and northern Kenya in dry bush country. The Teita Fiscal (*Lanius dorsalis*), 9 inches, differs from Somali Fiscal in lacking the white tips to the secondaries; it occurs in bush country, usually below 5,000 feet, in north-eastern Uganda, northern, eastern and southern Kenya and in northern Tanganyika.

RED-BACKED SHRIKE *Lanius collurio* (M) p. 229

Identification: 7″. Male identified by pale blue-grey crown and rump and contrasting chestnut back: broad black streak through eye to ear coverts; below pinkish-white; tail black with mainly white outer tail feathers. Tail often swung from side to side. Female dull rufous brown, buffish-white below with indistinct brown barring. Immature resembles female but more strongly barred below.

Voice: A harsh "chaaark," repeated once or twice.

Distribution and Habitat: Common winter visitor and passage migrant East and Central Africa. Frequents open areas with scattered trees and bush, and coastal scrub.

Allied Species: The Red-tailed Shrike (*Lanius cristatus*) has the upperparts grey and the crown and tail chestnut. It is a winter visitor and passage migrant to Kenya, Uganda and northern Tanganyika.

MAGPIE SHRIKE *Urolestes melanoleucus* p. 229

Identification: 14″. A very large black shrike with a long tail; white patch on each side of the mantle and a white wing-bar; rump grey. A most conspicuous bird which settles on the tops of bushes: occurs in family parties or pairs.

Voice: A loud, warbling two-note call, repeated several times: also a harsh, rasping call-note.

Distribution and Habitat: Local resident, widely but locally distributed south-eastern Kenya, Tanganyika, Nyasaland and the Rhodesias. Also in Angola and South Africa. Inhabits open country with scattered bush, neglected cultivation and acacia woodland. It specially favours black cotton-soil with scattered whistling thorn bushes in parts of Tanganyika.

BLACK-HEADED GONOLEK *Laniarius erythrogaster* p. 229

Identification: 8″. Upperparts jet black; underparts bright crimson-red; under tail-coverts buff. Immature barred buff and black below. A beautiful and unmistakable bird, rather skulking in habits and keeping to bushes and such-like cover.

Voice: A clear, two-note whistle "wee—oooo" frequently repeated and a harsher, rasping call which has been likened to someone tearing calico.

Distribution and Habitat: Local resident the Sudan, Ethiopia and Eritrea, south to Uganda, western Kenya and northern Tanganyika. Occurs in bush country, often near water, thick tangled vegetation and neglected cultivation. It is a common bird around Entebbe, Uganda and Kisumu, western Kenya, where it is a conspicuous species in gardens.

Allied Species: The Crimson-breasted Boubou (*Laniarius atro-coccineus*) is common in Matabeleland, Southern Rhodesia. It differs from the Black-headed Gonolek in having a white wing-bar.

SLATE-COLOURED BOUBOU *Laniarius funebris* p. 229

Identification: 7″. Entire plumage dark slate-blue to blackish on the head, wings and tail. Immature with indistinct tawny barring on upperparts. Skulking in habits, keeping to thick cover; found in pairs. In field, except in a good light, it appears as a completely black bird.

Voice: Male and female duet, one of pair uttering three or four bell-like whistles, followed immediately by the second bird giving a guttural croak. Also has various other whistles and churring notes and a harsh "krrrrr" alarm call.

Distribution and Habitat: Widespread resident, usually below 5,000 feet, southern Sudan, Ethiopia, Eritrea and Somaliland, south through Uganda and Kenya to southern Tanganyika. Inhabits dry bush country, keeping to thickets and stands of Salvadora bushes; also in coastal scrub and woodland where thick cover exists.

TROPICAL BOUBOU *Laniarius aethiopicus* p. 229

Identification: 9″. Upperparts, wings and tail glossy black, with or without a white wing-bar; below pinkish-white. Immature barred tawny on upperparts. Always found in pairs, skulking in undergrowth, thick bush, creepers and the thick foliage of trees. Attention drawn to presence by its clear bell-like whistles.

Voice: Varied and remarkable duet between male and female; one utters three rapid, clear bell-like whistles, answered immediately with a croaking "kweee." This second call is uttered so instantaneously that the whole call appears to be made by one bird. The notes vary very much and most localities seem to have their own local variety of whistles and croak. Birds also make a harsh churring call.

Distribution and Habitat: Widely distributed throughout suitable areas Ethiopian Region, including East and Central Africa: inhabits thick cover in forests, woodland, riverine thickets, gardens, bush and coastal scrub. Feeds sometimes on the ground in thick cover. Well known in gardens in towns, where it has the popular name of "bell-bird."

BLACK-BACKED PUFF-BACK *Dryoscopus cubla* p. 229

Identification: 6″. Male above glossy blue-black with conspicuous rump patch of downy white feathers; wing-coverts and flight feathers edged white; underparts white, greyish on breast and flanks. Female and immature have duller upperparts, rump grey and a white streak above the eye. Rump feathers often puffed out and conspicuous in field. Hunts insect food among foliage of trees and bushes in manner of warbler: usually in pairs and often members of mixed bird parties.

Voice: A loud, harsh "chik, weeooo—chik, weeooo" repeated over and over again: sometimes a double clicking note followed by a clear whistle. Often produces a loud "brrrrp" with wings when flying from branch to branch.

Distribution and Habitat: Widely distributed resident Uganda, and Kenya (except extreme north) south through Tanganyika to Nyasaland and the Rhodesias. Also in Angola and the eastern Congo. Inhabits forest areas, woodland, thickets, gardens, scrub and acacia country.

BLACK-HEADED BUSH SHRIKE *Tchagra senegala* p. 229

Identification: 8″. A brown bush shrike with striking chestnut-red wings, a black crown and a buff eye-stripe; tail black with white tips. Usually seen as it dives for cover into a bush, when red wings and white-tipped black tail noticeable.

Voice: A series of clear piping whistles and a churring alarm call. Has courtship flight, mounting sharply into air with crackling wings, then floating down in a spiral uttering a clear piping.

Distribution and Habitat: Widely distributed resident throughout most of Ethiopian Region and common throughout East and Central Africa. Inhabits desert scrub, bush, wooded areas, gardens and neglected cultivation, undergrowth and bush along rivers and mixed grass and bush.

Allied Species: The Brown-headed Bush Shrike (*Tchagra australis*) has the crown tawny brown, not black. It occurs locally from Kenya and Uganda south through Tanganyika to Nyasaland and Rhodesias. It is less common than the Black-headed Bush Shrike. The Blackcap Bush Shrike (*Tchagra minuta*) is smaller, 7 inches, with chestnut-red upperparts and a contrasting all black cap. It frequents lush grassy areas with scattered bush in marshes and at the margins of forests. It ranges through much of East and Central Africa but is local and uncommon.

SULPHUR-BREASTED BUSH SHRIKE

Chlorophoneus sulfureopectus p. 229

Identification: 7″. Rather a slim-looking shrike, pale grey above with bright yellowish-green wings and tail; forehead and stripe over eye bright yellow; breast bright orange merging to yellow on belly. A very striking bird found in pairs in thickly foliaged trees and bush.

Voice: A loud piping whistle of ten or twelve notes.

Distribution and Habitat: Widely distributed throughout most of the Ethiopian Region, local in East and Central Africa and uncommon. Frequents the tops of acacia trees, riverine forest, clumps of thickly foliaged trees, dense bush and coastal scrub. Rather skulking in its habits and in spite of its bright colours easy to overlook unless one hears its piping call.

FOUR-COLOURED BUSH SHRIKE *Telophorus quadricolor*

p. 229

Identification: 7″. A skulking species of great beauty, bright green above with a yellow forehead and eye-stripe; scarlet throat and black chest; belly rich yellow washed orange-red; flanks green.

Voice: Loud, clear bell-like whistles, which are difficult to locate in dense bush.

Distribution and Habitat: A not uncommon resident in coastal and south-eastern Kenya, south through eastern Tanganyika to Portuguese East Africa, Nyasaland and eastern Southern Rhodesia. Also in Natal and Zululand, South Africa. Owing to its shy and skulking habits it is often overlooked. It inhabits thick coastal scrub, dense riverine thickets and bush. In Kenya and Southern Rhodesia sometimes enters gardens.

DOHERTY'S BUSH SHRIKE *Telophorus dohertyi* p. 229

Identification: 7″. Bright green above with a crimson-red forehead and throat, followed by broad black breast-band and a yellow belly. Immature barred black above. A skulking species found in highland forest undergrowth.

Voice: A series of clear, bell-like whistles.

Distribution and Habitat: Local resident Kenya Highlands, including Mt. Elgon and Mt. Kenya, and also the highlands of south-western Uganda. Inhabits thickets near forest and dense forest undergrowth: often overlooked on account of its skulking habits.

GREY-HEADED BUSH SHRIKE *Malaconotus blanchoti* p. 229

Identification: 10″. A large, heavily-built bush shrike with a hooked black bill. Crown and nape grey; remainder upperparts, wings and tail bright green with yellow spots on tips secondaries and tail feathers; below bright yellow, washed orange-chestnut on chest. Immature has horn-coloured bill. Usually singly or in pairs: often in tops large acacia trees.

Voice: A loud two- or three-note whistle; sometimes utters a curious rattling chatter.

Distribution and Habitat: Ranges through much of the Ethiopian Region. Local and usually uncommon East and Central Africa. Inhabits any woodland but in East Africa favours acacia tree-tops in open riverine forest.

ROSY-PATCHED SHRIKE *Rhodophoneus cruentus* p. 228

Identification: 9″. A rather slim, long-tailed shrike with the general appearance of a babbler; pale pinkish-brown with a very conspicuous rosy-red rump and red on the throat and breast. Inhabits arid bush country where frequently seen on the ground at base of isolated bush. Red rump patch very striking in flight.

Voice: Various brief piping whistles: song very melodious, more thrush than shrike-like, four, five or six notes repeated over and over again.

Distribution and Habitat: Local resident, usually uncommon, Sudan, Ethiopia and Somalilands southwards through Kenya to northern Tanganyika. Not uncommon in bush country in Amboseli National Reserve, Kenya. Inhabits open bush country and arid scrub.

TITS: Paridae

A group of small, rather plump birds of distinct structure and habits: extremely active and acrobatic when feeding, often hanging upside down while searching for insects in foliage. Often members of mixed bird parties.

GREY TIT *Parus afer* p. 208

Identification: 4½″. Upperparts pale blue-grey; head and throat black, a broad white stripe from base of bill down sides of neck and white patch on nape; belly greyish-white. White streak down sides of neck best field character.

Voice: A harsh "chiss, tch-tch-tch" and a single "tsee."

Distribution and Habitat: Local resident, sometimes common, from Somaliland and Ethiopia southwards through Kenya and Tanganyika to Nyasaland and the Rhodesias; also in Angola and South Africa. In northern half of its range it inhabits dry bush and acacia country, especially acacia belts along dry river beds. Farther south, in Tanganyika and Central Africa, it is mainly a bird of brachystegia woodland.

WHITE-BREASTED TIT *Parus albiventris* p. 208

Identification: 5½″. A black tit with a contrasting white belly; wing feathers and wing coverts edged white. In pairs or family parties; very active and always on move.

Voice: A sharp "tss, tseee" or "tss, tss, tee"; song a repeated warbling "chee, chee, churr."

Distribution and Habitat: Locally common resident southern Sudan, Uganda, Kenya and Tanganyika: also Cameroons. Inhabits acacia country, woodlands, forests and coastal bush.

Allied Species: The Cinnamon-breasted Tit (*Parus rufiventris*) resembles a greyish edition of the White-breasted Tit with a rufous-cinnamon belly. It occurs in woodlands in Tanganyika, Nyasaland and the Rhodesias. The Black Tit (*Parus leucomelas*) is entirely glossy violet-black, with contrasting white shoulders and white edgings to flight feathers. It occurs very locally in bush, forest and woodland in Uganda, western Kenya, Tanganyika, Nyasaland and Southern Rhodesia. The Southern Black Tit (*Parus niger*) has very narrow white edgings to wing feathers and appears completely black in field, not black with white shoulders. It is found locally in scrub and woodland in Nyasaland and the Rhodesias. The Dusky Tit (*Parus funereus*), a common bird of forest tree-tops in western Kenya and Uganda, is entirely dark slate-grey with bright red eyes. Usually in small flocks, often associated with mixed bird parties.

AFRICAN PENDULINE TIT *Anthoscopus caroli* p. 208

Identification: 3″. A tiny, rather short-tailed grey bird with buff or buff-white underparts; forehead pale buff; bill short but tapering and sharp. Occurs in pairs or small parties in bush country. Recalls an Eremomela warbler, but the latter has yellow on belly.

Voice: A squeaky two-note call, often repeated.

Distribution and Habitat: Local resident in small numbers southern Uganda, Kenya, Tanganyika, Nyasaland and the Rhodesias. Also Portuguese East Africa and South Africa. Inhabits bush, scrub, stands of acacia and brachystegia woodland.

ORIOLES: Oriolidae

A group of active, thrush-sized birds, usually of brilliant yellow plumage, which inhabits tree-tops in woodland and forest. Calls loud, clear, melodious whistles.

AFRICAN GOLDEN ORIOLE *Oriolus auratus* p. 228

Identification: 9½″. Male brilliant yellow with black eye streak; wings black, broadly edged yellow on coverts and flight feathers; tail black and yellow; bill carmine. Female and immature yellowish-green with darker wings and tail; underparts yellow lightly streaked grey; eye-streak dark grey. Very rapid and direct flight, long undulations with upward sweep as it enters tree; shy, stays well concealed among foliage of tree-tops.

Voice: A clear, melodious whistle "weeka—wee-ooo" and other whistles and a mewing call.

Distribution and Habitat: Occurs in suitable areas throughout the Ethiopian Region. Local resident and partial migrant in East and Central Africa, breeding in Tanganyika and southwards. Frequents tall bushy woodland, open and riverine forest and brachystegia woodland.

Allied Species: The European Golden Oriole (*Oriolus oriolus*) is a winter visitor and passage migrant to East and Central Africa. Male differs in having black wings without yellow edges; female is pale grey below and lacks the dusky eye streak. Often abundant during April on migration along the Kenya coast. Inhabits bush, scrub, woodland and forest.

BLACK-HEADED ORIOLE *Oriolus larvatus* p. 228

Identification: 9″. A bright yellow oriole with a black head and throat; wing feathers edged greyish-white; male and female alike; immature greener with yellow streaks on head and throat.

Voice: A series of liquid, melodious whistles.

Distribution and Habitat: Common resident and partial migrant through-

ORIOLES, CUCKOO SHRIKES and SHRIKES

1. **AFRICAN GOLDEN ORIOLE** page 227
   Male: Wing feathers broadly edged yellow.
   Female: Dark grey streak through eye.
2. **BLACK CUCKOO SHRIKE** 215
   Male: Conspicuous yellow gape wattles.
   Female: Underparts barred black, yellow and white.
3. **BLACK-HEADED ORIOLE** 227
   Black head and throat; immature has yellow streaks on head and throat.
4. **GREY CUCKOO SHRIKE** 216
   Grey above and below.
5. **WHITE-BREASTED CUCKOO SHRIKE** 216
   Pale blue-grey, starling-like bird with contrasting white belly.
6. **DRONGO** 216
   Tail forked and " fish-tailed."
7. **WHITE-CROWNED SHRIKE** 218
   Contrasting brown mantle and white crown and rump.
8. **STRAIGHT-CRESTED HELMET SHRIKE** 217
   Distinctive black and white plumage and yellow eye wattle.
9. **NORTHERN BRUBRU** 219
   Chestnut flanks and white stripe over eye.
10. **RETZ'S RED-BILLED SHRIKE** 218
    Contrasting black breast and white abdomen; red eye wattle.
11. **ROSY-PATCHED SHRIKE** 225
    Rosy-red rump, throat and breast. Female has black markings on breast.

1
♀
♂
2
♀
♂
3
4
5
6
7
8
9
10
♀
♂
11

1
2
a
3
b
♀
♂
4
5
6
8
♀
7
♂
9
10
11
12
13

SHRIKES

1. **LONG-TAILED FISCAL** page 220
   Tail long and entirely black.
2. **FISCAL SHRIKE** 219
   a, *Immature:* Pale brownish with lightly barred belly.
   b, *Adult:* Conspicuous white patch on back.
3. **RED-BACKED SHRIKE** 221
   Male: Chestnut mantle, grey crown.
   Female: Rufous above; buff below with indistinct barring.
4. **MAGPIE SHRIKE** 221
   White patch each side of mantle and white wing bar conspicuous.
5. **SLATE-COLOURED BOUBOU** 222
   Entirely slate-black.
6. **BLACK-HEADED GONOLEK** 221
   Brilliant crimson-red underparts: immature has underparts barred buff and black.
7. **BLACK-BACKED PUFF-BACK** 223
   Male: Glossy blue-black upperparts; greyish-white rump " puff."
   Female: Rump grey; white streak above eye.
8. **BLACK-HEADED BUSH SHRIKE** 223
   Chestnut-red wings and black crown.
9. **GREY-HEADED BUSH SHRIKE** 225
   Pale grey crown; wash of orange-chestnut on chest.
10. **TROPICAL BOUBOU** 222
    Pinkish-white underparts; usually in pairs.
11. **SULPHUR-BREASTED BUSH SHRIKE** 224
    Yellow forehead and eye-stripe; bright orange breast.
12. **FOUR-COLOURED BUSH SHRIKE** 224
    Scarlet throat and black gorget; yellow forehead.
13. **DOHERTY'S BUSH SHRIKE** 224
    Crimson-red forehead and throat; black gorget.

out East and Central Africa and in South Africa. Inhabits forests, all types of woodlands, scrub and thick bush; often seen in gardens. Keeps to tree-tops but less shy than the two golden orioles.

CROWS: Corvidae

Plumage of many species black, or black and white. The largest of the perching birds: bills usually heavy with nostrils covered by forward-pointing bristles. Feed mainly on the ground: omnivorous.

PIED CROW *Corvus albus* p. 176

Identification: 18″. Black with a white breast and a white collar on hind neck.

Voice: A deep, guttural croak.

Distribution and Habitat: Widely but locally distributed throughout most of the Ethiopian Region. In East and Central Africa locally common; subject to erratic migrational movements. Inhabits open country, cultivated areas, refuse dumps, the vicinity of human habitations and margins of rivers, lakes and swamps, and the sea coast.

Allied Species: The White-naped Raven (*Corvus albicollis*) is larger, 22 inches, entirely black with a crescent-shaped white patch on the upper back. It occurs locally through East and Central Africa, frequenting rocky hills and escarpments, the vicinity of hunting camps and near human dwellings where it acts as a scavenger.

CAPE ROOK *Corvus capensis* p. 176

Identification: 17″. Entire plumage glossy black; feathers of throat lax; bill slender. Closely resembles a European Rook but throat feathered.

Voice: A guttural, high-pitched "kaaah."

Distribution and Habitat: Local resident, sometimes common, southern Sudan, Ethiopia and Somaliland, south to Uganda, Kenya and northern Tanganyika. In Northern Rhodesia occurs in Balovale district; widely distributed but uncommon in Southern Rhodesia. Also in Angola and South Africa. Frequents open plains country with scattered trees, cultivated and pasture land and sometimes lightly wooded areas.

Allied Species: The Indian House Crow (*Corvus splendens*) resembles a large slender jackdaw. It is an introduced species now abundant on Zanzibar Island and common at Mombasa, Kenya and Port Sudan. The Fan-tailed Raven (*Rhinocorax rhipidurus*), 18 inches, is an all-black raven with an extremely short tail, especially noticeable in flight. Its call is a shrill falsetto "pruk." It occurs in the vicinity of cliffs and gorges in northern districts of Kenya and Uganda.

PIAPIAC *Ptilostomus afer* p. 176

Identification: 18″. A blackish-brown, long-tailed magpie-like bird found in flocks in immediate vicinity palm trees: bill black, or pinkish-red with black tip. Occurs in small parties and feeds mainly on ground. In Uganda often associates with cattle, using the animals as animated perches and catching insects disturbed by them.

Voice: A deep piping call: alarm call a harsh scolding chatter.

Distribution and Habitat: A West African species which extends to western and northern Uganda. Common on the Semliki flats in Ankole. Inhabits open pasture country, always near palm trees: very gregarious.

STARLINGS: Sturnidae

A group of medium-sized usually gregarious birds: many species possess brilliantly metallic plumage, greens, blues and purples predominating. Most are noisy and conspicuous.

WATTLED STARLING *Creatophora cinerea* p. 236

Identification: 8½″. Gregarious pale grey bird with a prominent whitish rump and black wings and tail. In breeding season male's head bare of feathers, skin yellow and black ; a large fleshy black wattle on forehead above bill and another smaller wattle in centre of crown; double large pendulent wattle on throat. In non-breeding season wattles disappear and head becomes feathered. Immature resembles adult but browner.

Voice: A soft but rather squeaky whistle; less noisy than many species of starlings.

Distribution and Habitat: Widely distributed throughout East and Central Africa: also in Angola and South Africa. Extremely erratic in its appearances. Its movements appear to depend on the availability of an abundance of insect life. It breeds in East Africa where good rains have fallen and insects, often but not always locusts, are plentiful. It frequents thornbush and acacia woodland, open country, and especially pasture where it associates with horses and cattle and sheep, running between their feet and catching insects disturbed by the grazing animals.

VIOLET-BACKED STARLING *Cinnyricinclus leucogaster* p. 236

Identification: $6\frac{1}{2}''$. Also commonly called the Plum-coloured and Verreaux's Starling. Upperparts and throat brilliant violet-blue, changing in some lights to crimson-purple: belly white; eyes yellow. Female and immature quite different with mottled brown upperparts, below white streaked and spotted dark brown. A bird of the tree-tops, rarely seen on the ground. Appears when trees, especially figs, are in full fruit, disappears when crop over; very gregarious.

Voice: A soft, twittering whistle of three or four notes.

Distribution and Habitat: Distributed over the greater part of the Ethiopian Region. Local resident and migrant in East and Central Africa. Frequents forested and wooded areas, open park country with scattered trees and gardens where there are fruiting trees: also in dry country areas where there are fig trees.

Allied Species: Sharpe's Starling (*Pholia sharpii*) is a bird of high tree-tops in forest or wooded country, local in Uganda, Kenya and northern Tanganyika. It resembles a male Violet-backed Starling at a distance but upperparts and throat dark metallic blue-black; below pale buff, washed rufous on abdomen.

BLUE-EARED GLOSSY STARLING *Lamprocolius chalybaeus* p. 236

Identification: $9''$. A thickset metallic green starling, golden or bluish in some lights, with a bright orange-yellow eye. Throat and chest metallic green like upperparts, merging to metallic violet on belly. Ear coverts bluish but not conspicuously so. Often perches and feeds on ground. Immature sooty black with slight green gloss. Ruppell's Long-tailed Starling differs in having a white eye and a longer, graduated tail.

Voice: A variety of deep, musical whistles and high-pitched chattering notes.

Distribution and Habitat: Common and widespread resident and partial migrant greater part Ethiopian Region. Common East and Central Africa south to Transvaal, South Africa. A locally abundant species in Kenya and Tanganyika, found both in highland and in lowland localities. Inhabits open park-like country, cultivated areas, the vicinity of human habitations and all kinds of woodland.

Allied Species: The Lesser Blue-eared Starling (*Lamprocolius chloropterus*) closely resembles the Blue-eared Starling but is smaller, 7 inches. It occurs mainly in woodland country, especially brachystegia: gregarious. It has much the same distribution as the Blue-eared Starling but is generally uncommon in the north of its range, becoming locally abundant in southern Tanganyika, Nyasaland and the Rhodesias. The Purple Glossy Starling (*Lamprocolius purpureus*) is a larger bird, 10 inches, brilliantly violet-green, greener on mantle and wings, with a very large orange eye, which is conspicuously large even in the field. It is found in small flocks in open woodland, bush and park-like country in West Africa, eastwards to Sudan, Uganda and western Kenya.

SPLENDID GLOSSY STARLING *Lamprocolius splendidus* p. 236

Identification: 12″. A mainly forest tree-top species, brilliantly metallic-green and blue with a velvety black band across the closed wing; tail velvet violet-black, broadly tipped metallic blue-green: eyes yellow. Immature much duller with little metallic gloss. In flight produces a loud swishing noise with wings. In pairs or small flocks.

Voice: Loud single or double guttural "chark" or "chark, chark" and various whistling notes.

Distribution and Habitat: Local resident West Africa, eastwards through Congo and southern Sudan to western Ethiopia, Uganda, western Kenya, western Tanganyika and north-western Northern Rhodesia; also Angola. A forest species specially in evidence when figs and other fruiting trees are in bearing. Partial migrant; in Northern Rhodesia found mainly between August and October. At Entebbe, Uganda, it is very numerous and occurs alongside Ruppell's Long-tailed Starling.

Allied Species: The Purple-headed Starling (*Lamprocolius purpureiceps*) is small, 7 inches, and occurs from West Africa to Uganda. It frequents the same fruiting trees as the Splendid Glossy Starling. It is metallic green with the crown and nape covered with short velvety deep purple feathers. The Black-breasted Starling (*Lamprocolius corruscus*), 7 inches, is dark oily green, merging to violet and black on the belly; eye bright orange. This is a bird of coastal scrub and forests in eastern Kenya, Pemba, Zanzibar and coastal districts of Tanganyika south to eastern Cape, South Africa.

RUPPELL'S LONG-TAILED STARLING

Lamprotornis purpuropterus p. 236

Identification: 13-14″. Tail long and graduated; metallic violet-blue with head and throat washed bronze; eyes creamy-white. Immature duller. Best recognised by long tail and white eye. Usually in pairs or small parties; often alights and feeds on the ground.

Voice: Various chattering calls and whistles.

Distribution and Habitat: Local resident and partial migrant southern Sudan, Eritrea and Ethiopia, south through Uganda and Kenya to

Tanganyika. Replaced by closely allied Meve's Long-tailed Starling in Nyasaland and Rhodesias. Inhabits bush and acacia country, savannah and open woodland, and cultivated areas. A common and conspicuous bird at Entebbe, Uganda.

Allied Species: Meve's Long-tailed Starling (*Lamprotornis mevesii*) is a local resident, sometimes common, in mopane woodland in Nyasaland and the Rhodesias. It differs from Ruppell's Long-tailed Starling in having head dark blue and violet without bronze sheen; rump metallic coppery-gold.

GOLDEN-BREASTED or REGAL STARLING

Cosmopsarus regius p. 236

Identification: 12-14″. Slim with long graduated tail; brilliant green-blue upperparts and throat and contrasting rich golden-yellow belly; eyes white. Immature much duller. The most beautiful of the East African starlings and the easiest to identify in the field. Gregarious, in small flocks; usually very shy and wild.

Voice: Various loud whistling and chattering calls.

Distribution and Habitat: Local resident and partial migrant Eritrea, Ethiopia and Somaliland, south through eastern Kenya and northern half of eastern Tanganyika. Inhabits dry bush and thornbush country: locally common in the Tsavo National Park in Kenya.

Allied Species: A closely related, long-tailed species, but very different in colour, is the Ashy Starling (*Cosmopsarus unicolor*): 12 inches, entirely brownish-grey with a slight greenish tinge on wings and tail. It is a bush country species found locally in Tanganyika.

REDWING STARLING *Onychognathus morio* p. 236

Identification: 12″. Thickset starling with long tail; entire plumage glossy violet-black with flight feathers conspicuously rufous in flight. Female has head, neck and throat washed grey. Eyes red. Immature sooty-black with little gloss. Occurs in pairs or flocks.

Voice: Loud, drawn-out whistles "tee—jeeoooo" and shorter piping calls: often calls on the wing.

Distribution and Habitat: Local resident from Sudan and Ethiopia, south through East and Central Africa and Portuguese East Africa to South Africa. Occurs usually on rocky hills, precipices and cliffs, wooded and forest areas and in cultivation. In Nairobi, Kenya, it is found on buildings in the city centre.

SUPERB STARLING *Spreo superbus* p. 236

Identification: 7″. A plump, short-tailed starling; metallic blue and green, head blackish; belly bright rufous-chestnut; narrow white band across breast; under tail-coverts and below wings white; eyes pale yellow. Immature duller. Hildebrandt's and Shelley's Starlings also have chestnut-red bellies but lack white breast band and under tail-coverts and below wings rufous. Feeds mainly on the ground, often below or near acacia trees.

Voice: Various chattering and whistling notes: song a sustained warbling. Sometimes mimics other bird calls.

Distribution and Habitat: Widespread resident and partial migrant, often common, Somaliland and Ethiopia, south through Kenya to southern Tanganyika. Occurs in thornbush and acacia country and the vicinity of human dwellings. Gregarious and usually tame and fearless of man.

HILDEBRANDT'S STARLING *Spreo hildebrandti* p. 236

Identification: 7″. Dark metallic violet-blue with belly, under wings and under tail-coverts rufous. Eyes orange-red. Differs from Superb Starling in lacking white below. Its eye colour is also a good field character at close quarters.

Voice: Various melodious whistles; song a series of drawn-out double whistles.

Distribution and Habitat: Local resident southern half Kenya and northern Tanganyika: commonest in the Ukamba country of Kenya. Inhabits bush and wooded savannah, riverine acacia belts and cultivated areas. Usually gregarious and like the Superb Starling commonly feeds on ground.

Allied Species: Shelley's Starling (*Spreo shelleyi*) differs in having belly dark rufous chocolate. It is a local migrant to the northern districts of Kenya, south to Voi, breeding in Ethiopia and Somaliland. It inhabits acacia-bordered dry river beds and thornbush country.

RED-BILLED OXPECKER *Buphagus erythorhynchus* p. 236

Identification: 7″. Rather slim, ash-brown birds with thick red bills and a yellow eye-ring: associated with domesticated stock and large game animals, perching upon and climbing all over the animals searching for food—ticks and blood-sucking flies.

Voice: A hissing "tssssss" and a shrill chattering call, often uttered in flight.

STARLINGS

1. **VIOLET-BACKED STARLING** page 232
   Male: Upperparts brilliant metallic violet-blue; belly white. *Female:* Not metallic; above brown; below streaked and spotted dark brown.
2. **BLUE-EARED GLOSSY STARLING** 232
   Metallic green plumage and conspicuous yellow eyes.
3. **WATTLED STARLING** 231
   In breeding plumage the bare head and wattles of adult male distinctive: whitish rump and contrasting black wings and tail.
4. **SPLENDID GLOSSY STARLING** 233
   Velvety black bands across tail and wings; yellow eyes.
5. **RUPPELL'S LONG-TAILED STARLING** 233
   Long graduated tail; white eye.
6. **RED-BILLED OXPECKER** 235
   Associated game and domestic animals; red bill; yellow eye wattle.
7. **REDWING STARLING** 234
   Conspicuous rufous flight feathers; red eyes.
8. **HILDEBRANDT'S STARLING** 235
   Under tail coverts rufous; eyes orange-red.
9. **GOLDEN-BREASTED STARLING** 234
   Long graduated tail; golden-yellow belly.
10. **SUPERB STARLING** 235
    White breast band; white under tail-coverts; eyes creamy-white.

1
♀
♂
2
3
♀
♂
4
5
6
7
8
9
10

1
♀
♂
2
♀
♂
3
♀
♂
4
♀
♂
5
♀
♂
6
♂
7
♂
8
♂
9
♀
♂
10
♂
11
♀
♂
12
♂

SUNBIRDS

1. MALACHITE SUNBIRD page 239
Male: Long central tail feathers; emerald green plumage.
Female: Below yellowish, unstreaked.

2. TACAZZE SUNBIRD 242
Male: Long central tail feathers; appears black; metallic violet above and on breast.
Female: Whitish streak each side of throat; below greyish.

3. GOLDEN-WINGED SUNBIRD 243
Male: Long central tail feathers; wings and tail edged golden-yellow.
Female: Wings and tail edged yellow.

4. BRONZY SUNBIRD 242
Male: Long central tail feathers; appears black; metallic bronze-green on body and head.
Female: Below yellowish, streaked dusky.

5. BEAUTIFUL SUNBIRD 243
Male: Long central tail feathers; scarlet breast patch bordered yellow; belly black, not metallic green, in race found East of Rift Valley.
Female: Whitish eye-stripe; yellowish-white below with trace of streaking on chest.

6. GREEN-HEADED SUNBIRD 246
Male: Metallic green head and grey belly.
Female: Like male but throat grey.

7. COLLARED SUNBIRD 247
Male: Metallic yellowish-green; violet breast band.
Female: Like male but throat yellow or greyish.

8. MARIQUA SUNBIRD 244
Male: Maroon breast band. *See* text.
Female: Greyish with buff eye stripe; heavy dusky streaks on breast.

9. EASTERN DOUBLE-COLLARED SUNBIRD 245
Male: Scarlet breast band; yellow pectoral tufts and violet or blue upper tail coverts.
Female: Dusky olive-green.

10. VARIABLE SUNBIRD 244
Male: Plumage metallic blue-green; broad purplish breast patch. Belly may be white, yellow, orange or red; *see* text.
Female: Greyish; yellowish or whitish below, unstreaked.

11. SCARLET-CHESTED SUNBIRD 246
Male: Thickset, square-tailed; cap metallic green; breast scarlet.
Female: No pale eye-stripe.

12. AMETHYST SUNBIRD 245
Male: Throat rosy-purple; cap metallic green.
Female: Pale eye-stripe.

Distribution and Habitat: Local resident and partial migrant from Somaliland and Ethiopia, south through East and Central Africa to Natal, South Africa. Numerous in many parts of Kenya, Uganda, Tanganyika and Northern Rhodesia, but very uncommon and local in Nyasaland and Southern Rhodesia. Frequents open country and farmlands; associated with domestic cattle and horses and big game.

Allied Species: The Yellow-billed Oxpecker (*Buphagus africanus*) is larger, 9 inches, with a contrasting and conspicuous pale buff rump and a heavy chrome yellow, red-tipped bill. It has a more restricted range in East and Central Africa, being absent from eastern Kenya except in the Isiolo and Nanyuki districts, and from eastern Tanganyika. Like the Red-billed Oxpecker it associates with game and domestic stock.

WHITE-EYES: Zosteropidae

A group of small greenish or yellowish-green warbler-like birds with conspicuous white rings around their eyes. Gregarious, in flocks even during the nesting season. Often associated with mixed bird parties. The classification of these birds is still unsatisfactory: different populations vary greatly and the status of some races and species is uncertain.

YELLOW WHITE-EYE *Zosterops senegalensis* p. 208

Identification: 4″. Best recognised by its very yellow underparts, powdery yellowish-green upperparts and narrow white eye ring. Immature birds slightly darker. The Green White-eye and the Kikuyu White-eye are much greener above with very broad white eye-rings and greenish flanks.

Voice: A weak, peeping flock call: song a series of soft warbling notes.

Distribution and Habitat: Local resident and partial migrant from Cameroons and Senegal, eastwards to Ethiopia and Eritrea, south through East and Central Africa to Portuguese East Africa, eastern Transvaal and Zululand, South Africa and South-West Africa. Inhabits open thornbush country and acacia and savannah woodland, brachystegia woodland, cultivated areas and gardens.

KIKUYU WHITE-EYE *Zosterops kikuyuensis* p. 208

Identification: 5″. Above bright green with a broad yellow forehead; white eye-ring large and conspicuous: below yellow on throat and centre of breast to yellowish-green on flanks. Immature duller and darker. Yellow White-eye smaller with narrow white eye-ring and very yellow below. Gregarious.

Voice: High-pitched, piping flock call; song a soft clear warble.

Distribution and Habitat: A local resident highland areas of southern half of Kenya to highlands of northern Tanganyika—Mt. Hanang, Ngorongoro, Longido, Oldeani, and Ufiome. In Kenya very common in forests of Aberdare Mts. and Mt. Kenya, and in forests around Nairobi. Inhabits highland forests, bamboos and gardens.

Allied Species: The Green White-eye (*Zosterops virens*) has a wide distribution in East and Central Africa, south to South Africa. It differs from the Kikuyu White-eye in having a very restricted yellow forehead and a smaller white eye-ring, but not a narrow eye-ring as in the Yellow White-eye.

SUNBIRDS: Nectariniidae

A distinct family of small birds with slender curved bills and, in most species, brilliant metallic plumage in males. In some species male has dull, female-like non-breeding plumage. Some females are difficult to identify in field and are best recognised by their associated males. Flight very erratic and rapid. Most species visit flowering trees, such as *Erythrina*, in which they may be observed at close quarters. The best way in which several of the rarer forest species may be seen is to wait in the vicinity of a flowering tree for the birds to appear.

MALACHITE SUNBIRD *Nectarinia famosa* p. 237

Identification: Male 9″, female 5″. Male unmistakable, bright emerald-green with long central tail feathers and yellow pectoral tufts, the latter conspicuous when bird displays. In non-breeding plumage pale brownish-grey but with long tail and green wing coverts and rump. Female and immature brownish-grey, paler, yellowish and unstreaked below. Female Golden-winged Sunbird has yellow-edged wings and tail; female Bronzy Sunbird is lightly streaked olive below.

Voice: A rapid "chiii" or a harsher "chee, chee." Song a rapid, jingling warble, often of short duration.

Distribution and Habitat: Local resident with restricted migrations, highland areas Eritrea, Ethiopia and southern Sudan, south through highlands of eastern Congo, Uganda, Kenya and Tanganyika to the montane grasslands of Nyasaland and Northern Rhodesia, and the eastern border of Southern Rhodesia. Also in South Africa to the Cape

SPARROWS and WEAVERS

1. BUFFALO WEAVER page 248
Large; black; wings margined white. Female and immature paler, streaked below. Gregarious.

2. WHITE-HEADED BUFFALO WEAVER 249
Large; orange-red rump and under tail.

3. GREY-HEADED SPARROW 250
Unstreaked; rufous rump and shoulders.

4. GREY-HEADED SOCIAL WEAVER 250
Short tail; pale grey cap. Immature lacks grey cap.

5. WHITE-BROWED SPARROW-WEAVER 249
White eyebrow and rump conspicuous. Gregarious and noisy.

6. KENYA RUFOUS SPARROW 250
Upperparts streaked; black or grey chin; rufous rump.

7. CARDINAL QUELEA 260
Small, short tail, sparrow-like, male with red head. Gregarious; rank grasslands.

8. RED-BILLED QUELEA or SUDAN DIOCH 259
Sparrow-like; red bill. Very gregarious.

9. VIEILLOT'S BLACK WEAVER 255
Male: Black with pale yellow eyes.
Female and Juvenile: Dusky olive; streaked upperparts.

10. RED-HEADED WEAVER 259
Pink bill; male head and chest red. Arboreal; not gregarious.

1
♂
♀
2
3
4
5
6
♀
♂
7
♀
♂
8
♀
♂
9
♂
♀
10
♂
♀

1
2
3
4
5
6
7
8
9
10
11
12
13

WEAVERS

1. **BLACK-HEADED WEAVER** page 250
Male: Head not completely black; nape chestnut.
Female: Dull olive-brown, indistinctly streaked; below yellowish-white.

2. **LAYARD'S BLACK-HEADED WEAVER** 251
Male: Head black; no chestnut on nape.
Female: Greyish-brown with indistinct streaking; below whitish.

3. **SPEKE'S WEAVER** 251
Male: Yellow crown and mottled back.
Female: Slightly mottled olive-brown; below whitish.

4. **VITELLINE MASKED WEAVER** 252
Male: Very narrow black frontal band.
Female: Olive-yellow, streaked dusky; below yellowish.

5. **MASKED WEAVER** 252
Male: Front half of crown black.
Female: Olive; below yellowish to white on abdomen.

6. **SPECTACLED WEAVER** 255
Male: Green back; black patch around eye; black throat.
Female: No black on throat.

7. **HOLUB'S GOLDEN WEAVER** 255
Large, thickset greenish-yellow weaver, brighter yellow below with orange wash on throat.

8. **BLACK-NECKED WEAVER** 254
Black above; sides of face yellow.

9. **REICHENOW'S WEAVER** 258
Male: Black above; front half crown yellow; sides of face black.
Female: Crown completely black.

10. **GOLDEN PALM WEAVER** 254
Male: Brilliant orange head.
Female: Unstreaked greenish-yellow; below yellow.

11. **GOLDEN-BACKED WEAVER** 253
Male: Golden-yellow back and black head; no contrasting yellow collar.
Female: Streaked olive-brown; below yellowish.

12. **YELLOW-COLLARED WEAVER** 253
Male: Greenish mantle and contrasting yellow collar.
Female: Pale brown, streaked dusky; cinnamon on breast.

13. **CHESTNUT WEAVER** 253
Male: Chestnut body plumage and black head.
Female: Sparrow-like; below tawny-buff.

where it descends to sea level. In East and Central Africa inhabits bushy moorlands over 5,000 feet, montane grasslands where there are protea bushes, edges of forest and forest glades and montane scrub. In East Africa much attracted to the orange-flowered *Leonotis* bush and to red-hot pokers.

Allied Species: The Scarlet-tufted Malachite Sunbird (*Nectarinia johnstoni*) is larger (12 inches and 6 inches) with much longer tail feathers and bright red pectoral tufts in both sexes. It is confined to the alpine moorlands and upper forest edge of Mt. Kenya and the Aberdare Mts. in Kenya, Mts. Kilimanjaro and Meru and the Crater Highlands in northern Tanganyika, the Ruwenzori Mts. and the Birnga Volcanoes in Uganda and the eastern Congo, and the Nyika plateau in Nyasaland and Northern Rhodesia.

TACAZZE SUNBIRD *Nectarinia tacazze* p. 237

Identification: Male 9″, female 5½″. Large, thickset sunbird with long central tail feathers: appears black, changing in certain lights to brilliant metallic violet, glossed copper on head. Female dusky olive-grey, paler below with whitish streak down sides of throat. Immature like female but with dusky throat. Male Bronzy Sunbird appears blackish but metallic upperparts and breast coppery-green, not violet. Female Bronzy Sunbird has yellowish underparts streaked with olive.

Voice: Loud single or double "tssssp," and a sustained warbling song usually delivered from high in a tree.

Distribution and Habitat: Resident in mountain areas over 7,000 feet in Eritrea, Ethiopia, southern Sudan, eastern Uganda, Kenya and northern Tanganyika. Inhabits mountain forests and marshy glades in forest, and in gardens and the vicinity of human habitations at high levels. Much attracted to the flowers of red-hot pokers and often visits flowers in gardens. Common in the Kenya Highlands on both sides of the Rift Valley.

BRONZY SUNBIRD *Nectarinia kilimensis* p. 237

Identification: Male 9″, female 5½″. Black-looking sunbird with long central tail feathers. Appears metallic bronze-green in a good light. Female olive-grey with dark ear-coverts and streaky yellowish underparts: immature like female but throat dusky. Tacazze Sunbird male is metallic violet, not bronze-green, and female is unstreaked pale grey below. Malachite Sunbird female is yellowish below without streaks.

Voice: A very distinct, loud "chee—choo, wee" usually uttered twice: also a brief warbling song.

Distribution and Habitat: Resident, locally common, north-eastern Congo, Uganda, and the highlands of Kenya, Tanganyika, Nyasaland, Northern Rhodesia, the eastern border of Southern Rhodesia and Angola. In Uganda occurs as low as 2,500 feet, but elsewhere a highlands bird, commonest between 5,000 and 7,000 feet. Occurs in wooded areas, cultivation, gardens, near human habitations and in mountain scrub. Much attracted to flowering *Erythrina* trees. A common garden bird in Nairobi and Entebbe, East Africa.

BEAUTIFUL SUNBIRD *Nectarinia pulchella* p. 237

Identification: Male 6″, female 4½″. A small long-tailed sunbird, shining metallic green with a scarlet breast patch bordered on each side by yellow; belly entirely black in race found east of Rift Valley, metallic green in that which occurs west of the Rift. Male in non-breeding plumage drab grey, whitish below with retained metallic wing-coverts and rump, and long tail feathers. Female ash-grey with whitish eye-stripe; below yellowish-white with trace of streaking on breast. Immature like female but throat blackish.

Voice: A sharp, clear "tsp" and a soft warbling song.

Distribution and Habitat: Local resident, with restricted migratory movements, from Senegal and Sierra Leone, eastwards to Sudan, Eritrea, Ethiopia and Somaliland, southwards through Uganda and Kenya to southern Tanganyika, but not in coastal districts. Inhabits bush country, savannah and open woodlands and stands of acacia. Especially attracted to flowering *Acacia* and *Delonix elata* trees.

Allied Species: The Red-chested Sunbird (*Nectarinia erythrocerca*) 6 inches, 5 inches, is long-tailed in male, metallic greenish-blue with a maroon red breast-band and a black belly; female greyish-brown with heavy chest streaks. Occurs in vicinity of water, for example around Lake Victoria where it is a common sunbird, in western Kenya, Uganda, the southern Sudan, eastern Congo and northern Tanganyika west of the Rift Valley.

GOLDEN-WINGED SUNBIRD *Nectarinia reichenowi* p. 237

Identification: Male 9″, female 6″. Male unmistakable, brilliant metallic reddish-bronze and copper with yellow-edged wings and tail; long tailed: non-breeding male has most of metallic body plumage replaced by dull black. Female olive above, yellowish below, also with yellow edged wings and tail; immature like female but underparts darker. Yellow-edged wings and tail distinguish species in all plumages.

Voice: A variety of liquid, clear "tweep" and "tssssp" calls and a warbling song.

Distribution and Habitat: Local resident highlands over 5,000 feet in Kivu district of Congo, Mt. Elgon, Uganda and the highlands of Kenya and northern Tanganyika. Inhabits moorland, mountain bush and edges of forest: much attracted by stands of the bushy orange-flowered *Leonotis*. Males have curious slow, zig-zag display flight among bushes, when yellow wings and tail are very conspicuous.

VARIABLE SUNBIRD *Cinnyris venustus* p. 237

Identification: 4″. Male bright metallic blue-green with broad purplish-blue chest patch; belly yellow more or less washed orange (white in Kenya Northern Frontier and coastal race; orange-red in western Uganda and Congo race); pectoral tufts yellow and orange-red. Female and immature olive-grey, white or yellowish-white below, unstreaked. The Collared Sunbird is yellowish-green and lacks the broad purplish chest patch.

Voice: Short "tssp" calls and a longer churring call. Song a soft warble.

Distribution and Habitat: Local resident and partial migrant from sea level to over 8,000 feet, Somaliland, Eritrea, Ethiopia, southern Sudan, south through eastern Congo, Uganda, Kenya and Tanganyika, Portuguese East Africa, Nyasaland, Northern Rhodesia and locally in Southern Rhodesia. Also in West Africa and Angola. A common species in East African gardens. Frequents bush country of all sorts, edges of forests, cultivation and gardens, and rank vegetation near water. Attracted especially to flowers of orange *Leonotis* and to various flowering *Acacias*.

MARIQUA SUNBIRD *Cinnyris mariquensis* p. 237

Identification: 5½″. Male metallic green, slightly coppery in tint with maroon breast band and black belly. Female greyish-brown with pale buff eye-stripe; below yellowish with heavy breast streaks; immature like female but throat black. The Red-chested Sunbird resembles this species but has bluish-green upperparts and elongated central tail feathers.

Voice: A clear, loud "tssp, tssp" and a warbling song.

Distribution and Habitat: Local resident with restricted migratory movements Ethiopia, Eritrea, and Somaliland south through Uganda, Kenya and Tanganyika to the Rhodesias and the drier areas of Zululand and Transvaal, South Africa. Mainly a bird of savannah and acacia woodlands, cultivated areas and scrub.

Allied Species: The Little Purple-banded Sunbird (*Cinnyris bifasciatus*) closely resembles the Mariqua Sunbird but is smaller, 4 inches. It occurs locally in East and Central Africa, south to Zululand: also Angola. It is common in coastal districts of Kenya, Tanganyika and Portuguese East Africa.

EASTERN DOUBLE-COLLARED SUNBIRD

Cinnyris mediocris p. 237

Identification: Male bright metallic green; upper tail coverts blue or violet-blue; narrow line violet-blue at base of throat, followed by scarlet band across chest; belly olive; conspicuous yellow pectoral tufts. Female and immature dusky olive-green, darker below.

Voice: A clear, sharp "tssp, tssp, tssp," frequently uttered; a clear warbling song.

Distribution and Habitat: Local resident highland areas over 5,000 feet Kenya, Tanganyika, south to mountain ranges of Nyasaland, Northern Rhodesia and western Portuguese East Africa. A highlands species frequenting forest, scrub and gardens: much attracted to flowers of *Leonotis* and red-hot pokers.

Allied Species: The Tanganyika, Nyasaland, Rhodesian and Angola races of the Southern Double-collared Sunbird (*Cinnyris chalybeus*) are found in brachystegia woodland and scrub, and not in mountain forest: best recognised by pale wings and non-metallic grey rump; upper tail coverts may be grey or metallic green or violet. It is possible that these birds constitute a full species and that the South African races of *Cinnyris chalybeus*, which have metallic backs, are conspecific with *Cinnyris mediocris*. The Northern Double-collared Sunbird (*Cinnyris reichenowi*) is a small forest species, 4 inches, found below 7,500 feet. It may be recognised by its very wide and dark scarlet breast-band which extends on to the belly; upper tail coverts violet. It occurs locally on mountains southern Sudan, eastern Congo, Uganda and western Kenya east to Mt. Kenya. The Olive-bellied Sunbird (*Cinnyris chlorophygius*) is a West African species which is common in the forests of southern Sudan, Uganda and north-western Tanganyika. It has a broad bright scarlet breast band and very large and conspicuous yellow pectoral tufts.

AMETHYST SUNBIRD *Chalcomitra amethystina* p. 237

Identification: 5″. A square-tailed, velvety black sunbird with a metallic green cap and a rosy-purple throat: female olive-brown with whitish eye-stripe, heavily streaked on breast and flanks; immature like female but has black throat. Female scarlet-chested Sunbird has no eye-stripe, and is browner above and heavily mottled rather than streaked below.

Voice: A variety of loud "cheep" or "tsssp" calls and a loud warbling song.

Distribution and Habitat: Local resident and partial migrant southern Sudan, Kenya, Tanganyika, Portuguese East Africa, Nyasaland and the Rhodesias: also in Angola and South Africa. A common species, often called the Black Sunbird, found in a variety of habitats from mountain forest to coastal scrub and mangrove swamps, savannah and brachystegia woodland, bush country and cultivation.

SCARLET-CHESTED SUNBIRD *Chalcomitra senegalensis* p. 237

Identification: 6″. A rather thickset, square-tailed velvety brown or black sunbird with a metallic green cap and throat and a vivid scarlet chest. Female brown without eye-stripe, heavily mottled below; immature like female but throat dusky. Female Amethyst Sunbird has pale eye-stripe and is streaked below.

Voice: A variety of loud, clear notes, the commonest of which is a descending "tssp, teee, tee": song a loud trilling warble.

Distribution and Habitat: Local resident and partial migrant Senegal eastwards to Sudan, south through eastern Congo, Uganda, Kenya, Tanganyika, Portuguese East Africa, Nyasaland and Rhodesias: also in Angola and Natal and eastern Cape, South Africa. A common and conspicuous species found in a variety of habitats from edges of forests, wooded areas, savannah and park-like country to bush, river line acacias and cultivated areas: often visits gardens.

Allied Species: The Somali Scarlet-chested or Hunter's Sunbird (*Chalcomitra hunteri*) differs in having a velvet-black, not metallic green, throat and a metallic violet rump. It occurs in bush country in Somaliland, eastern Ethiopia, eastern Kenya and north-eastern Tanganyika.

GREEN-HEADED SUNBIRD *Cyanomitra verticalis* p. 237

Identification: 6″. A mainly non-metallic olive-green sunbird with a grey belly and a metallic green head and throat: female resembles male but has throat grey like remainder underparts. Immature resembles female but lacks metallic green crown and throat is dusky.

Voice: A double note call "tee-cheek, tee-cheek": also a soft warbling song.

Distribution and Habitat: Local resident Uganda, western Kenya east to Mt. Kenya, south through Tanganyika to Nyasaland and Northern Rhodesia. Also in West Africa and Angola. Inhabits evergreen forests, wooded areas and riverine forest and cultivation near forests. Much attracted to flowering *Erythrina* trees.

Allied Species: Many races of the Olive Sunbird (*Cyanomitra olivacea*) occur in East and Central Africa in forested and woodland country. This is a medium-sized, rather slim sunbird, 5-6 inches, with entirely non-metallic olive-green plumage, paler below, usually with yellow pectoral tufts. It occurs both in tree-tops and in forest undergrowth: one of its best field characters is its habit of constantly flicking its wings when perched.

COLLARED SUNBIRD *Anthreptes collaris* p. 237

Identification: 4″. A tiny, thickset sunbird with a short tail; metallic yellowish-green above and on throat, a narrow violet breast band and yellow underparts. Female and immature are also metallic on upper-parts but not on throat. The male Variable Sunbird resembles this species but has the plumage metallic blue-green and a very broad dark violet breast patch.

Voice: A weak "tsssp," frequently uttered and a soft warbling song.

Distribution and Habitat: Widely distributed throughout most of the Ethiopian Region in suitable localities. In East Africa very common in Uganda and in coastal districts of Kenya and Tanganyika. Equally common locally Nyasaland and Rhodesias. Frequents forests, woodland, scrub, bush country and in coastal districts common in mangrove swamps: often visits gardens.

Allied Species: The Kenya Violet-backed Sunbird (*Anthreptes orientalis*), 6 inches, occurs in dry bush country of Somaliland, southern and eastern Ethiopia, Kenya and Tanganyika. The male is metallic violet-blue above and on chin; underparts white with pale yellow pectoral tufts: looks not unlike a tiny Violet-backed Starling: female grey above with white eye-stripe and violet-black tail. The Violet-backed Sunbird (*Anthreptes longuemarei*) is larger and greyish below in male, yellowish below in female. It is a West African species which occurs eastwards to Uganda, western Kenya, western Tanganyika, Nyasaland and the Rhodesias.

TREE CREEPERS: Certhiidae

A group of small tree-climbing birds of white or buff spotted brown plumage. Very woodpecker-like in their general actions. Only one species found in Africa.

SPOTTED CREEPER *Salpornis spilonota* p. 145

Identification: 6″. A small woodpecker-like bird with white-spotted brown plumage and white-spotted wings and tail; bill thin and curved. Obtains its food from bark of trees, flying to the base and climbing upwards; single or in pairs.

Voice: A shrill whistle of several notes run together and a single "tseee," not unlike a tit's call.

Distribution and Habitat: An uncommon local resident East Africa, Nyasaland and the Rhodesias; also Portuguese East Africa, Angola, northern South Africa and West Africa. Inhabits park-like country, savannah and acacia bush and brachystegia woodland: very uncommon Kenya and Uganda, more frequent in the brachystegia country of Tanganyika and the Rhodesias.

WEAVERS, SPARROWS, WAXBILLS and Allies: Ploceidae

This is one of the largest bird families in Africa. Most but not all are seed-eaters with short heavy bills. They resemble true finches in general appearance but have ten, not nine primaries. Finches build open nests; weavers and allies build domed structures with a side, top or bottom entrance. Many species highly gregarious, nesting in colonies. Some have female-like non-breeding plumage.

BUFFALO WEAVER *Bulbalornis albirostris* p. 240

Identification: 10″. A very large thickset weaver, black except for white-margined flight feathers and white bases to feathers of body plumage. Bill dull red or whitish-horn; eye brown. Female and immature with streaky underparts. Gregarious, building large stick nests close together in baobab or acacia trees. Male of Vieillot's Black Weaver also black but much smaller and with a conspicuous creamy-white eye.

Voice: Very noisy birds, especially at nesting colonies, with a variety of loud, falsetto croaking and chattering calls.

Distribution and Habitat: Local resident and partial migrant from Nigeria and Senegal, eastwards to Sudan, Ethiopia, Eritrea and Somaliland, south through Uganda, Kenya and Tanganyika to the Rhodesias; also in Angola and South Africa. Inhabits acacia woodland, savannah country especially where there are baobab trees and thornbush country. Locally common in the arid Northern Frontier district of Kenya.

WHITE-HEADED BUFFALO WEAVER *Dinemellia dinemelli*

p. 240

Identification: 9″. A large, heavy brown and white weaver, rather parrot-like in general appearance, with a most conspicuous orange-red rump and under tail coverts, especially noticeable during flight. Usually seen in pairs or small flocks; frequently feeds on ground below acacia trees and often associated with Superb and Hildebrandt's Starlings.

Voice: A harsh, parrot-like call and a series of chattering notes.

Distribution and Habitat: Local resident Somaliland, Ethiopia and Sudan, south through Uganda and Kenya to Tanganyika. Inhabits acacia woodland, dry bush and thornbush scrub. One of the most conspicuous birds of the dry thornbush country of Kenya.

WHITE-BROWED SPARROW WEAVER *Plocepasser mahali*

p. 240

Identification: 6″. Also called the Stripe-breasted and Black-billed Sparrow Weaver. Upperparts light brown, darker on crown with conspicuous white eyebrow and white rump; below white. Gregarious in small flocks and colonies. Immature resembles adult.

Voice: Noisy birds, especially at nesting colonies, uttering a "chuk, chuk" call and various loud chatterings: male's song not unlike that of Superb Starling.

Distribution and Habitat: Local resident, often common, Ethiopia, southern Sudan and southern Somaliland, south through Uganda, Kenya and Tanganyika to Nyasaland and the Rhodesias. Also in Portuguese East Africa, Angola and South Africa. Found in dry bush and acacia country and in Rhodesia in thorn scrub and mopane country. Locally very common in Northern Frontier Province of Kenya.

Allied Species: Donaldson-Smith's Sparrow Weaver (*Plocepasser donaldsoni*), 6 inches, is an uncommon bird of northern Kenya and southern Ethiopia, inhabiting dry bush and acacia country. It is buff-brown, paler below, with a white rump. It is abundant in the vicinity of Isiolo, northern Kenya.

GREY-HEADED SOCIAL WEAVER *Pseudonigrita arnaudi* p. 240

Identification: 5″. A rather short-tailed greyish-brown weaver with a pale dove-grey cap. Immature browner and has cap buff.

Voice: A short piping call and a rather squeaky chatter.

Distribution and Habitat: Local resident western and southern Sudan and southern Ethiopia, south through Uganda and Kenya to northern and central Tanganyika. Inhabits dry thornbush and acacia country; gregarious, nesting in scattered colonies.

KENYA RUFOUS SPARROW *Passer rufocinctus* p. 240

Identification: 6″. Resembles brightly coloured house sparrow; male with grey crown, streaked back, black chin and bright rufous rump; female and immature paler and duller. Grey-headed Sparrow has no streaks on upperparts.

Voice: Typical sparrow type chirp.

Distribution and Habitat: Local resident, common, from central Kenya to north-eastern Tanganyika. Inhabits upland open country where there are whistling thorn bushes in which it nests: often around human habitations and cattle sheds. Habits much the same as a house sparrow.

GREY-HEADED SPARROW *Passer griseus* p. 240

Identification: 6″. Head grey; mantle tawny brown, not streaked; rump and shoulders bright rufous. Immature duller with trace of streaking on back.

Voice: Typical sparrow type chirping.

Distribution and Habitat: Local resident Kenya, Uganda and Tanganyika to Nyasaland and Northern Rhodesia; also in West Africa, Angola, the Congo and Portuguese East Africa. Usually associated with human dwellings, but also occurs in bush country and in cultivated areas.

Allied Species: The Chestnut Sparrow (*Sorella eminibey*) is a very small sparrow, 4½ inches, the male of which is entirely dark chestnut; female greyish with indistinct streaks on mantle. It occurs in arid bush and acacia country in the Sudan and Ethiopia, south through eastern Uganda and Kenya to northern Tanganyika.

BLACK-HEADED WEAVER *Ploceus cucullatus* p. 241

Identification: 7″. A thickset black-headed yellow weaver with chestnut hind crown and nape; broad yellow collar on hind neck; mantle mottled black and yellow; below, throat black, remainder underparts yellow, washed rufous on breast and flanks. Layard's Black-headed Weaver is smaller and has head and nape completely black, with no chestnut on crown or nape. Female and immature olive-brown above, indistinctly streaked; yellowish-white below. Gregarious, breeding in colonies in trees and palms, often alongside human dwellings: frequently associated with Vieillot's Black Weaver and mixed colonies of the two species are not uncommon.

Voice: A noisy chatter at nesting colonies.

Distribution and Habitat: Local resident, often abundant, West Africa eastwards to Sudan, Congo, Eritrea, Ethiopia, Uganda and western Kenya. Occurs in forested and cultivated areas, nesting nearly always in vicinity of human habitations. Abundant in many parts of Uganda.

LAYARD'S BLACK-HEADED WEAVER *Ploceus nigriceps*

p. 241

Identification: 6½″. Sometimes called Spotted-backed Weaver. A black-headed yellow and black weaver without chestnut on hind crown and nape; otherwise resembles Black-headed Weaver with which it may be conspecific. Female and immature brownish-grey with indistinct streaking; below dull yellowish-white. Gregarious, breeding in colonies. This species and the Golden Palm Weaver are the two common weavers on the Kenya coast.

Voice: A loud chattering at nesting colonies; also a single harsh "zeet."

Distribution and Habitat: Local resident and partial migrant southern Somaliland south through Kenya and Tanganyika to Portuguese East Africa, Nyasaland and the Rhodesias. Also in south-western Uganda, the eastern Congo and South Africa. Frequents coastal bush, open woodland, vegetation near water and the vicinity of human dwellings.

SPEKE'S WEAVER *Ploceus spekei*

p. 241

Identification: 6″. Yellow, with a dusky mottled back, a yellow crown and contrasting black face and chin. Female and immature upperparts olive-brown slightly mottled; below white, washed yellowish-buff on throat and breast. Gregarious, breeds in colonies, often in acacia trees.

Voice: Usual weaver chatter at nesting colonies and a sharp "teep."

Distribution and Habitat: Local resident and partial migrant Somaliland and Ethiopia, south through Kenya to north-eastern Tanganyika. Inhabits lightly wooded areas, cultivation, riverine acacias and vicinity buildings and houses. A common bird in the eastern highlands of Kenya, including Nairobi.

MASKED WEAVER *Ploceus intermedius* p. 241

Identification: 5½″. Mainly yellow weaver with an olive-green, indistinctly streaked mantle; face and front half of crown black. The closely allied Vitelline Masked Weaver has the black on the crown restricted to a very narrow frontal band. Female, male in non-breeding dress and immature lack black on head, upperparts more olive and a yellow stripe over eye; below yellowish to white on abdomen. Gregarious, breeding in dense colonies; nest construction very different from that of the Vitelline Masked Weaver, made of grass stems, spherical with a short spout. The Vitelline Masked Weaver is less gregarious and its onion-shaped nest, constructed of blades of grass, has a large bottom side entrance and no spout.

Voice: The usual weaver chattering calls at nesting colonies but less noisy than many other weavers.

Distribution and Habitat: Local resident, with restricted spasmodic migrations during non-breeding season; occurs south-eastern Sudan, Ethiopia, Somaliland, south through Uganda, Kenya and Tanganyika to Nyasaland and the Rhodesias. Also in Portuguese East Africa, Angola and South Africa. In north of range generally a bird of dry thornbush country but also occurs in acacia woodland and savannah; in the south it is largely confined to the vicinity of water.

VITELLINE MASKED WEAVER *Ploceus vitellinus* p. 241

Identification: 5½″. Male closely resembles Masked Weaver but crown mainly chestnut with very narrow black frontal band. Female, male in non-breeding dress and immature olive-yellow above, distinctly streaked on mantle; below yellowish. Much less gregarious than Masked Weaver and single pairs often nest alone. Nest construction a good field character for distinguishing these two weavers—see under Masked Weaver.

Voice: Soft chattering calls and a "tsssp" call-note.

Distribution and Habitat: Local resident and partial migrant in non-breeding season from Senegal eastwards through Sudan to Ethiopia, Eritrea and Somaliland; south through Uganda and Kenya to northern Tanganyika. A bird of thick bush and arid thorn scrub, visiting cultivated areas in non-breeding season. This is one of the common dry country weavers in Kenya.

Allied Species: The Little Weaver (*Ploceus luteolus*) has much the same distribution and habitat preference as the Vitelline Masked Weaver. It is a small weaver, 4½ inches, yellowish-green, yellower below, with the front half of the crown, face and throat black; female and immature lack the black face and are less yellow.

YELLOW-COLLARED WEAVER *Ploceus capitalis* p. 241

Identification: 6″. Male, head and throat black; conspicuous yellow hind neck band and yellowish-green mantle; below, chestnut on breast and flanks to yellow on belly. The Golden-backed Weaver has black extending from crown to nape and entire mantle is yellow. Female and immature pale brown above, streaked dusky; below white, washed cinnamon on breast and flanks. Gregarious, nearly always near water, especially papyrus and reed beds.

Voice: Various churring call-notes, typical of weavers in flocks.

Distribution and Habitat: Local resident Eritrea, western Ethiopia and southern Sudan, Uganda, western Kenya and north-western Tanganyika: also occurs in West Africa. Inhabits swamps and lake-shore and adjacent cultivation and forest edge. A common bird around Lake Victoria where it nests in colonies in reed beds alongside the closely allied Golden-backed Weaver.

GOLDEN-BACKED WEAVER *Ploceus jacksoni* p. 241

Identification: 6″. Male, a black-headed weaver, the black extending on to the nape, with a golden-yellow mantle; chestnut and yellow below. In the Yellow-collared Weaver black does not extend on to nape; a well-defined yellow hind collar contrasts with the yellowish-green mantle. Female and immature upperparts olive-brown, streaked dusky; below yellow to white on belly. Gregarious, breeding in colonies over or near water.

Voice: Usual weaver type calls at nesting colonies.

Distribution and Habitat: Local resident south-eastern Sudan, Uganda, western Kenya to central Tanganyika. Frequents shores of lakes, swamps and larger rivers. Common locally on Lake Victoria and breeds in mixed colonies alongside Yellow-collared Weaver.

CHESTNUT WEAVER *Ploceus rubiginosus* p. 241

Identification: $6\frac{1}{2}$″. Male very distinct, bright chestnut with black head and throat. Female and male in non-breeding plumage sparrow-like, brownish-grey streaked black above; below tawny buff to white on throat and belly. Immature like female but tinged rufous. Very gregarious, breeding in dense colonies in acacia trees.

Voice: Usual weaver type chattering calls at nesting colonies.

Distribution and Habitat: Local resident, partial migrant in non-breeding season, Ethiopia, Eritrea, Somaliland and south-eastern Sudan, south through north-eastern Uganda and Kenya to central Tanganyika. Common in dry bush country in Kenya but appearances spasmodic. Inhabits arid bush country and acacia woodlands, entering cultivated areas where wheat is grown during non-breeding season.

GOLDEN PALM WEAVER *Ploceus bojeri* p. 241

Identification: 6″. An entirely yellow weaver with a brilliant orange head; washed chestnut on chest. Female unstreaked greenish-yellow; below yellow; eye dark brown. Gregarious but sometimes encountered in single pairs.

Voice: A low-pitched weaver chattering.

Distribution and Habitat: Local resident southern Somaliland, south through extreme eastern Kenya to north-eastern Tanganyika. A common species and one of the most noticeable weavers on the Kenya coast, breeding in small colonies in coconut palms and in bushes in coastal scrub.

Allied Species: The Taveta Golden Weaver (*Ploceus castaneiceps*) lacks the brilliant orange crown, which is washed chestnut with a patch of chestnut on the nape: female olive-brown with dusky mantle streaking; yellowish-buff below. It occurs in south-eastern Kenya and north-eastern Tanganyika. The Golden Weaver (*Ploceus subaureus*) resembles a dull edition of the Golden Palm Weaver, the head being pale dull chestnut, not bright orange. Female yellowish-olive streaked darker above, lemon-yellow below; eyes pink. Found in eastern Kenya and Tanganyika, south through Portuguese East Africa and Nyasaland to South Africa. The Orange Weaver (*Ploceus aurantius*) is an orange-yellow weaver with an olive back and a black spot in front of the eye. Female olive above, faintly streaked, whitish below. A water-frequenting species common locally on Lake Victoria. It ranges from West Africa to Uganda, Kisumu in Kenya and north-western Tanganyika.

BLACK-NECKED WEAVER *Hyphanturgus nigricollis* p. 241

Identification: 6″. Upperparts, wings and tail black, contrasting with yellow underparts. Male has crown and face yellow and chin black; female has crown black and a yellow eye stripe; entire underparts yellow. Immature like female but greenish above. Occurs usually in pairs; not gregarious, shy and retiring. Reichenow's Weaver is also black above but has sides of face black, not yellow.

Voice: A curious vibrating "teee, teee."

Distribution and Habitat: Uncommon local resident West Africa eastwards to Ethiopia, Uganda and Kenya, south to south and central Tanganyika. Found both in forest country and in thick bush and scrub.

SPECTACLED WEAVER *Hyphanturgus ocularis* p. 241

Identification: 6″. A green-backed weaver with yellowish-green wings and tail, yellow underparts and a black patch around eye: male has black chin, female orange-rufous. Occurs singly or in pairs, shy.

Voice: Usually a silent bird, sometimes calling weakly "tss, tss, tss, tss, tss, tss" or a single metallic "peeet."

Distribution and Habitat: Local resident in small numbers West Africa to Ethiopia, south Uganda, Kenya, Tanganyika, Portuguese East Africa, Nyasaland and the Rhodesias to South Africa. Inhabits forested areas, acacia woodland, riverine forest and rank vegetation near streams and lakes.

HOLUB'S GOLDEN WEAVER *Xanthophilus xanthops* p. 241

Identification: 8″. A large thickset greenish-yellow weaver, brighter yellow below and washed orange on throat and upper breast. Female and immature slightly duller than male; eye pale creamy-yellow. Found singly, in pairs or small parties, not gregarious.

Voice: A harsh, sparrow-like chirping call.

Distribution and Habitat: Local resident West Africa, Angola and Congo to Uganda, Kenya, Tanganyika, northern Portuguese East Africa, Nyasaland, the Rhodesias and South Africa. Inhabits a variety of country where there is plenty of rank vegetation, including cultivation and gardens, woodlands, the vicinity of swamps and marshes.

VIEILLOT'S BLACK WEAVER *Melanopteryx nigerrimus* p. 240

Identification: 7″. Male entirely black with conspicuous creamy-white eye; female and immature dusky-olive, streaked on upperparts. Gregarious, nesting in colonies in trees, often near human habitations.

Voice: A typical weaver chattering at nesting colonies.

Distribution and Habitat: A West African species resident eastwards to southern Sudan, Uganda, western Kenya and western Tanganyika. Inhabits forested and wooded areas and cultivation.

GROSBEAK, WEAVER, MALIMBES, BISHOPS and WIDOW-BIRDS

1. LONG-TAILED WIDOW-BIRD page 263
Male: Long tail and red and buff shoulders.
Female: Sparrow-like, streaked dusky above and below.

2. JACKSON'S WIDOW-BIRD 263
Male: Black plumage and thick, black decurved tail.
Female: Sparrow-like, streaked dusky above and below.

3. GROSBEAK WEAVER 259
Male: Black plumage, heavy bill, white wing and forehead patches.
Female: Rusty-brown with dark streaks on breast.

4. RED-COLLARED WIDOW-BIRD 262
Male: Black plumage and straight tail. NOTE: Red absent or restricted to crescent-shaped breast patch in some races.
Female: Sparrow-like; washed yellowish on chest.

5. WHITE-WINGED WIDOW-BIRD 262
Male: Moderately long tail, black plumage and white wing patch.
Female: Sparrow-like.

6. YELLOW BISHOP 261
Male: Bright yellow rump and shoulders; crown black.
Female: Sparrow-like with yellowish-brown rump.

7. CRESTED MALIMBE 258
Chest deep crimson-red.

8. BLACK-WINGED BISHOP 261
Male: Black wings and tail.
Female: Sparrow-like; yellowish eye-stripe.

9. FAN-TAILED WIDOW-BIRD 262
Male: Black with orange-red shoulders and bluish-white bill.
Female: Sparrow-like with black shoulders.

10. ZANZIBAR RED BISHOP 261
Male: Black underparts.
Female: Sparrow-like.

11. RED-HEADED MALIMBE 258
Underparts completely black, no red on chest.

12. RED BISHOP 260
Male: Pale brown wings and tail; black forehead.
Female: Sparrow-like.

1
2
3
4
5
6
7
8
9
10
11
12
♂
♂
♂
♂
♂
♂
♂
♂
♂
♂
♂

1
2
3
4
5
6
7
8
9
10
11
12
13
14
15
16

WHYDAHS, WAXBILLS, FINCHES and BUNTINGS

1. **PIN-TAILED WHYDAH** page 274
   Male: Black and white plumage, long black tail and red bill.
   Female: Buff band down centre of crown and red bill.
2. **FISCHER'S STRAW-TAILED WHYDAH** 267
   Male: Long, straw-like central pairs tail feathers and cream cap.
   Female: Reddish-brown crown and pink bill.
3. **PARADISE WHYDAH** 268
   Male: Unmistakable tail and black, chestnut and buff plumage.
   Female: Cream or white band down centre of crown and black bill.
4. **GREEN-WINGED PYTILIA** 264
   Male: General green upperparts; red face; dark red tail.
   Female: Green above with deep red rump and tail; no red on face.
5. **AFRICAN FIRE FINCH** 265
   Male: Bill blue-grey; black under tail coverts.
   Female: Duller and greyer; bill grey.
6. **RED-BILLED FIRE FINCH** 265
   Male: Bill rosy-red; under tail coverts pale brown.
   Female: Duller and browner; bill pink.
7. **CUT-THROAT** 264
   Male: Conspicuous crimson band on throat.
   Female: Lacks throat band.
8. **RED-CHEEKED CORDON-BLEU** 266
   Male: Conspicuous crimson cheek patch.
   Female: Duller; lacks crimson cheek patch.
9. **BRONZE MANNIKIN** 264
   Dusky head and pale-grey bill.
10. **YELLOW-BELLIED WAXBILL** 266
    Black and red bill; crimson rump.
11. **WAXBILL** 266
    Red bill and red streak through eye.
12. **BRIMSTONE CANARY** 268
    Pale coloured bill and bright yellow underparts.
13. **YELLOW-RUMPED SEED EATER** 269
    Yellow rump.
14. **STREAKY SEED EATER** 269
    Conspicuous whitish eye-stripe; rump same colour as remainder upperparts.
15. **GOLDEN-BREASTED BUNTING** 270
    Rufous back; golden-yellow breast.
16. **CINNAMON-BREASTED ROCK BUNTING** 270
    Reddish-brown belly.

REICHENOW'S WEAVER *Othyphantes reichenowi* p. 241

Identification: 6". Upperparts blackish; male with front half of crown rich golden-yellow; ear-coverts black; female has crown and ear-coverts black; underparts both sexes bright yellow. Immature like female but upperparts dusky-olive with dark streaks. Usually in pairs or small parties, not gregarious. The Black-necked Weaver has a black mantle, but face yellow and male with a black throat patch.

Voice: A sparrow-like chirp and a brief chattering song.

Distribution and Habitat: Local resident highlands over 4,000 feet southern Ethiopia, Kenya west to Mt. Elgon and northern Tanganyika. Inhabits edges of forests, moorland scrub, wooded areas, cultivation and the vicinity of human habitations.

CRESTED MALIMBE *Malimbus malimbicus* p. 256

Identification: 7". A thickset, black forest weaver with a square-crested head and throat deep crimson-red; female resembles male but crest shorter: immature duller. The Red-headed Malimbe is black with orange-red on the crown, not deep crimson, and its underparts are completely black. Inhabits tree-tops in forests, singly or in pairs: not gregarious but often members of mixed bird parties.

Voice: A low musical whistle and various short chirping calls.

Distribution and Habitat: A West African species which extends to western Uganda where it is resident and locally common in the rain forests. Relatively abundant in the Bwamba forest, western Uganda.

RED-HEADED MALIMBE *Malimbus rubricollis* p. 256

Identification: 7". Crown, nape and sides of neck bright scarlet red; remainder plumage black. Female resembles male but has black forehead; immature like adult but duller. The Crested Malimbe has dark crimson-red crown and throat and a square crest. Forest tree-top bird, hunting among branches like a large tit; not gregarious, usually in pairs but often members of mixed bird parties in forest.

Voice: Low wheezy and chirping call-notes, but usually silent.

Distribution and Habitat: Local resident forest areas southern Sudan, Uganda and western Kenya in the Kakamega forest. A West African species also distributed through Congo and northern Angola. Inhabits forest tree-tops and the vines and creepers hanging from forest trees.

GROSBEAK WEAVER *Amblyospiza albifrons* p. 256

Identification: 7″. A large, heavy swamp-haunting weaver with a thick bill. Male slate-black with white patch on forehead and white wing patch; southern and western race brownish on head. Female and immature rusty-brown with dark streaked underparts. Often seen perched on bulrushes in swamps and marshes. In small parties.

Voice: A short, low whistle and a brief bubbling song.

Distribution and Habitat: Local resident and partial migrant throughout East and Central Africa, but uncommon Southern Rhodesia: also in West and South Africa, Angola and Portuguese East Africa. Inhabits swamps and dense vegetation near water and swampy forests; visits cultivation.

RED-HEADED WEAVER *Anaplectes melanotis* p. 240

Identification: 6″. Male easily recognised by bright red head, mantle and chest, and black face; bill pink. Female greyish with red or yellowish edgings to wings and tail; bill pale pink. Immature like female but washed buff and bill dusky. Not gregarious; occurs singly, in pairs or in family parties.

Voice: Usually silent, but utters a high-pitched chatter at nest.

Distribution and Habitat: Widely distributed local resident, partial migrant in non-breeding season, Senegal eastwards to Somaliland, south through Uganda, Kenya and Tanganyika to Portuguese East Africa, Nyasaland, the Rhodesias and South Africa. Widely distributed but not common in savannah woodland, scrub and brachystegia woodlands. Frequents the tops of trees, creepers and bushes, mainly insectivorous.

RED-BILLED QUELEA or SUDAN DIOCH *Quelea quelea* p. 240

Identification: 5″. A streaky, sparrow-like weaver with pink-red bill and legs: male in breeding plumage has black face and is suffused pink on crown and breast. Female, non-breeding male and immature lack black face and pink suffusion. Extremely gregarious, sometimes in flocks numbering hundreds of thousands of birds. The Cardinal and Red-headed Queleas are smaller with dark red heads and black, not pink, bills.

Voice: A constant but low murmuration of chatter from flocks and breeding colonies.

Distribution and Habitat: Resident and spasmodic migrant from Senegal eastwards through Sudan to Ethiopia, Eritrea and Somaliland, south through Uganda, Kenya and Tanganyika to Portuguese East Africa, Nyasaland, the Rhodesias and South Africa. Inhabits dry thorn-bush, scrub and acacia country, at times entering cultivation where it is very destructive to wheat crops.

CARDINAL QUELEA *Quelea cardinalis* p. 240

Identification: 4″. A small, short-tailed sparrow-plumaged weaver with a crimson head and throat and a black bill. Female and immature lack crimson head. Occurs in loose colonies of a dozen or so pairs, and in larger flocks during the non-breeding season.

Voice: A soft "zeet, zeet" call-note.

Distribution and Habitat: Local resident, migratory during the non-breeding season, southern Sudan, Eritrea and Ethiopia south through Uganda, Kenya and Tanganyika to Northern Rhodesia. Inhabits open bush country where there is rank grass.

Allied Species: The Red-headed Quelea (*Quelea erythrops*) differs in being larger, 5 inches, with a blackish-crimson throat; bill black. This is a widely distributed but local species inhabiting rank grasslands and marshes. It is found from West Africa to Ethiopia, south through East Africa to Nyasaland and Northern Rhodesia and South Africa.

RED BISHOP *Euplectes orix* p. 256

Identification: 5″. One of the several species of brilliant red and black bishop weavers. Male distinguished by pale brown wings and tail, orange-red under tail-coverts and black forehead. Female, non-breeding male and immature sparrow-like, streaky above. The Zanzibar Red Bishop is smaller with a scarlet crown and black underparts. The Black-winged Red Bishop has the wings and tail black. Not highly gregarious, but often in small flocks and breeds in small scattered colonies. All male bishop weavers are very conspicuous during breeding season, making display flights over grass with rump feathers fluffed up.

Voice: Various twittering calls.

Distribution and Habitat: Local resident, migratory in the non-breeding season, Eritrea, Somaliland and Ethiopia, south through Kenya, Uganda and Tanganyika to Portuguese East Africa, Nyasaland, the Rhodesias and South Africa. Inhabits tall rank grass, sugar cane and maize cultivation, and rank herbage often near water. Wanders to open plains and short grass bush country after nesting.

ZANZIBAR RED BISHOP *Euplectes nigroventris* p. 256

Identification: 4″. A small black and red bishop distinguished by its brown wings and tail, red crown and completely black underparts. Female, non-breeding male and immature sparrow-like, streaked above and distinguished in field from Red Bishop only by its smaller size. Usually in small flocks; breeds in small scattered colonies.

Voice: A sharp twittering call.

Distribution and Habitat: Local resident, partial migrant in non-breeding season, eastern Kenya, Zanzibar and Pemba Islands, eastern Tanganyika and northern Portuguese East Africa. Common in coastal areas of Kenya where it is the most conspicuous bishop weaver. Inhabits bush and scrub where there is an abundance of rank grass and herbage.

BLACK-WINGED BISHOP *Euplectes hordeacea* p. 256

Identification: 5½″. A large red and black bishop with contrasting black wings and tail and buff or white under tail-coverts. Female, non-breeding male and immature buff with streaked mantle, black wings and tail and yellowish eye-stripe. Black wings and tail distinguish this species from the other black and red bishops. In pairs or small loose flocks.

Voice: Various twittering calls but often silent.

Distribution and Habitat: Local resident and partial migrant West Africa eastwards to Sudan and Ethiopia, south through Uganda, Kenya, Pemba and Zanzibar Islands, and Tanganyika to Portuguese East Africa, Nyasaland and Rhodesias: also in Angola and south-west Africa. Inhabits maize and sugarcane fields and rank grass.

Allied Species: The Black Bishop (*Euplectes gierowii*) is a large thickset species, 6 inches, black with an orange-red chest band, nape, mantle and rump. It occurs in elephant grass, swamps, and sugarcane and maize cultivation, in central Ethiopia south to southern Sudan, Uganda, western Kenya and northern Tanganyika; also in Angola.

YELLOW BISHOP *Euplectes capensis* p. 256

Identification: 6″. Male black with shoulders and rump bright yellow. Female and immature sparrow-like with an olive rump; male in non-breeding plumage also sparrow-like but retains yellow rump. Not gregarious; usually in pairs or single.

Voice: A series of brief cheeping and twittering calls.

Distribution and Habitat: Local resident and partial migrant, often common, throughout East and Central Africa. It inhabits grassy bush country, savannah woodland, the edges of forest and woodland and overgrown, neglected cultivation.

FAN-TAILED WIDOW-BIRD *Coliuspasser axillaris* p. 256

Identification: 6½″. Longer tailed than the bishop weavers, black with orange-red shoulders and a bluish-white bill. Most conspicuous when it perches on reeds or bushes or flies in display over breeding ground. Female and immature sparrow-like, with shoulders black, edged with orange or buff. Male in non-breeding dress like female but shoulders orange-red.

Voice: Various twittering calls.

Distribution and Habitat: Local resident and partial migrant West Africa to Ethiopia, south through Kenya, Uganda, eastern Congo and Tanganyika to Nyasaland, the Rhodesias, Portuguese East Africa and South Africa. Inhabits swamps and marshes and the edges of lakes and rivers where there is tall, rank grass.

WHITE-WINGED WIDOW-BIRD *Coliuspasser albonotatus* p. 256

Identification: Male 7″, female 5″. Black species with moderately long tail; white wing patch very conspicuous in flight. Female and immature streaky, sparrow-like, best identified by associated males; male in non-breeding plumage like female but retains white wing patch. Gregarious, found in scattered colonies when nesting and in flocks when not breeding.

Voice: Various brief twittering notes.

Distribution and Habitat: Local resident and partial migrant West Africa to southern Ethiopia south through East and Central Africa, and Portuguese East Africa to South Africa. Inhabits rank tall grass and bush and grass, usually on dry ground, but sometimes in swampy hollows: much attracted to artificial dams in agricultural land; common in the Kenya Highlands. Often associates with Yellow Bishops and Red-collared Widow Birds.

RED-COLLARED WIDOW-BIRD *Coliuspasser ardens* p. 256

Identification: Male 11″, female 5″. Entire plumage black with crescent-shaped scarlet patch on upper breast. The Kilimanjaro, Kenya Highlands and Ethiopian Highlands race has the crown and nape scarlet in addition to the red breast patch. Some birds in Uganda, Tanganyika, Nyasaland and Portuguese East Africa, which occur alongside normal males, have plumage all black, without a red breast patch. Female, male in non-breeding plumage and immature streaked black and tawny on upperparts; below buff, washed yellow on throat and chest. Breeds in loose colonies of scattered pairs; in small flocks in non-breeding season and when feeding.

Voice: Various chirping calls and a metallic rasping song.

Distribution and Habitat: Local resident and partial migrant West Africa to Ethiopia, south through Uganda, Kenya and Tanganyika to Portuguese East Africa, Nyasaland, the Rhodesias and South Africa. Inhabits areas of rank grass and mixed grass and bush.

LONG-TAILED WIDOW-BIRD *Coliuspasser progne* p. 256

Identification: Male 24-30″, female 6″. This is one of the most striking African birds, jet black with a neck ruff, a tail two feet or more long and bright red and buff shoulders. Flies slowly with slow jerky wingbeats and tail spread, a few feet above nesting ground. Female and immature pale tawny buff, heavily streaked: male in non-breeding dress like female but larger and retains red shoulder patches. Forms flocks in non-breeding season when frequents and roosts in swamps and reedbeds.

Voice: A loud sharp chirping call.

Distribution and Habitat: Local resident in the highlands of central and western Kenya, over 6,000 feet. Elsewhere found in the highlands of Angola and in South Africa. Frequents open high-level grasslands and moorland, the vicinity of dams and marshes and cultivation. In Kenya common on the Kinangop Plateau and in the Nanyuki district.

JACKSON'S WIDOW-BIRD *Drepanoplectes jacksoni* p. 256

Identification: Male 13-14″, female 5½″. Male entirely black with contrasting olive-brown shoulders and a thick, long decurved tail. Female, male in non-breeding dress and immature tawny, streaked dark brown. When nesting, males construct circular dancing rings on which they display by repeatedly springing two or more feet into the air.

Voice: A soft "chee" uttered during display and a brief clicking song.

Distribution and Habitat: Local resident highlands over 5,000 feet in western and central Kenya and the Loliondo and Crater Highlands in northern Tanganyika. Gregarious; found during breeding season in highland grasslands. Forms flocks in post-breeding period, when it visits cultivated areas.

BRONZE MANNIKIN *Spermestes cucullatus* p. 257

Identification: $3\frac{1}{2}''$. Tame, gregarious little birds feeding on grass seeds and on ground like miniature sparrows. Above dusky with oily-green gloss, darker on head, throat and breast; rump and flanks vermiculated black and white; belly white; bill pale blue-grey. Immature brown with black tail.

Voice: A sharp, low "tik, tik."

Distribution and Habitat: A common resident from West Africa to East Africa, southwards to Central Africa, Portuguese East Africa and South Africa. Found in bush country, coastal scrub, cultivation, grasslands, edges of swamps and lakes and among rank herbage and grass.

Allied Species: The Rufous-backed Mannikin (*Spermestes nigriceps*) has the mantle bright chestnut-brown. It occurs in scrub, edges of forest and mixed bush and grass from southern Somaliland, south through eastern and central Kenya, Tanganyika, Portuguese East Africa, Nyasaland and the Rhodesias to South Africa.

CUT-THROAT *Amadina fasciata* p. 257

Identification: $4\frac{1}{2}''$. Small finch-like bird of speckled brown appearance, paler below with a rufous belly; male with very conspicuous crimson band on throat. Immature resembles female. Gregarious in small flocks; often associated with cordon-bleus and other waxbills.

Voice: Sparrow-like chirping calls.

Distribution and Habitat: Local resident and partial migrant Senegal and Nigeria eastwards to Sudan, Ethiopia and Somaliland, south through Uganda, Kenya and Tanganyika to Portuguese East Africa, Nyasaland, the Rhodesias and Transvaal, South Africa. Inhabits dry thornbush and acacia country; often noticed around waterholes and dams. Common in the arid northern districts of Kenya.

GREEN-WINGED PYTILIA or MELBA FINCH *Pytilia melba* p. 257

Identification: $5''$. A red-billed, green, finch-like bird with a red face, throat, rump and tail; breast golden-orange. Female and immature lack red on face and throat and are vermiculated grey and white below. Shy, usually in pairs or family parties. When disturbed the birds dive into the nearest thicket, leaving a fleeting impression of a green bird with a dark red rump and tail.

Voice: Usually silent, but sometimes utters weak chirping calls.

Distribution and Habitat: Local, sometimes common, resident Senegal eastwards through Sudan to Eritrea, Ethiopia and Somaliland, south through eastern Congo, Uganda, Kenya, Zanzibar and Tanganyika to Portuguese East Africa, Nyasaland, the Rhodesias, Angola and South Africa. Inhabits bush country, coastal thickets, thorn scrub, neglected cultivation and rank grass and bush.

AFRICAN FIRE FINCH *Lagonosticta rubricata* p. 257

Identification: 4½″. Small, deep red and brown finch-like birds, the female and immature paler, greyer and duller. Best distinguished from Red-billed Fire Finch by its blue-grey bill. Occurs in pairs and feeds largely on the ground; shy, disappearing into undergrowth when disturbed, showing a flash of its crimson rump. Much less common in gardens than the Red-billed Fire Finch.

Voice: A bell-like trill, followed by several chirping notes.

Distribution and Habitat: Resident West Africa, eastwards to Eritrea and Ethiopia, south through eastern Congo, Uganda, Kenya and Tanganyika to Portuguese East Africa, Nyasaland, Northern Rhodesia and eastern Southern Rhodesia. Also in Angola and South Africa. Inhabits thick, lush bush and rank grass, margins of forests, thick bush along streams and overgrown cultivation.

Allied Species: The very closely allied Jameson's Fire Finch (*Lagonosticta jamesoni*) also has a blue-grey bill but is pale above, washed with rose pink. It inhabits more arid localities than the African Fire Finch, favouring thickets in dry thornbush country.

RED-BILLED FIRE FINCH *Lagonosticta senegala* p. 257

Identification: 4″. A small, pinkish-red waxbill with a distinct rosy-red bill. Female and immature browner and duller. The African and Jameson's Fire Finches have blue-grey bills. Feeds mainly on the ground, in pairs or family parties. It is a tame and confiding little bird much at home around human habitations and in gardens. It is well known as the "animated plum," a not inappropriate name.

Voice: A distinctive, weak "tweet, tweet": does not appear to trill like the African Fire Finch.

Distribution and Habitat: A common resident in suitable localities throughout most of the Ethiopian Region. Widespread and often abundant East and Central Africa. Usually seen feeding on open or bare ground near human dwellings; also in scrub, thickets and riverine undergrowth.

YELLOW-BELLIED WAXBILL *Coccopygia melanotis* p. 257

Identification: 3½″. A tiny greenish waxbill with a buff belly, black tail and crimson rump; bill colour distinctive and a good field character, upper mandible black, lower mandible red; sexes alike; immature duller and bill dusky. The South African and Angola race has a black face. Usually in small flocks in lush undergrowth.

Voice: A weak "swee, swee."

Distribution and Habitat: Local resident Ethiopia, Eritrea and southern Sudan, south through eastern Congo, Uganda, Kenya and Tanganyika to Portuguese East Africa, Nyasaland, the highlands of Northern Rhodesia and the eastern border of Southern Rhodesia: also in Angola and South Africa. Occurs in rank undergrowth along forest margins and streams and in grassy areas in wooded and forest country.

WAXBILL *Estrilda astrild* p. 257

Identification: 4½″. Pale brown waxbill with a conspicuous and vivid red bill and a red streak through the eye; brown, not red, on rump and tail; immature duller with dusky bill. In small flocks in lush grass.

Voice: Constant weak twittering flock calls.

Distribution and Habitat: Resident, often abundant, throughout greater part of Ethiopian Region, including East and Central Africa. Occurs in flocks in neglected cultivation, lush grasslands and in rank grass and bush, often near water.

Allied Species: The Crimson-rumped Waxbill (*Estrilda rhodopyga*) differs in having a crimson rump and crimson-edged tail feathers. It occurs in similar haunts as the Waxbill, favouring small marshes where there is thick grass and undergrowth. It ranges from the Sudan to Ethiopia and Somaliland, south through Uganda, Kenya and Tanganyika to Nyasaland.

RED-CHEEKED CORDON-BLEU *Uraeginthus bengalus* p. 257

Identification: 5″. Male easily recognised: a mainly azure blue waxbill with crimson cheek patches; female and immature duller and lack crimson on face. In pairs or family parties: tame and confiding.

Voice: Weak, squeaking call-note and a three-note song "ts, ts, tseeee" repeated over and over again.

Distribution and Habitat: Resident, sometimes common, from West Africa eastwards to Eritrea, Ethiopia and Somaliland, south through eastern Congo, Uganda, Kenya and northern half Tanganyika.

Frequents thornbush and acacia country, savannah, neglected cultivation, edges of forest and in gardens and around human habitations. Feeds largely on the ground.

Allied Species: The Angola Cordon-bleu (*Uraeginthus angolensis*) is found in southern half Tanganyika and in Central Africa, Angola and South Africa. Frequents thickets, woodlands and rank vegetation: feeds on ground. Differs from Red-cheeked Cordon-bleu in having no red on cheeks, which are blue. The Blue-capped Cordon-bleu (*Uraeginthus cyanocephalus*) is easily recognised by its blue, not fawn-brown, crown; this species also lacks the red cheek patches. It occurs in dry bush country of southern Somaliland, Kenya and Tanganyika. The Purple Grenadier (*Granatina ianthinogaster*), 5½ inches, is a rich cinnamon-brown waxbill with a black tail and a conspicuous cobalt blue-rump and a red bill. It occurs in scrub and thornbush country in Ethiopia and Somaliland, northern Uganda, Kenya and northern Tanganyika.

PIN-TAILED WHYDAH *Vidua macroura* p. 257

Identification: Male 12-13″, female 4½″. A red-billed, black and white whydah with a long, narrow black tail. Female and immature streaked and sparrow-like with a buff band down centre of crown and a pink bill. Male in non-breeding dress like female but larger with much white in wings. Flight erratic and jerky; has characteristic display flight, the male hovering and "dancing" in the air over the female perched below.

Voice: Various chirping calls and a sustained twittering song.

Distribution and Habitat: Widely distributed and common resident throughout the Ethiopian Region in suitable localities. Common in East and Central Africa. Inhabits all types of grassland and light bush and scrub and in cultivation. Usually in small parties, the males greatly outnumbered by females and immature birds.

Allied Species: The Steel-blue Whydah (*Vidua hypocherina*) is an uncommon and local species in dry bush country of Somaliland, Ethiopia, northern Uganda, northern and eastern Kenya and northern Tanganyika. Male glossy blue-black with long narrow tail feathers. Female and immature resemble female Pin-tailed Whydah but white below, not buff.

FISCHER'S STRAW-TAILED WHYDAH *Vidua fischeri* p. 257

Identification: Male 11″, female 4″. Male unmistakable, a small black and cream-coloured whydah with two central pairs of tail feathers pale yellow, very thin and elongated, resembling straws. Female and male in non-breeding plumage sparrow-like, streaked above, with a reddish-brown crown; bill red. Immature like female but duller and with bill dusky. In pairs or small flocks. Male has remarkable display; settling on topmost twigs and leaves of bush or small tree immediately above female it flaps wings, at the same time holding on by its feet to prevent itself from flying.

Voice: A sharp "tssp" and a brief three- or four-note song repeated over and over again.

Distribution and Habitat: Local resident Ethiopia and Somaliland south to Kenya and Tanganyika: inhabits dry bush and scrub country.

PARADISE WHYDAH *Steganura paradisaea* p. 257

Identification: Male 15-16″, female 5″. Male unmistakable, recognised by its black, chestnut and buff plumage and remarkable tail. Perches frequently on tops of thorn trees and flies in a curious undulating, jerky manner. Non-breeding male and female sparrow-like with black bill and a broad white stripe down centre of crown. Immature dull tawny-brown with white belly.

Voice: A rather shrill, metallic "teeet" call, but usually silent.

Distribution and Habitat: Local resident in suitable localities throughout most of Ethiopian Region; widely distributed but local in East and Central Africa. Inhabits bush and acacia country, and savannah woodlands.

Allied Species: The Broad-tailed Paradise Whydah (*Steganura orientalis*) differs in having the central tail feathers broad along entire length, not tapering to a point. It occurs in the Sudan, eastern Congo, Eritrea, Kenya, Tanganyika and locally in Central Africa to Portuguese East Africa, Angola and South Africa.

FINCHES: Fringillidae

The finches are thick-billed, seed-eating birds which resemble weavers but have nine visible primaries only. Nests unlike those of weavers, open and cup-shaped.

BRIMSTONE CANARY *Serinus sulphuratus* p. 257

Identification: 6″. A thickset greenish-yellow canary with a stout horn-grey bill and bright yellow underparts; greenish-yellow rump does not contrast with rest of upperparts. Immature like adult but duller. Occurs in pairs or small parties. Holub's Golden Weaver has somewhat similar colour pattern but is larger, with a black bill and an orange wash on the breast.

Voice: Rather harsh chirping calls and a varied but typical canary song.

Distribution and Habitat: Local resident highlands of Kenya, Uganda and eastern Congo, south through Tanganyika to Nyasaland and the Rhodesias; also in Angola and South Africa. Inhabits scattered bush in open country, mountain moorland and bush, riverine thickets and vegetation near water, and cultivated areas and gardens. Less gregarious than most other species of canary, found in pairs or small parties.

Allied Species: The Yellow-fronted Canary (*Serinus mozambicus*), 4½ inches, is olive above with dusky streaks; forehead and streak above eye bright yellow; rump bright yellow, contrasting with rest of upperparts; below yellow with a dark moustache stripe separating yellow cheeks from yellow chin. This is a bird of lightly wooded country, cultivation and savannah bush; often associated with baobab trees in East African coastal districts. It occurs locally, sometimes abundant, throughout East and Central Africa, but not usual in highland areas over 6,000 feet.

YELLOW-RUMPED SEED EATER *Serinus atrogularis* p. 257

Identification: 4″. A tawny-grey seed-eater with whitish underparts and a bright lemon-yellow rump which contrasts strongly with remainder upperparts when bird in flight. Found in pairs or small flocks.

Voice: Usual canary type song and a double "tssp" call-note.

Distribution and Habitat: Local resident, often common, Sudan, Ethiopia, Eritrea and Somaliland south through eastern Congo, Uganda, Kenya and Tanganyika to the Rhodesias: also in Angola and in South Africa. Inhabits most types of woodlands, especially brachystegia, and open bush, grasslands and park-like country.

STREAKY SEED EATER *Serinus striolatus* p. 257

Identification: 6″. Tawny-brown with dark streaked upperparts and crown; whitish eye-stripe; below tawny white or buff, streaked dark brown on throat, breast and flanks: immature duller. A common species best recognised by streaky plumage, the rump being the same colour as rest of upperparts and the conspicuous white eye-stripe.

Voice: A high-pitched three-note call and a bubbling canary type song.

Distribution and Habitat: Common resident highlands Ethiopia, Kenya, Uganda, eastern Congo, northern Tanganyika and the mountain highlands of Nyasaland and Northern Rhodesia. Inhabits moorland bush, the edges of forests, mixed grass and bush, cultivation and gardens. A very common bird in the highlands of Kenya.

BUNTINGS: Emberizidae

Mainly ground-feeding finch-like birds found singly, in pairs or in small parties. Distinguished from finches by bill formation, the cutting edge of the upper mandible being sinuated.

GOLDEN-BREASTED BUNTING *Emberiza flaviventris* p. 257

Identification: 6″. Best recognised by rufous back, white-tipped wing-coverts and golden-rufous breast: crown and sides of face black with a white stripe down centre of crown and a white band on each side of the face: white tips to outer pairs tail of feathers conspicuous when bird flies. Immature has buff streak on crown and is duller.

Voice: A trilling "zizi, zizi" and a bubbling song "tee, wee—cheee—te—tweee" repeated over and over again.

Distribution and Habitat: Resident, widespread and locally common, over most of the Ethiopian Region; common in East and Central Africa. Inhabits dry forest, woodlands—including brachystegia and mopane—and bush and acacia country; usually single or in pairs.

Allied Species: The Somali Golden-breasted Bunting (*Emberiza poliopleura*) differs in having the feathers of the upperparts margined white and with more white on the underparts, giving the bird a generally brighter appearance. It occurs in dry thorn scrub in the south-eastern Sudan, north-eastern Uganda, Ethiopia, Somaliland and Kenya to northern Tanganyika.

CINNAMON-BREASTED ROCK BUNTING
Fringillaria tahapisi p. 257

Identification: $5\frac{1}{2}$″. A slim, reddish-brown bunting with crown, sides of face and throat and chest black; white streak down centre of crown and white streaks above and below eye. Female has crown dark tawny, streaked black, and is greyish on throat and chest. Immature like female but duller and head stripes tawny not white. Usually found in pairs on rocky ground.

Voice: A drawn-out two-note call "tee, eeeee"; song a bubbling "chi, chi—cheeeee, che che" repeated over and over again.

Distribution and Habitat: Widely distributed in the Ethiopian Region from Nigeria eastwards to Ethiopia, south to South Africa. Local but not uncommon in East and Central Africa. Inhabits rocky, stony ground and hillsides where there is scattered bush and short grass: also frequents brachystegia and mopane woodland. Usually tame and confiding. Feeds mainly on ground.

APPENDIX

Institutions and Societies: The following Institutions and Societies are listed for the convenience of visitors who may wish to make contacts with local naturalists and to refer to ornithological collections and libraries.

Kenya: The Coryndon Museum, P.O. Box 658, Nairobi. Extensive exhibition and research collections. The Belcher Ornithological Library and the Natural History Society's Library are housed in the museum.

The East Africa Natural History Society, c/o The Coryndon Museum, P.O. Box 658, Nairobi.

Uganda: The Uganda Museum, Kampala. No extensive zoological collections at present.

The Uganda Society, Private Bag, Kampala. Small reference collections of birds are kept at the headquarters of the Queen Elizabeth National Park and the Murchison Falls National Park.

Tanganyika: King George V Memorial Museum, P.O. Box 511, Dar es Salaam. A small exhibition collection of birds is being built up.

The Tanganyika Society, c/o P.O. Box 511, Dar es Salaam. A small reference collection of birds is kept at the headquarters of the Serengeti National Park at Seronera.

Portuguese East Africa: Museu Dr. Alvaro de Castro, C.P. 598, Lourenço Marques. Exhibition and reference bird collections.

Nyasaland: The Nyasaland Society, P.O. Box 125, Blantyre.

Northern Rhodesia: Rhodes-Livingstone Museum, P.O. Box 124, Livingstone. Limited bird collections being built up.

Lusaka Natural History Club, P.O. Box 844, Lusaka.

Southern Rhodesia: National Museum of Southern Rhodesia, P.O. Box 240, Bulawayo. Extensive exhibition and research bird collections and library facilities.

Rhodesian Ornithological Society, c/o P.O. Box 240, Bulawayo.

Bibliography. The following books are suggested for reference purposes:

ALEXANDER, W. B., *Birds of the Ocean*, New York and London.

ARCHER, G. F. and E. M. GODMAN, *Birds of British Somaliland and the Gulf of Aden*, 4 vols., London.

BANNERMAN, D. A., *The Birds of West and Equatorial Africa*, 8 vols., Edinburgh and London.

BATES, G. L., *Handbook of the Birds of West Africa*, London.

BENSON, C. W. and C. M. N. WHITE, *Checklist of the Birds of Northern Rhodesia*, Lusaka.

BENSON, C. W., *Checklist of the Birds of Nyasaland*, Blantyre.

BELCHER, C. F., *Birds of Nyasaland*, London.

CAVE, F. O. and J. D. MACDONALD, *Birds of the Sudan*, Edinburgh.

CHAPIN, J. P., *The Birds of the Belgian Congo*, 4 vols., New York.

DELACOUR, J. and PETER SCOTT, *The Waterfowl of the World*, 3 vols., London.
FRIEDMANN, H., *The Parasitic Cuckoos of Africa*, Washington.
FRIEDMANN, H., *The Honey-Guides*, Washington.
FRIEDMANN, H., *The Parasitic Weaverbirds*, Washington.
JACKSON, F. J., *The Birds of Kenya Colony and the Uganda Protectorate*, 3 vols., London and Edinburgh.
LYNES, H., " Review of the genus Cisticola," *Ibis*. ser. 12, vol. 6, supp., London.
PETERSON, R. T., G. MOUNTFORT and P. A. D. HOLLOM, *A Field Guide to the Birds of Britain and Europe*, London.
MACKWORTH-PRAED, C. W. and C. H. B. GRANT, *Birds of Eastern and North-eastern Africa*, 2 vols., London.
ROBERTS, A., *The Birds of South Africa*, revised edition by McLACHLAN and LIVERSIDGE, London.
SCLATER, W. L., *Systema Avium Aethiopicarum*, London.
SMITHERS, REAY H. N., M. P. STUART IRWIN and M. PATERSON., *Checklist of the Birds of Southern Rhodesia*, Cambridge, England.
VAURIE, CHARLES, *The Birds of the Palearctic Fauna*, London.

INDEX

Numbers in bold type refer to pages facing illustrations